M000049693

195 LAKES
of the
FRASER VALLEY

195 LAKES
of the
FRASER VALLEY

Volume I
West Vancouver to Stave Falls

Ed Rychkun

hancock

house

ISBN 0-88839-339-3
Copyright © 1995 Ed Rychkun

Cataloging in Publication Data
Rychkun, Ed.
    195 lakes of the Fraser Valley

    Contents: Vol. 1. West Vancouver to Stave Falls—v. 2.
Dewdney to Hope.
    ISBN 0-88839-339-3 (v. 1)—ISBN 088839-377-6 (v. 2)

    1. Lakes—British Columbia—Fraser River Valley—Recrea-
tional use—Guidebooks. 2. Outdoor recreation—British Columbia—Fraser River Valley—Guidebooks. 3. Fraser River Valley
(B.C.)—Guidebooks. I. Title. II. Title: One hundred and ninety-
five lakes of the Fraser Valley.
GV191.46.B7R92 1995   917.11'75044   C94-0910312-8

All rights reserved. No part of this publication may be reproduced, stored
in a retrieval system or transmitted, in any form or by any means, elec-
tronic, mechanical, photocopying, recording, or otherwise, without the
prior written permission of Hancock House Publishers.
Printed in Canada-Webcom

Edited: Suzanne Chin
Production: Ed Rychkun

Cover photo and maps by author
Hoover Lake on cover

Published simultaneously in Canada and the United States by

HANCOCK HOUSE PUBLISHERS LTD.
19313 Zero Avenue, Surrey, B.C. V4P 1M7
(604) 538-1114   Fax (604) 538-2262

HANCOCK HOUSE PUBLISHERS
1431 Harrison Avenue, Blaine, WA 98230-5005
(604) 538-1114   Fax (604) 538-2262

CONTENTS

ACKNOWLEDGMENTS

When you take on a project like this book there are many times you begin to question your sanity. This is because of the incredible effort required to find, compile, assemble, then validate the type of information required in this type of book. What began as an exciting exploration adventure transformed into a nightmare of notes, maps and conflicting information. It became a battle to determine what information was correct. It is a tremendous effort. There are also times when those close to you also begin to question your wisdom when your project becomes an obsession. But you tell yourself that, in the end, it will be worth it. The people who will be able to share these secret spots will appreciate it. I can not tell you how often I bugged people for maps and details, for every little tidbit of information. In looking back, however, the one who has persevered the most is my back roads partner and wife, Hope. Without her I would have never taken on such a venture and, without her support, I would certainly never have finished this book. Her tenacious navigating abilities got us to places that would have tested the best of explorers. Her almost infinite tolerance of my stubbornness to seek out every lake is a tribute to her sturdy character. It is to her that I dedicate this book and acknowledge her quiet efforts. It is her support that allowed me to steal the time to finish it...and there were many times where I just did not see an end.

There were also many others who deserve to be mentioned. Although most of them did not know their constant caller was writing a book, their cooperation and willingness to provide information should not go unnoticed. The Forest Service was exceptional in their support, providing maps of logging roads and trails. The Greater Vancouver Regional District was very helpful, as was the Ministry of Parks. Even BC Hydro helped. The Department of Fisheries and Oceans were outstanding, opening their office files and allowing me to gain a mass of fishing information. I owe a special acknowledgment to them for allowing me the use of their water-depth contour maps.

INTRODUCTION

This is not just another hiking book, nor is it another day-trip guide. This is a recreation guide to *all* the lakes in the lower Fraser Valley. You will not be disappointed. My purpose is to share with you the secrets of 195 freshwater lakes in the lower valley. So whether you are a fisherman, hiker, camper, nature lover, boater or four-wheeler, the detailed information presented between these covers will be of interest.

This book is also the result of an endless quest to find the many hidden lakes and valleys so common to the area but so difficult to find. I have always been frustrated by the numerous rough sketches presented in various guide books. So many times I have tried to find those places one is being 'guided' to only to end up having to chart my own course. Lakes are usually a good size so one would normally believe they would be reasonably easy to find—even if you *were* using someone's rough sketch of the location...wrong! So many times there are numerous roads not plotted and so many times the area is not what you expected. So many times you just burn gas and waste valuable recreation time. Have you ever tried to find a lake from an unscaled sketch? I don't mean to belittle some of the attempts and perhaps a sketch is better than *nothing* but sometimes an accurate map would be helpful. Further, while descriptions of scenery are nice, sometimes a bit more hard information would be a welcome addition.

Well, this book is a bit different. I have spent much time consolidating facts and recreational details, providing explicit directions and maps...*plenty* of maps to guide you to some of the most unbelievable places in the valley, all within a few hours' drive from Vancouver—excluding some of the hikes, that is!

Being interested in fishing, hiking and recreation in general, I have always had the urge to find a new secret place or private space involving water. Judging by the masses who head to the waterways of the valley, most outdoor people appear to have a similar urge. For one reason or other the more appealing spots seem to involve water; lakes and streams have an almost magnetic attraction. In reality the Fraser Valley has a vast supply of such appealing bodies of water but access to the water is not always easy to find. The major lack is always information on how to find the lake, the difficulty of access and the type of facilities. As a result, I have focused on these very issues, attempting to cover everything recreationally relevant about a lake and its surrounding landscape. For each publicly accessible lake (regardless of difficulty) I have provided information and maps on several crucial elements:

- **Features** Every lake is unique, offering a different landscape and features. Typically these features support unique recreational activities. Where one area may be a great place for fishing, another may be great for hiking. In many cases, the facilities are developed to take advantage of these key natural features. So *knowing* what the area is famous for or what the attraction is, would indeed be a nice thing to know *ahead* of time.
- **Location** Every lake is situated in different terrain. The area use and roughness also varies dramatically, directly affecting the accessibility. The lakes in the valley vary from city park to remote glacial settings. Most of the lakes are in remote wilderness, accessible only by rough roads, many with steep foot-trails and only a small portion of shoreline accessible. No one wants to hassle other's privacy, destroy their vehicles on rough roads or have a hassle getting lost in the wilderness. So *how to find* the lake easily *without frustration* would be a nice change. This means accurate maps are essential.
- **Facilities** There are quite a staggering variety at these lakes. Some have just evolved naturally through use, while others have been developed to some degree. Others have been well organized by the Parks Board. The type, quantity and quality of all these recreational *facilities* are of special interest to anyone thinking about a visit, *before* the visit.
- **Recreational details** Each lake and its surrounding area supports a different set of recreational activities. While some have fantastic camping facilities, others have fantastic scenery. For example fishing, boating, hiking, riding, four-wheeling and camping are all different activities requiring different detailed information. What each area has or does not have, for *recreational purposes* would be very helpful information to have *before* the venture is taken.

This is precisely what this book is about; not a lot of effort has gone into the descriptions of scenery since the focus is on lakes and recreation. What is presented is how to find all the lakes in the valley and what to expect when you get there. This is done through an incredible number of *accurate* maps and through a summary of relevant information.

A RECREATIONAL PARADISE

It may come as a surprise to many that the lower Fraser Valley is actually an incredible paradise of recreational opportunities. The valley has true wilderness, mountains, waterways, lakes and an astounding variation in terrain. Since the lakes are so numerous, they have a tendency to be situated in a rather dramatic range of terrain making visiting each a unique adventure. The greater surprise is that the vast majority are accessible, some requiring a bit more effort than others, but nevertheless open for public use. Even more of a surprise is that the vast majority even have some type of recreational facilities—some more rugged than others, of course. Many have unbelievable settings carved into the wilderness by the efforts and the boots of outdoor adventurers.

You may find it quite amazing that there are over 195 lakes in the Fraser Valley between Vancouver and Hope and every lake has its own unique character. More often than not the drive to the lake or the hike to it also has its unique qualities. To anyone interested in the outdoors this means an almost never-ending supply of alternative places to explore—a fantastic situation that has not always been the case.

The Ministry of Forests has opened up previously inaccessible areas through logging roads and have recently been assigned the task of development on Crown land. As a result they have been responsible for creating many recreational facilities at many of the lakes that were never before easily accessible. Even BC Hydro is in the recreation business, providing new access and formal facilities at their sites, even developing fisheries. The Ministry of Parks, the Greater Vancouver Regional District Parks Department and even the Ministry of the Environment have all played some role in opening up and developing the area. What may be most surprising is that there are very few totally inaccessible lakes or many that have restricted access. While they may have use restrictions, the vast majority are available for public use.

MAPS ARE IMPORTANT

Without a doubt, any hiker or outdoor enthusiast must rely heavily on good maps—the most crucial aid to anyone spending time in the outdoors—but, in many cases, good-quality maps do not exist. I am personally doomed without a map which is the reason this book has so many...*three levels* to be exact because you need three levels to get to the spot you have chosen. These are detailed for each lake, typically including a *regional*, a *local* and a *detailed* lake map.

- **Regional maps** First, you need to look at a *regional map* to get perspective on how to get to a specific area allowing you to drive there. Then you need to drop down to the next level.
- **Local map** This is what you need to identify the specific *local* roads, landmarks and details allowing you to get to the lake itself. Typically, this level of detail cannot be shown on a regional map since it would have to be enormous to show the details. Now that you are near the lake you need the next level of detail.

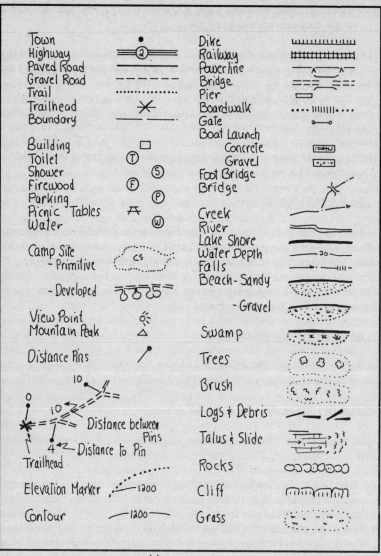

Town	•	Dike	⊥⊥⊥⊥⊥⊥⊥⊥⊥⊥⊥
Highway	═══⓶═══	Railway	┼┼┼┼┼┼┼┼┼┼┼
Paved Road	───────	Powerline	──∧──∧──
Gravel Road	─ ─ ─ ─	Bridge	═╪═ ═╪═
Trail	··············	Pier	▭
Trailhead	✶	Boardwalk	···‖‖‖‖‖‖···
Boundary	────┼────	Gate	o──●
		Boat Launch	
Building	▢	Concrete	
Toilet	Ⓣ	Gravel	
Shower	Ⓢ	Foot Bridge	
Firewood	Ⓕ	Bridge	
Parking	Ⓟ		
Picnic Tables	⊼	Creek	
Water	Ⓦ	River	
		Lake Shore	
Camp Site		Water Depth	──→ 20
– Primitive	CS	Falls	──┄┅‖‖‖
		Beach – Sandy	
– Developed			
		– Gravel	
View Point	☼		
Mountain Peak	△	Swamp	
Distance Pins	⁄	Trees	

Distance between Pins

Distance to Pin

Trailhead

| Elevation Marker | ⋰─1200 |
| Contour | ─1200─ |

Brush	
Logs & Debris	
Talus & Slide	
Rocks	⟀⟀⟀⟀
Cliff	⌒⌒⌒⌒⌒
Grass	

Map conventions

- **Detailed map** Once at the lake take a look at the *detailed* picture, the one that tempted you here in the first place. This means you need a concise presentation of relevant information depending on what you want to do. If you are an angler, you want to know lake depths, access points, boat launch, streams, bays and such. If you are a hiker, you want to know the trails, facilities, features and so on.

In either case, the three levels of detail are quite essential and useful. To many the map presents a concise picture that puts the area in perspective. These maps are presented here for the majority of lakes. The regional map will get you to the area within which there will be several lakes and is provided at the beginning of each region. The local map amplifies the area around the lake so you can get there. It is provided for just about every lake working like a moving magnifying glass. Most lakes will also have a detailed map of the area near the lake. A detailed map is not presented where the lake is tiny or inaccessible and in many cases I have included a picture of the lake.

MAP CONVENTIONS

I have used many of the typical conventions of other professional cartographers. The conventions are usually a symbol resembling the real thing so you will get used to reading them. These are illustrated in the map convention picture.

To be consistent, a map convention has been used that helps to identify the type of surface. Distance markers are used in most cases (a little marker pin) to indicate the cumulative distance from an access point (if beside the pin) or to indicate the incremental distance (if between pins). Where streets or roads are well named (as in the city) distances are not used and street names are more practical. In addition, a scale is provided to give an indication of distance but the most important feature is that *all* maps are drawn with north at the top!

THE LOWER FRASER VALLEY

The Fraser Valley is shown in the next illustration. It includes the area from the Pacific Ocean at Vancouver to the area known as Hope. The region of interest is 130 by 60 kilometers carved out by the massive Fraser River on its final journey to meet the Pacific Ocean. This vast valley is bounded by the US border to the south and the Coast Mountains to the north. It includes an abundance of water areas in both lowlands and the higher lands along the north of the valley. South of the river, you typically find flatter lands making up the floodplain, slowly being devoured by the eastward march of the metropolitan areas along the coast. To the north of the river the lateral moraine plateau areas quickly give way to sharply rising Coast Mountains, beyond which you find very remote wilderness where the city has not been able to march northward because of the rugged nature of the area. Much of the northern area has been reserved as park, watershed or is still Crown land being actively logged.

In looking more closely at the lakes within this vast area, the majority stretch along the northern plateau all the way from West Vancouver to the Hope area. To best present these lakes, the book is divided into specific regions that project above and below the Fraser River.

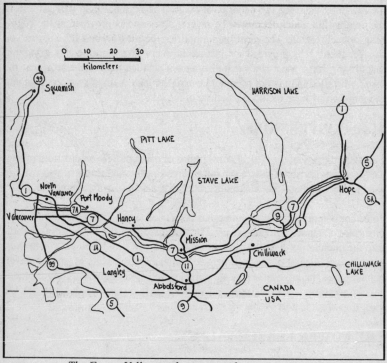

The Fraser Valley roads, towns and major waterways

REGIONS, HIGHWAYS and ACCESS

As mentioned, the best way to present the Fraser Valley is to divide it into a series of 'regions'. It should be noted that these regions have nothing to do with any other map system and are used here for convenience only. The vast majority of lakes are strung out in northerly chains and are accessible through a key access point along the middle of the valley. These access points are spread along the main highways that parallel the river up the valley. On the northern side of the river, the main artery is *Highway 7* and on the south side of the river *Highway 1* or the *Trans-Canada Highway* is the main roadway. These two actually converge in Burnaby as they approach the north shore of Vancouver. These two highways and a few of their main branches are all you need to enter the regions that contain the lakes. Since the northern terrain alternates between valleys (with major lakes) and mountains, the access points represent points from which you would normally drive into the northern valleys or along the mountains to gain access to the lakes.

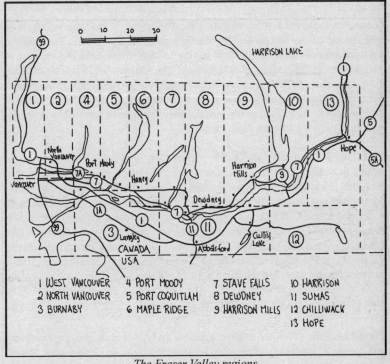

The Fraser Valley regions

Along the northern part of the Fraser Valley these regions represent strips and are shown on the map.

Each strip is a region forms a chapter. These are typically ten to 20 kilometers wide and 35 to 45 kilometers long, all adjacent to the Fraser River. For example the Maple Ridge region covers an area just north of Haney, which is on a major highway and is therefore a major access point from which you would proceed into the Alouette Park area where several lakes could be visited in sequence proceeding north.

Each access point has been described, allowing you the easiest access into the region. From this point the lakes can usually be driven or hiked to. In many cases there may be several access points which may require a hike, a four-wheel drive, a truck or a car, depending on road quality.

15

It is always a difficult task to consolidate such a quantity of information as discussed earlier into a form concisely suitable to a wide range of recreational needs. For this reason a format has been chosen that uses maps, tables and descriptions, working eastward from the first region at West Vancouver.

Because of the sheer volume of information compiled, it has been necessary to split the valley into two parts. This has been done for two reasons. First, we did not want to create a massive volume too big to carry. Second, we did not want to compromise on the amount of information. The solution was to create two volumes. The first, Volume 1, covers West Vancouver to Stave Falls. The second, Volume 2, continues east covering the rest of the valley from Dewdney to Hope. For the sake of convenience, the introduction, the table of contents, and the index have been replicated in both volumes.

Each lake is discussed individually within each region but these are usually treated in a chain sequence—as if you were conducting a reconnaissance to visit each site. Each lake will then contain detailed descriptions of the setting, access points, facilities, trails, roads, fish types and whatever recreational information is deemed relevant. Where available, water depth contours are also provided. A scenic picture of the lake helps you get your own idea of the scenery. Each lake has been given a reference number reflecting the region and the lake number in the sequence. For example 7-3 reflects Region 7, Lake 3 (Hayward Lake). These can be referenced through the summary tables in the index.

FINDING and ACCESSING the LAKES

The lakes of the valley are situated in a vast array of terrain, ranging from very difficult, as in mountainous areas, to those which lie in residential areas. Needless to say, the roads, trails or highways can be equally as variable in quality and each will typically dictate the type of vehicle required. In this book, I have used six means of access, *4X4, truck, car, hike, boat or plane*. In some cases a combination is required, i.e. you may need a 4X4 before hiking up to the lake.

The convention used in this book includes one for roads as shown on the symbol and convention map described earlier. These show the road type so where you see a **solid** line it is *paved*. A **dashed** road is *gravel* and a **dotted** line means you need to hike. If any other classification (i.e. horse trails) is needed, these are shown individually. In several cases a boat is required and in a few others there is no way in except by float plane. One would like to think that the road type would also give you a clue as to whether you require a car, truck, 4X4 or hiking boots but it is not always so. For this reason I have always stated separately what *type* of vehicle is required for each journey. Typically road type will relate to the transportation method in the following way:

- **Car** This is any normal paved or gravel road which can be driven on by a car. The assumption is that you do not want to destroy your vehicle and potholes are typically the major obstacle.
- **Truck** Many gravel roads will typically be navigated by a car but a great many roads are secondary roads used for logging. These will usually be rough enough to require higher clearance so a truck is recommended.
- **4X4** These roads are also typically gravel secondary roads that require a four-wheel drive for some portion of the journey. These roads will be steep, narrow and rough, requiring good clearance and good traction.
- **Hike** This means that you must walk to the lake simply because the trail is too narrow, rough, designed for goats or vehicles are prohibited.
- **Boat** There are a few cases where only a boat will get you through part of the journey, simply because there is no other way.
- **Float Plane** In a few cases the lakes are accessible only by flying in.

When I suggest that a 4X4 is required this means that part of the journey (usually the last part) demands it. This is because the last part is typically the *worst* part, even though you may be able to drive a car most of the distance. This is of course *my* opinion and I am reasonably conservative since I do not like to destroy my vehicle.

In general the logging roads (and back roads) are particularly rough in the spring and many turn into waterways in the winter and spring. The water washes loose gravel away to leave huge boulders and rough areas. In the fall, thanks to Goodyear rubber, you will find the roads are much smoother so leave the rougher ones for the fall if your vehicle is wimpy. The other considerations are whether the area is open to the public and whether there are access restrictions. Some of the access is restricted because of active logging activities. In other cases the area itself may simply be restricted because it is part of a protected area such as a watershed. Where possible, these are all described.

FOR THE ANGLERS

Each year the Ministry of the Environment stocks many of the lakes in the lower mainland region. While most of the stocked fish are either cutthroat and rainbow trout, sometimes they like to place kokanee, salmon and even char into certain lakes. The program has been in effect since 1984 and often new fisheries are created by stocking waters not previously containing fish. The program is designed to stock lakes with specific fish sizes at regular intervals. Programs are carefully determined from the potential of the lake to grow the fish, the presence or absence of spawning streams, number of anglers fishing the lake and the type of angling experience the fisheries manager wishes to provide. Sometimes they will stock large numbers of small fish or small numbers of large fish.

Some lakes are stocked every year while others are stocked during alternate years. In certain cases lakes are stocked to rejuvenate barren lakes or assist those with diminishing populations. The frequency of stocking does not necessarily indicate the quality of angling. Often the best angling is in the remote infrequently stocked lakes or in previously barren lakes a few years after the stocking.

The program, being run from the Surrey office, is quite impressive. It should be noted that many of the lower mainland lakes are not stocked simply because they are already sufficiently endowed with trout. Many of the larger lakes fall into this category.

SIZE CLASS	SIZES	AGE	WHEN CATCHABLE
fry	4 cm	less than a year	need two years in lake
yearling	10 cm	1 year	need a year in the lake
fingerling	10 cm	1 year	need a year in the lake
catchables	20 cm	2 years	ready for angling

The formal stocking program began in 1984 covering the vast majority of lakes in the Fraser Valley. The table above details the class, size and age of the fish being stocked. Considering the program began almost ten years ago and the fry and fingerlings will grow to 'catchable' size in two to four years, you can see there are quite an impressive number of lakes that should be well-endowed with excellent angling opportunities. For this reason, the stocking details are provided for each year.

In addition to the stocking program the government also provides a variety of useful maps and survey information for the angler, boater, hiker or nature-lover. The Ministry of the Environment is particularly prolific, providing information in many different forms. To an angler the information on roads, lake features, water depth and land features are all useful. In this respect, two sources of map information are particularly useful, mainly the lake survey information and topographic maps. I have provided these and where available, I have made a point to provide this for the keen angler who would like to know more about the under water features and water depths. The topographic series are also very useful to show changes in elevation and various terrain structures. It is nice to know, for example, that you may need to climb 500 meters if a simple hike is suggested. These are included on the maps and described when relevant.

FACILITIES INFORMATION

There are really four categories of camping and other recreational facilities available. I have classified these into *Developed, Primitive, Natural* and *Nothing*, describing the type of campsites, the quality of the facilities and the type and quality of the trails. A description is given below. These by no means should be taken as absolute since the variation can be significant. For this reason a detailed description of the area, roads, campsites, facilities, trails and other relevant items are provided for each lake. In general, however, the terms infer certain details:

- **Developed** These are typically found at provincial parks where good demarcated campsites, toilets, showers, water, fire pits, wood and other developed, organized facilities are available. Typically boat ramps are usually good concrete or gravel with parking for trailers. The sites have had serious thought go into them and are accessible via car in most cases.

- **Primitive** These are in a class of their own and typically are a result of some effort on the part of BC Forest Services (BCFS) to create a recreation site. Some provincial sites can also be included in this category. These 'primitive' sites are left as natural as possible. Most of the effort has been placed on accommodating nature and providing *basic* facilities only. These sites will typically not be easily accessible by car and will include gravel road access (sometimes truck or 4X4) with clearings in the bush or trees, typically close to the lake. These are rougher in that they may not have wood, water and fire pits available, but typically these are demarcated areas cleared (or beaten bare) set in the woods on or close to the lake. A toilet (or biffy), garbage can and maybe picnic tables will typically be provided but there is a tendency for 'tough guys' to destroy these tables for firewood so you may find them in rough shape. The site will provide some water access for a cartop boat, small trailer or a canoe but you may need to carry the boat for up to 200 meters in some cases. The launch area will therefore be cleared but primitive to say the least. These may sound pretty rough but they can be incredibly beautiful. A lot of thought has gone into leaving the environment alone—and into selecting the prettiest spots. The focus is on providing limited basics, leaving that which is natural intact and many times the trails are maintained footpaths. If you want to get away from the provincial park crowds, British Columbia Forest Service (BCFS) sites are indeed the place.

- **Natural** The other type is where there is nothing formally developed. Rather than categorize this as *nothing,* I prefer to refer to the area as *natural.* In this case there has been no planned effort to create public facilities. Ironically, these natural places have some of the finest settings and natural facilities around thanks to that unwritten ethic with ardent anglers and nature lovers who always seem to find the nicest spots and have each left behind as their little contribution another little clearing, a little rock fire pit, bits of firewood and little odds and ends for the next adventurer to enjoy. The next trail-blazer usually will return the favor. In such cases, a hike is typically required and trails are footpaths through the bush, beaten by the boots of keen anglers and the paws of wildlife.

- **Nothing** There is no visible sign of any open area or campers. A better description would be *virgin bush*. I have seldom found such a place. It is rare in the valley.

The information presented in this book varies quite significantly from lake to lake. Where some lakes have extensive recreational value a fair amount of information is available and given here. Other lakes have little value and have sparse information, particularly as the information relates to fish or facilities. In fact some lakes have no fish at all since they may be too small, too high or just barren. In other cases the lakes may be private or restricted (as in a watershed). In other situations the lakes may be in special areas where camping or fishing are not allowed (such as the University of British Columbia Research Forest). Others are just plain inaccessible. Regardless of the situation each of the lakes are still described here since they each have their own unique recreational value. I have actually included *all* lakes that are called 'lakes' regardless of their size or accessibility. I feel it is useful to know that certain lakes are off limits.

AREA USE RESTRICTIONS

Since we are dealing with lakes and the recreational demand is heavy there are many restrictions to be considered. The most notable relate to the fish while others are more subtle, being imposed indirectly, like a rough road, tough hike, limited camping, day use only and so on. In many cases the lakes in the Fraser Valley have been classified as barren. In other cases, the fish have been depleted simply as a result of the population density relative to the available lakes. In the last decade access to the lakes has increased quite dramatically through new roadways, the popularity of the 4X4 and the opening up of a vast network of logging roads. This all means that pressure on the ecosystem may be a problem with many lakes in recovery status, habitat development or those still in much of a virgin state. The difficulty with this is that to allow the fish to grow and multiply, there must be an effective fisheries management program in place or the lake will simply be over-fished. In coming to the call, the Fisheries Department has placed restrictions on certain lakes varying from age restrictions in popular urban lakes to boat and barbless hook restrictions in other areas. Some of the smaller lakes have restrictions on boats and motors. In conjunction with this program, the forest service has contrived a variety of lake facilities and access arrangements to support the program. For example, many of the lakes have primitive facilities and purposely limit boat access to limit fishing activity. Carrying a boat for a two-kilometer hike is quite a deterrent to the average angler.

In this book the restrictions are listed as published at the time of this writing. These are included where they apply for each lake. The key restrictions are:

- **Age** In certain lakes, simply because of the urban population intensity relative to the size of the lake, it is necessary to restrict fishing by the age of the fisherman. Typically this is designed to reserve the lake for the younger people.
- **Motors and boats** On certain lakes, there are either heavy urban demands or the lake fishery has not been well established. There are natural reasons for restricting motors and boats. Many of the smaller urban lakes need these restrictions or they would be covered with oil slicks, water skiers and an aqua-traffic problem.
- **Size and catch limits** There is normally a restriction on the size of the fish that may be taken but there may also be a restriction on the number of fish that may be taken out. In several cases the size restriction may vary depending on the status of the program, the lake demands or other factors. For example at Sayres Lake only two trout can be taken out, simply because of their larger size.
- **Angling methods** There are many lakes that have restrictions on the ways in which you are allowed to catch the fish. For example, some lakes require the use of barbless hooks. Other lakes may have a restriction on the type of bait (i.e. no live bait).
- **Times** There may be seasonal restrictions or there may be a need to temporarily close the lake to fishing activity.

Although there may appear to be many restrictions they have been put in place with considerable thought, designed to protect the fisheries and their habitat. Consideration is made to keep the lake's natural ecosystem from being strained or even destroyed. The rules can change quickly so you should always get the latest information when you get your fishing license. Also bear in mind that fisheries authorities have some rather impressive powers and have a tendency to consider you guilty until proven otherwise. Ignorance of the restriction is not a justifiable excuse so it is best to take the initiative and seek out the rules first.

FOR THE RECREATIONAL ENTHUSIAST

Finally, the information in this volume should not be considered as favoring the angler. Each lake has certain features and highlights, catering to different recreational needs. These are classified into recreational 'activities' in this book. Where relevant, the following activities and supporting information are detailed.

- **Back-road activities** Although not discussed directly, detailed local maps are included to cover recreation details other than for providing directions.

Dirt-biking and four-wheeling have become popular so I have shown up-to-date logging roads for those so inclined. Also included are distance markers, stream and mountain features.

- **Fishing** For the fisherman lakeshore features and other details including estuaries and stream exit/entry points are included. Water depth contours, shore access and even suggested hot spots are shown, along with stocking tables to entice you. Restrictions are discussed and the type of fish are listed along with size reports.
- **Hiking** is common to most lake areas with many trails reaching into interesting terrain away from the lake. Access trails and roads are all shown with steepness/elevation markers shown when required. Trails are shown with trail features and distances. In several cases interpretive nature trails are also detailed.
- **Horse and bike trails** Several of the lakes in the valley have been developed to provide excellent equestrian facilities. These include trails, staging areas, corrals and parking, all for public use. These trails, also commonly used by bikers and hikers are detailed in the area as well as the facilities.
- **Boating** Every (almost) lake attracts boaters. The suggested boating types, shore access points, launching facilities and boating restrictions are discussed.
- **Camping** The information includes a detailed layout of campsites and related facilities. A map of the surrounding area and the shoreline characteristics are included and the quality of facilities is discussed. Where they exist, swimming, beaches, firewood, toilets, water, parking and picnicking details are provided.
- **Crucial amenities** In many cases the lakes are remote so one needs to be prepared. Gas, groceries, sporting goods, fishing gear, services and even local pubs are indicated where the trips reach into isolated areas.

Finally, I have included an index in the back that consists of a table of the 195 lakes, summarizing all of the key statistics, recreational features and access details. You can quickly scan the information for crucial criteria then go directly to the section describing the details.

A FOOTNOTE

The problem with guide books is that information changes. Roads change, rules change, area ownership changes and even the terrain changes. Please be aware of this in your travels. Some areas and access will improve while others will become worse. Fishing regulations are perhaps the most changeable. Every effort has been made to make the information presented here as accurate as possible at the time of writing. There is no guarantee that all the information will remain accurate. Phone numbers to key information sources are provided at the back of the book. If you are in doubt, please call these numbers.

REGION ONE
WEST VANCOUVER

THE WEST VANCOUVER REGION is the first area covered by our Fraser Valley excursion. It starts at the northwestern extent of the Fraser Valley right against the Pacific Ocean and covers a coastal strip of the Coast Mountains of about 12 kilometers by 30 kilometers. From the south where you find the city of Vancouver, our region projects north to include West Vancouver then the massive area containing the Vancouver watershed. The most accessible part, despite the rugged mountainous terrain, is an L-shaped area which has the city of West Vancouver at the bottom of the L and Howe Sound to the east. On this western side, the strip of mainland forms an escarpment climbing quickly from the ocean to reach elevations of 1200 to 1500 meters forming a long ridge paralleling Howe Sound. At the south end in West Vancouver the climb is not quite as pronounced, allowing residential developments to encroach half-way up the mountains. At the top inside the ridge, the gigantic drainage basin formed by the Capilano River makes up the Greater Vancouver watershed and contains some of the most incredible wilderness in the valley. Access is mostly restricted with very little open for recreational use simply because of its rugged quality and its importance as the water supply area. The West Vancouver watershed, another area closer to West Vancouver, is also restricted from public use.

However, much of the area along the coastal fringe is reserved for recreational use. In fact all the areas that slope away from the watershed have some form of recreational feature and several parks reach to the watershed's boundary providing a variety of recreational facilities within easy reach of the metropolitan area. The major park system in the region is Cypress provincial park, famous for hiking and winter activities and involving a northern and southern section joined by the Howe Sound Crest, a long thin area along the ridge of the watershed. To the north, Crown land controlled by the forest service makes up the balance. Within this vast wilderness are many lakes and rivers but unfortunately the larger lakes are in the watershed and restricted from use.

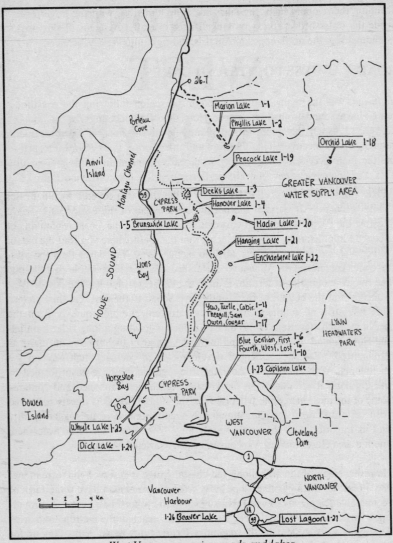

West Vancouver region roads and lakes

Most of the lakes are typically less than a few hectares, shallow and accessible through park hiking trails only. In this respect, fishing is not the feature attraction but summer hiking and winter sports activities are most definitely the highlight.

24

Scanning the regional map, the lakes are quite numerous with the larger ones inside the watershed. Cypress provincial park is really the focus of this area, extending from the north opposite Anvil Island right into West Vancouver.

ROADS, ACCESS POINTS AND LAKES

Highway 99 is the main roadway through the region following the coastline along Howe Sound from Squamish to Horseshoe Bay, meeting *Trans-Canada Highway 1* which then cuts inland along the north shore of Burrard Inlet through West Vancouver. This highway and the *Cypress Bowl Parkway* constitute the main access arteries leading to a maze of mountain trails and small lakes. Starting our journey from the north the first few lakes; **Marion Lake (1-1)** and **Phyllis Lake (1-2)** are southwest of Squamish, accessed by a long hike along logging roads that lead almost eight kilometers southeast of Furry Creek toward the watershed.

Continuing south along *Highway 99*, the next set of lakes, also accessible from the highway, requires some vigorous hiking up the escarpment into the mountain range overlooking Howe Sound. **Deeks Lake (1-3)**, **Hanover Lake (1-4)** and **Brunswick Lake (1-5)** are within the northern extension of Cypress provincial park.

Continuing south around the bend at Horseshoe Bay and east toward West Vancouver, *Highway 99* now joins *Highway 1* and we come to the first major access road into the Coast Mountains; the *Cypress Bowl Parkway*. This paved road climbs up to the southern extension of Cypress provincial park where skiing is the focus in winter but hiking and scenery take the spotlight the rest of the year. From here it is possible to hike through a network of mountain trails leading to many small lakes including **First Lake (1-6)**, **Fourth Lake (1-7)**, **West Lake (1-8)**, **Blue Gentian Lake (1-9)** and **Lost Lake (1-10)** in the southeast area of the park. You can get to another set of small lakes around a hectare in size in the middle of the park accessed from the main ski parking area including **Yew Lake (1-11)**, **Turtle Lake (1-12)**, **Cabin Lake (1-13)**, **Theagill Lake (1-14)**, **Sam Lake (1-15)**, **Owen Lake (1-16)** and **Cougar Lake (1-17)**.

Six more lakes are in the same region just over the ridge in the Vancouver watershed are; **Orchid Lake (1-18)**, **Peacock Lake (1-19)**, **Macklin Lake (1-20)**, **Hanging Lake (1-21)**, **Enchantment Lake (1-22)** and **Capilano Lake (1-23)**, all restricted from use. If you are fit enough to hike the Howe Sound Crest Trail you may catch a glimpse of these lakes but that's it.

The next two, **Dick Lake (1-24)** and **Whyte Lake (1-25),** overlook Horseshoe Bay and West Vancouver but are situated in the West Vancouver watershed, also restricted from use.

Finally, **Beaver Lake (1-26)** and **Lost Lagoon (1-27)** are two more lakes right in the downtown Vancouver area in Stanley Park.

At first glance this appears to be a spectacular number of lakes but the fact is that only a small number are large enough to be considered lakes and should more appropriately be classified as *ponds*. Actually there are many more ponds in the area than I have noted but these are tiny and unnamed. They are literally scattered everywhere but are very small and, in most cases, the lakes are very shallow and muddy so do not contain fish and you most definitely cannot boat.

MARION and PHYLLIS LAKES are two high-elevation lakes snuggled in the mountains high above Porteau Cove on Howe Sound. The lakes make a 1.5 kilometer chain of water squeezed between a valley formed by the Capilano Mountain and Deeks Peak. Marion is the first lake, four hectares and 520 meters high. A long thin lake 600 meters long, it is only a slight distance below its twin Phyllis Lake at six hectares and 530 meters. Phyllis Creek, the access route, flows northwest toward the ocean, having carved a massive gash into the Britannia Range. Phyllis Lake is actually at the headwaters just a few hundred kilometers from the Greater Vancouver water supply area. Just over the divide is the headwaters of the Capilano River which flows in the opposite direction. So this is an interesting area, taking you deep into the wilderness. The two lakes are a mere 500 meters apart, providing an excellent day's outing if you hike along the old logging roads.

FINDING the LAKES

Access this area from Highway 99 and onto the logging road cutting off the main road. After crossing the bridge at Furry Creek (about three kilometers north of Porteau provincial park) begin the climb up a long stretch of highway. On the right at 26.7 kilometers from the Horseshoe Bay gate, a logging road turns back into the valley on the right. It has a gate across it to keep vehicles like yours out. Access to the lake is becoming more of a problem each year as a private golf course is being developed at the entrance area. Persevere—the trip is worth it! With the excep-

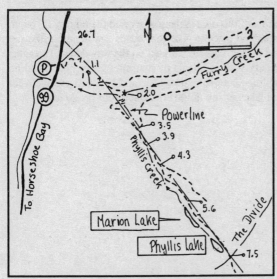

Finding Marion and Phyllis Lakes

tion of the development the land is Crown forest beyond. After parking at the gate get your best boots out for a good hike.

The total elevation gain is 460 meters from the highway and the distance is about seven kilometers to the end of Phyllis Lake. As an estimate one way, allow three hours at a steady pace. Once through the gate you will start at 60 meters in elevation and curve around to the left climbing quickly to 180 meters at .8 kilometers. From here the road flattens, paralleling Furry Creek until the junction at 1.1 kilometers. Take the right branch (the left one takes you up the north side of Furry Creek) and at two kilometers (after crossing the bridge across Furry Creek) you will have climbed to 300 meters and turned due south. Here you loop around to cross Phyllis Creek. From here you will loop down across the power-line and back toward Phyllis Creek then parallel to it on the south side at a more graceful climb following the power-line. At 3.5 kilometers keep right (straight through) and continue to parallel the creek. You will be at about 400 meters and 3.9 kilometers when you come to the next bridge. At 4.3 kilometers (460 meters elevation) keep right and continue to parallel the east side of the creek. Marion Lake will be the first lake on your right at just over 5.6 kilometers and an elevation of 520 meters. Phyllis is at 6.5 kilometers. The road continues to the divide (at 7.5 kilometers) marking the Vancouver watershed where entry is restricted.

RECREATION

The most impressive feature of this area is the scenery and the hiking. If you are a mountain-biker this is a good place to give your quads a workout on the way up and your knuckles and brakes a decent workout on the way down. The valley is impressive for its scenery with remnants of campsites along the shoreline. There are no formal facilities here so expect little and you will receive a lot. Fish are reported in these lakes so you might even catch your breakfast.

DEEKS LAKE   1-3
HANOVER LAKE   1-4
BRUNSWICK LAKE   1-5

DEEKS, HANOVER and **BRUNSWICK LAKES** are set high on the ridge overlooking Howe Sound in the northern section of Cypress Park, above Highway 99 to Squamish. The north section forms a small part of the total 3000 hectare Cypress provincial park, the main section of which is in the upper reaches of the North Shore Mountains above West Vancouver. The park is divided into two distinct areas; one overlooking Vancouver and the other smaller area to the north overlooking Howe Sound. The two areas are joined by a thin strip paralleling the ridge of the escarpment. This thin strip contains the almost ten-kilometer Howe Sound Crest Trail. The north section of the park is situated high up in the forest overlooking Howe Sound providing a rich variety of alpine and sub-alpine scenery and vista views. Without a doubt this is a place to experience an incredible hiking and camping adventure if you are up to it.

Although there are several lakes in the area only three are really accessible. There is no easy way to get to these since you need to climb to 1080 meters and walk 6.7 kilometers from the highway just to get to the first one, Deeks Lake. The three lakes form a chain that parallels the mountain tops, offering a good look at sub-alpine vegetation and Howe Sound. Deeks is the largest of the three, at an elevation of 1080 meters, the first in line on the hike. From here the trail heads southeast to Hanover Lake at a lofty 1170 meters. Then another climb to 1270 meters will get you to Brunswick Lake in an alpine setting.

FINDING the LAKES

These lakes are not for the unprepared hiker. The trailhead is directly across from the paved parking lot at 21.4 kilometers from the intersection of Highways 99 and 1 at Horseshoe Bay (use the traffic control gate on the highway as zero). The parking lot is on the left and the trailhead is directly across the road.

The hike is a tough one with a suggested time of two to three hours to the outlet end of Deeks Lake if you are in good shape. The ascent is significant (i.e. 1.2 kilometers vertical in 6.7 kilometers) so you want to make sure you are up to the challenge. *To be safe, double the time on the uphill route.* You should be prepared to camp overnight *just in case* so take the appropriate gear. As a word of caution, the weather changes very quickly and gets rough.

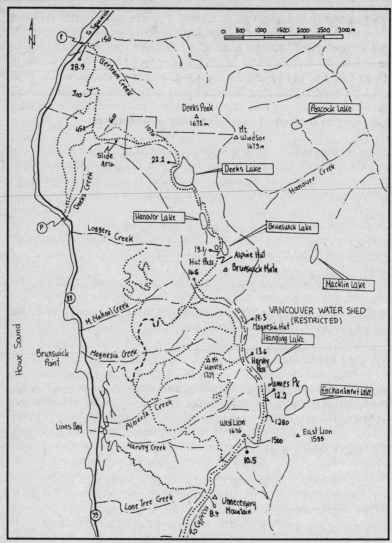

North Cypress Park roads and trails

The clouds bump against the ridge as they blow inland so they can cover the ridge with rain and fog—a bit unnerving for the unprepared. At times you may not be able to see more than ten meters, so take care and be prepared. This is *not* a casual afternoon hike, even for the experienced! Every year several hikers get lost in this area and are never found. Keep this in mind when you consider this hike.

Starting from the trailhead at the highway you will climb briskly then cross Bertram Creek. This is actually a side trail connecting with the main trail about two kilometers after Bertram Creek. You will undertake some steady climbing in a southerly direction under some impressive rock bluffs. Take a left on the Deeks Lake trail and avoid a dangerous slide area along the lower route. Signs mark the problem indicating the bypass route to the north. You will eventually get back on the logging road after 1.5 kilometers and begin a decline to Deeks Lake, the first and largest lake at an elevation of 1080 meters.

To get to Hanover Lake, the next in the chain, you need to climb to 1170 meters and hike another 2.2 kilometers from the north end of Deeks. The trail follows the southern shoreline to the creek, then parallel to it for 500 meters. It then crosses the creek within a half kilometer of the lake.

As the final climax you will climb a three-meter rope up a rock ledge before finally reaching Hanover Lake at 1170 meters. The total distance from the highway will be 8.9 kilometers.

To reach Brunswick Lake you will need to continue another kilometer. This time you will begin a final ascent of another 100 meters into an alpine wilderness at 1270 meters in elevation. You will cross the stream again before reaching the lake for a total distance of 9.9 kilometers.

FACILITIES

Don't go up here hoping to find a Hilton hotel; facilities are definitely not for the faint-hearted nor are they designed to compete with other provincial park camping facilities. These are primitive and rough though select areas have been cleared by dedicated campers who have all contributed a bit of shoe-leather and ingenuity to wear out open campsites. As you approach the final lake you gain considerable elevation; 1270 meters which is about as high as the trail will take you and this area is exposed to harsh elements. Just beyond Brunswick Lake you can continue along the Crest Trail to climb another 100 meters and visit the alpine shelter if you need it.

DEEKS LAKE You will arrive here by following the north side of Deeks Creek. Deeks is the lower lake sitting at 1080 meters and is the largest at 25 hectares. As you approach the lake the area just along the north shoreline provides open grounds and lake access. A little trail parallels the shore to another open spot on the north end of the lake. The main trail crosses Deeks Creek at the outlet and parallels the lakeshore through the woods all the way around to the south inlet where a few more campsites can be found. Sheer rock cliffs comprise the eastern shoreline so the side trail stops at the bluff.

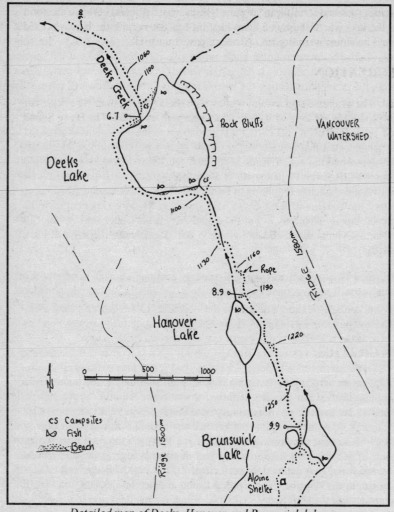

Detailed map of Deeks, Hanover and Brunswick lakes

HANOVER LAKE is a smaller lake of three hectares about midway sitting at 1170 meters. The trail follows the north shore then continues up the east creek to Brunswick. A little footpath leads to an open fishing spot near the north end at the creek outlet.

BRUNSWICK LAKE at 1270 meters is also about three hectares with some decent spots with remnants of fire pits. The area is much more open with characteristic rock and scrub alpine terrain. The campsite is found between the pond and the lake where there is a short side trail to the north end. If it gets cold there is an alpine warming hut up the hill past Brunswick.

RECREATION

Trails The extensive trail system is shown on the adjoining map. The scale bar shows the trails are long with considerable gains in elevation. The Howe Sound Crest Trail is the main one. Part of it is used to get to the lakes. This is a rugged 30-kilometer trail that actually begins at the south part of Cypress Park off the main upper parking lot. It leads north past the Lions to Deeks Lake before dropping to Highway 99 just south of Porteau Cove provincial park. So if you *really* want a challenge try hiking to Deeks Lake from the other end. Sections of the trail are rough and it's easy to lose your way so only experienced well-equipped experts should try it. For the record, here is the whole journey (refer to the North Cypress roads and trails map a few pages back...the distances are marked):

South Cypress Park Trailhead to Strachan Meadows This section is 2.6 kilometers taking about .75 hour offering good photo opportunities at Lions View Lookout. A short side trail to the west leads to the Bowen Island look-out and provides a glimpse of Howe Sound. Be sure to fill your water bottles here as the next fresh water source may be well beyond the Lions.

Strachan Meadows to St. Marks Summit This section is 2.9 kilometers (5.5 kilometers total) taking 1.25 hours (two hours total). The trail climbs 275 meters vertically to the summit of St. Marks Mountain and a short side trail to the west provides an expansive view of Howe Sound.

St. Marks Summit to Unnecessary Mountain (South Peak) The next section is 2.9 kilometers totaling 8.4. This will add 1.25 hours for a total of 3.25 hours. The developed trail continues a short distance down the north side of St. Marks Mountain but beyond this point the trail is undeveloped although flagging marks the next section. This is a fairly steep climb of 200 meters to the ridge of Unnecessary Mountain. Once on the ridge, the route narrows and the trail is easy to follow. Watch for the flags and remember to stay on the ridge.

Unnecessary Mountain (South Peak) to Base of the West Lion This section is 2.1 kilometers (10.5 total) adding 1.25 hours (4.5 hours total). Allow yourself time to enjoy the spectacular scenery but watch your footing. Often the trail splits into multiple paths resembling braids, so please stay on the flagged route to prevent further damage to the sub-alpine vegetation. Just past the south peak of Unnecessary Mountain a trail from Lion's Bay to the west links up with the Howe Sound Crest Trail. Be sure to stay on the ridge. The trail then descends the north side of Unnecessary Mountain and leads toward the base of the Lions. Be careful on several short but steep sections, particularly if the rock is wet. Closer to the base of the west Lion the route branches. To the east the trail switchbacks down and across to take you between the Lions toward Porteau Cove. A side trail to the west descends a short distance before climbing the steep and tough rock face of the west Lion. This is recommended for climbers and advanced hikers only and the views are spectacular.

West Lion to James Peak The short jaunt is 1.7 kilometers (12.2 kilometer total), taking two hours (6.5 hours total). North of the Lions the marked route drops quickly, skirting the east base of Thomas Peak along an open slope of large boulders. The trail climbs again to Enchantment Pass then follows the steep southern ridge leading to the summit of James Peak. Use caution when crossing the short rope section of the ridge. James Peak offers splendid views in all directions.

James Peak to Harvey Creek Saddle is 1.40 kilometers (13.6 kilometers total) taking one hour (7.5 hours total). The route follows down the northwest slope of James Peak onto a meadow in the saddle between James and David peaks. Beyond the meadow the trail drops quickly to avoid the east-facing cliffs of David Peak. Directly north of David Peak the trail climbs rapidly, traversing more large boulder fields until reaching the saddle on the ridge between David Peak and Harvey Pass. Watch carefully for trail markers on open slopes.

Harvey Creek to Magnesia Meadows Hut is a short .7-kilometer hike (14.3 kilometers total), adding about ten minutes. The developed trail begins again at Harvey Creek and climbs a logged and burned slope to the head of the Harvey Creek Basin at Harvey Pass. The gentle route to the hut passes a small lake and offers dramatic views of Mt. Harvey, Howe Sound and Magnesia Meadows.

Magnesia Meadows Hut to Brunswick Mountain Trail. This is a 2.3-kilometer (16.6 kilometers total), one hour (9.5 hours total) trail that climbs slightly through the meadows before entering the forest then remains fairly level as it crosses the southern and western slopes of Brunswick Mountain before intersecting with the Brunswick Mountain Trail. Periodic views to the south feature Horseshoe Bay and Bowen Island.

Brunswick Mountain Trail to Brunswick Lake is 2.5 kilometers (19.1 kilometers total), one hour (10.5 hours total). The trail continues northeast to Hat Pass then begins the long descent to the Brunswick Lake hut. The views of Brunswick Mountain, Brunswick Lake, Mt. Hanover and the Deeks Lake Valley are superb. Take care not to disturb the vegetation in this remarkable area.

Brunswick Lake to Deeks Lake (Outlet) is another 3.2 kilometers (22.2 kilometers total), 1.5 hours (12 hours total). This section parallels the creek connecting the two lakes, crossing it twice. Use extra caution when crossing. Enjoy the waterfall and views of Middle Lake and Deeks Lake. A cleared area suitable for camping is located just beyond the Deeks Lake outlet.

Deeks Lake (Outlet) to Highway 99 is 6.70 kilometers (28.9 kilometers total), 2.5 hours (14.5 hours total). From Deeks Lake the trail climbs at first then quickly drops through a mature forest and connects with a logging road. Farther along a marked trail to the north provides the recommended higher-elevation bypass route of 1.5 kilometers avoiding a dangerous slide area along the lower route. Signs mark a short-cut trail along the bypass route to the west that winds northward to Howe Sound. A side trail to the south leads to the mouth of Deeks Creek. As the road approaches Highway 99 a marked trail to the west leads to the trailhead.

Fishing Deeks Lake is the best fishing bet with good access to lakeshore at the areas marked on the map. The woods open at the stream exit and entry areas so will provide a better alternative for throwing a line out. The fish are reportedly small but the thrill lies in catching your own breakfast! Hanover Lake has an access point just off the trail at the north end where you can scramble to water's edge for a cast into the clear water. At Brunswick, there is access near the campsite and where the stream enters at the south end. A little side trail takes off just past the pond.

SCATTERED within the south portion of Cypress Park are several little 'lakes' less than a hectare in size. Overlooking metropolitan Vancouver, this south section is much more accessible than its northern counterpart.

South Cypress Park is readily accessible via a good paved road allowing quick access into a rich variety of alpine and sub-alpine wilderness. Due to this proximity to Vancouver and its easy access the park has been the focus of extensive recreational developments expertly integrated into the landscape. In the winter the feature is downhill or cross-country skiing while hiking, mountaineering and the spectacular scenery are the summer highlight.

There are several 'lakes' in this section of the park, the first found in the cross-country skiing area once known as Hollyburn Lodge. Several picturesque sub-alpine lakes are within easy walking distance from the cross-country parking lot. These include First, West, Fourth, Blue Gentian and Lost Lakes, all in the southeast corner of the park. Although they are called lakes, they are actually just *ponds*, most under a hectare in size, many not suitable for fish because of the poor water circulation, depending on tiny little brooks. In addition, the ponds are also shallow and muddy and typically a dark brackish color resulting from accumulations of resins leached from conifers. The water has effectively reached a saturation point where the ponds are naturally polluted causing problems for fish. This dark water and the shallow depth make it easy for the sun to warm the waters in summer so fish would have extreme temperature, poor oxygen and toxic resins to deal with. In winter the cold typically freezes the shallower lakes solid, giving fish an even greater obstacle. So these pretty darkwater lakes provide homes for salamanders and frogs. The lakes are picturesque and the trail system is excellent so if you want a terrific look at sub-alpine vegetation, this place is for you. All the lakes could be walked to in one day if you wished, with picnic facilities at First and Blue Gentian.

RECREATION

Facilities The park is particularly focused on winter activities with commercial facilities including three chair lifts, double tow ropes and numerous ski runs in this open sub-alpine area. There are rentals, a ski school, licensed lounge and a cafeteria at the main parking area. You will find toilets and a first aid hut right at the main parking lot. There are also a variety of well-groomed and maintained ski-touring or cross-country trails. At the main site you will find a ski school and a place to rent equipment. Large paved parking lots are scattered throughout the area providing ample parking.

Camping is restricted in the immediate area but wilderness camping is permitted at higher elevations beyond the Alpine and Nordic ski areas and along the Howe Sound Crest Trail. They are not designated campsites so you may choose your own site. Picnic grounds are located at the Highview Lookout on the access road overlooking Vancouver and near the old Hollyburn Lodge on First Lake. Picnic facilities are also being put in at Blue Gentian Lake. Mountain bikes are permitted only on the main access road.

Skiing The park is particularly focused on providing good facilities for the cross-country and downhill skier. The trail maps provided here show the trail system and skiing facilities.

Trails The park has an excellent trail system with a fair amount of traffic, particularly in the southerly sections. The trails penetrate deeply into wilderness areas essentially networking sub-alpine terrain in some very rugged sections offering you a wide variety of panoramic views. The degree of difficulty varies considerably as does the vegetation. With reference to the trail map, the main trails are as follows:

Baden Powell Centennial Trail This is one of the more lengthy trails in the region, extending 41.7 kilometers from Horseshoe Bay to Deep Cove along the North Shore Mountains. Two sections pass through Cypress provincial park.

Black Mountain Loop Trail is a 2.5-kilometer, 1.75-hour round-trip trail. The elevation change is 100 meters not including the distance and time for access along Baden Powell Trail to the Black Mountain Loop Trail that winds through sub-alpine meadows, skirting several little lakes. For a detailed look at this trail, see the next cluster of lakes 1-12 to 1-17.

Lodge Trails These are a network of trails varying in length and difficulty linking the areas surrounding Hollyburn Lodge accessed via the Hollyburn cross-country parking lot. For details see the lakes 1-6 to 1-10

Hollyburn Mountain Trail is a six-kilometer, 2.5-hour round-trip trail with an elevation change of 440 meters beginning north of the power-line road in the Hollyburn Ridge parking area. From here proceed either along the trail or via the Hollyburn Lodge route at the east end of the parking lot. The trails meet farther along the ridge then climb to the peak at 1325 meters.

Horseshoe Bay to Cypress Bowl This is a *brutal* 8.5-kilometer, one-way trail that will cost you 6 hours and the 1040-meter climb is tough. The western start is in the parking lot at the north end of Eagle Ridge Drive (just off Highway 1) overlooking Horseshoe Bay. This first segment is the steepest on the entire trail which then goes up to Eagle Ridge, over Black Mountain, then into the Cypress Bowl Ski area.

Hollyburn Ridge-British Properties takes 9.5 kilometers one way. This trail will take 3.75 hours but the elevation change is only 70 meters. The trail's second access point is in Cypress provincial park either from the alpine or the cross-country ski area parking lot. From Cypress Bowl the trail follows the road to the cross-country area along the Burfield Trail to Hollyburn Lodge then down to Blue Gentian Lake. From here the trail follows Lawson Creek to the BC Hydro right-of-way and the British Properties.

Yew Lake Trail This 1.5-kilometer loop will take only 45 minutes. It is a self-guiding trail that begins across from the ticket office and is highlighted by forest, meadows and small lakes, returning to the base of the Black Mountain chair lift. See Yew Lake 1-11 for details.

Howe Sound Crest Trail This is a rugged 30-kilometer trail that begins in the upper parking lot and leads north via the Lions and Deeks Lake before dropping to Highway 99 just south of Porteau Cove provincial park. Sections of the trail are rough and easy to lose so only experienced well-equipped experts should try it. See the section on Trails under Deeks Lake 1-3 to 1-5.

FINDING the LAKES

The easiest way to get to this cluster of lakes is to take exit 8 onto the Cypress Parkway from Highway 1. This is an easy climb up Hollyburn Mountain into Cypress Bowl. The paved road climbs gracefully making several switchbacks. At 13 kilometers take a sharp turn onto the right fork taking you to cross-country parking lot number 4. From here you can visit all five lakes following good walking trails.

FIRST LAKE is at 960 meters and less than a hectare in size. Take the hiking trail at the south end of parking lot number 4 to the fire access road, about 500 meters into the tall trees. You will dead-end on this road so take a left and follow it to the old Hollyburn Lodge site, about 350 meters more. Take a right between the old lodge and ahead you will see a picnic site overlooking First Lake with an interesting old ski lodge. The sub-alpine conifers and the lake setting are the prettiest in the area. Total walking distance is .9 kilometers.

WEST LAKE is the larger of the lakes but not as interesting as First Lake. It sits at around a hectare and 870 meters in elevation. From First Lake follow the Old Forks Trail along the lakeshore to the dam and the bridge at the south end. The ranger's cabin just to right of the bridge is where you'll find local maps and information. Continue over the bridge onto the Grand National Trail for about 160 meters, passing the Sitzmark intersection, on to the Jack Pratt Trail, an additional 250 meters. Take a left onto Jack Pratt Trail and follow it down an easy slope to West Lake, 650 meters more. You can sit at the east end on the gravel dike near the dam for a rest. Total walking distance is about two kilometers from the lot.

BLUE GENTIAN LAKE is a bit more exciting at less than a hectare and 810 meters high. Starting from West Lake you will take a much rougher trail that plunges down into the gully just a bit west of the dam. This trail follows the creek for about 220 meters where you will encounter a left fork to Blue Gentian. This trail continues for another 220 meters plunging into the lush gully even farther down through the woods to finally emerge at this little lake of less than a hectare. Total distance from the car is 2.5 kilometers. A new boardwalk goes half-way around the lake and there are a few new picnic tables to rest at. The lake is small and shallow, giving way to lilies and marsh, but a pretty site.

LOST LAKE is another 700 meters east of Blue Gentian, dropping to an elevation of 770 meters and just under a hectare. Take the trail that continues from the north end of Blue Gentian Lake. It drops to the creek. Take the foot-bridge across the creek here and continue through the rock bluffs and canyon. The trail enters the lake at the horseshoe at the south end. From here you trek all the way back just over 3.2 kilometers in total.

FOURTH LAKE is 1010 meters, also less than a hectare in size best accessed from the top end of parking lot 4 near the information sign. You can park near the information board before the first hut near the power-line. From the parking lot, take the power-line road up the hill, past both the Burfield and Sitzmark Trails (about 500 meters to the bottom of the hill) and continue up the hill, keeping to the right on the bypass. At about 600 meters you will pass the warming hut and the Baden Powell Trail. Fourth Lake is a short distance along the latter. Fourth Lake is the fourth (would you believe) of a small chain that parallels the power-line. A set of ponds is named First (Elsvik), Second, Third, Fourth and Fifth. Sixth and Seventh are farther up but are really tiny ponds. There are no facilities at these lakes, but you can rest on the rocks on Fourth Lake. If you were ambitious and wanted to continue the trek from Lost Lake you would backtrack to Blue Gentian then back to West Lake.

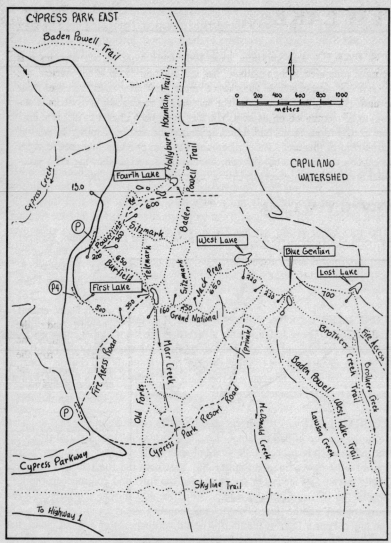

East Cypress Park lakes and trails

From there head back toward First Lake taking the Baden Powell Trail just before First Lake and heading north to reach Fourth. Either way needs a bit of steady climbing to reach the power-line road at the crest of the hill. From the car using the short route it is 1.1 kilometer to the lake.

YEW LAKE is long and thin, about 300 meters long. At two hectares it is enormous compared to its neighbors. Set at a high elevation of 930 meters, the lake is about dead-center of the south Cypress Park area easily accessed from the main parking lot. This little lake has such a fascinating ecosystem it deserves to be mentioned on its own. Yew has aptly been chosen to describe how water in its various forms has played an important part in shaping the natural environment of this area. The trail around the lake provides interpretive signs that explain the features but the lake itself is the surprise, showing off a spectacular array of seldom-seen sub-alpine vegetation and aquatic life.

FINDING YEW LAKE

Yew Lake is reached from the main parking lot at the Cypress Bowl ski area

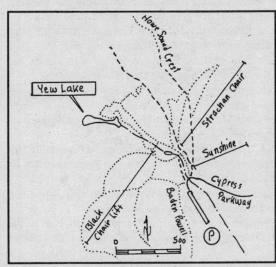

Finding Yew Lake

15.2 kilometers from Highway 1. Take the Yew Lake Interpretive Trail which loops around the north end of the lake to follow the lakeshore. From the main parking lot take the gravel walk slightly up the hill toward the Black Mountain chair lift, about 400 meters away. Keep left after the Baden Powell Trail, past the small pond on the right to reach the lift. The Yew Lake trail is just past the chair lift where you should pick up an interpretation pamphlet. This trail is described in detail later on.

RECREATION

Facilities at the lake are simple, designed for the nature-lover with two picnic tables, one at the north end of the main lake where the trail curves down to the lakeshore with a small gravel area overlooking the lake. The second table is at the east end of the lake where it is set carefully by itself on a little gravel area. That's it! The plan here is to provide you with a chance to *observe* nature and not to sleep with it. This is an excellent place to just stroll and ponder the many life forms here.

Interpretive Trail The Yew Lake Trail is the highlight beginning past the ticket office following the babbling brook up to the lake. The trail, a full 1.4 kilometers, is easy flat walking, returning to the base of the Black Mountain chair lift. A total of 15 interpretive markers, each noting a particular natural feature of the area, follow the trail. Starting from the first marker just past the Black Mountain chair lift, the features are as follows:

Marker 1 The interest here is the water and the deer cabbage, a semi aquatic plant that flanks the stream. It is found only at high altitudes and its rather rank smelling white blossoms will be easy to find.

Marker 2 Trail-side snacks are the issue here, identifying the billberry, huckleberry and raspberry plants that grow naturally in the area.

Marker 3 The buzz of insects will verify that Yew Lake has more bugs (especially mosquitoes) per cubic meter of air than anywhere else!

Marker 4 The pungent odor of skunk is sure to allow you to identify the large leafed lily known as skunk cabbage—the feature here.

Marker 5 Rotting rock is decomposed granite. The process of running water helps to transform the granite to soil.

Marker 6 The yellow water lily is prolific in this area acting like green islands which harbor a multitude of aquatic insects.

Marker 7 The bogbean, a juicy meal for deer, also acts as a "dragon fly ladder" for the aquatic dragonfly nymph to climb up in preparation for its transformation into an adult.

Marker 8 The first plant, mainly algae, is identified in this area. If you look close, you will see this prolific fish food, but no fish!

Marker 9 A glacial boulder deposited by the last glacier sits here in the swamp. It looks much like a foreign object that doesn't belong here, creating a very odd sight.

Marker 10 The main inhabitant of these little ponds is the northwestern salamander. His life is explained and you may even see one.

Marker 11 The deadly trap, the bog plant or Round-Leafed Sundew is found in this area, attracting insects and eating them. They should be well fed around here.

Marker 12 Sway-backs or bent tree trunks, a slow deformation of the tree trunks caused by the weight of heavy snow, are explained here.

Marker 13 Mosses are abundant at this stop. The many varieties in the bog are covered at this stop.

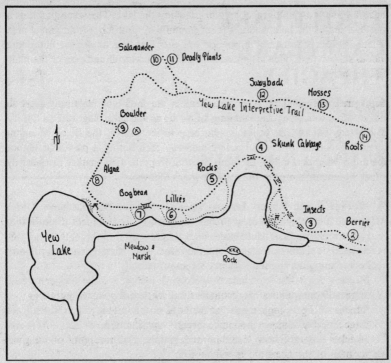

Detailed map of Yew Lake

Marker 14 How roots branch down to pick up water is the highlight here. Their plight to reach downward into the water table is clearly illustrated.

Marker 15 Lichens that hang from the trees, with no roots, but with yellow threads, are common in this area, with several examples. The uniqueness of this plant is explained here.

Fishing is inadvisable since you are more likely to catch a salamander or a lily pad stem and the lake is shallow with a mud bottom, not supportive of fish life.

ANOTHER set of small lakes is situated elegantly near the top of Black Mountain at an elevation of 1217 meters, just west of the main Cypress Park parking lot. These little lakes make up a cluster scattered throughout the timbered rock slopes near the peak. The terrain in this area is characteristically rocky, varying quite significantly in vegetation.

A completely different set of sub-alpine lakes, these are quite a contrast to their neighbors, sitting as high up as you will get in this region. The cluster has a good trail system looping around to cover Cougar, Owen, Theagill, Sam and Cabin lakes around Black Mountain and Yew Lake to the north of the main section. All of the lakes are less than a hectare in size, but each has its own striking character.

There are actually several other little lakes scattered here, sitting in little swampy basins formed from the annual melting snow. Water is effectively trapped in the rock outcrop gullies found everywhere, forming a terrain of smooth flat rocks, little meadows, marshes and conifers lining the lakes. Little gurgling streams join the lakes adding to the postcard-quality scenes. The lakes are typically shallow and marshy, except for Cabin Lake which is the featured swimming hole.

FINDING the LAKES

There are several ways to reach these lakes, two of which need a brisk climb. First, from the Cypress parking lot, face straight north toward the main ski areas. Now take a look to your left over your shoulder. That is Black Mountain at an elevation of 1217 meters, some 200 meters higher than you are.

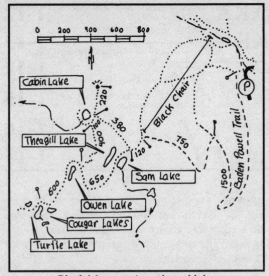

Black Mountain's trails and lakes

You can take the Baden Powell Trail that snakes up the mountain from the end of the parking lot. You will see the scar on the hill—it is about 2.2 kilometers of solid climbing or you can walk to the foot of the Black Mountain chair lift and climb up the open areas used for skiing. They swing back and forth under the lift. This route is about a kilometer shorter but it is much steeper.

A much faster alternative is to take the lift for $2.00 one way and get to the top in about ten minutes. Since it runs year round, it is certainly the easiest method. With reference to the trail map, get to the top where the Black Mountain Loop Trail begins just behind the lift where you plunge down into the lush forest. Here the trail will allow you to visit all the lakes within two hours. The following excursion takes you on a tour of the lakes, assuming you have taken the chair lift to the summit. To get to the start of the loop trail from the summit you need to hike 120 meters into the gully. The Loop Trail goes left to Theagill and the Baden Powell Trail while the right fork goes to Cabin Lake and the Black Mountain Summit (1217m). Take the left fork.

THEAGILL LAKE at 1150 meters elevation is less than one hectare in size. Get to the Loop Trail by hiking 120 meters to the junction then take a right and within 100 meters and a few minutes Theagill, a cigar-shaped lake, will appear on the right. A side trail takes you to a view of the lake just about five meters above the shore. The lake is set in a bit of a hole, disguised by the browny-brackish water but is in a particularly pleasant setting with rocks on either side. Continuing along the trail there is a small side path to take you down to the south end where a little stream spills out into neighboring Sam Lake where you will find a favorite spot to rest and sun on the shoreline.

SAM LAKE is also at an elevation of 1150 meters, under one hectare just opposite the trail past Theagill. It is a bit larger with some great sunning rocks just on the left shore as you approach the lake. This lake looks a bit deeper and is not quite as brown. As you cross the creek, another side path takes you to the south shore for a good view of the lake.

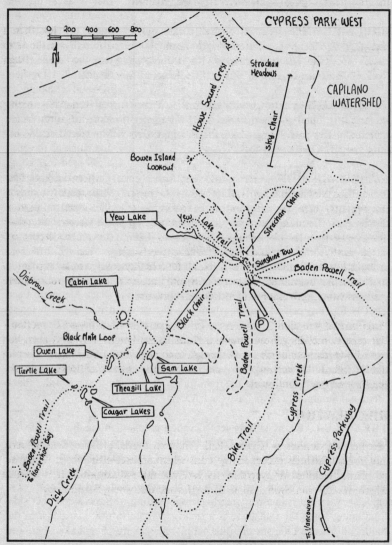

West Cypress Park lakes and trails

OWEN LAKE is also less than a hectare set in another hole at 1160 meters and open to the south. Just before Owen leave the Black Mountain Loop Trail that takes you right and back up the mountain to Cabin Lake and back to the chair lift. This marks 650 meters from the last trail intersection. As you come down and around the Baden Powell Trail you will find shoreline access along the trail. This is about .8 kilometers from the chair lift.

COUGAR LAKES are a set of small ponds at 1120 meters, all less than a hectare in size forming a cluster of lakes about 500 meters from the trail fork to Black Mountain. The trail passes by the main ponds giving you an excellent look at sub-alpine vegetation. This is 1.0 kilometers from the lift.

TURTLE LAKE is a tiny pond situated at 1130 meters in elevation, less than a hectare. It is found at total distance of 1.2 kilometers from the lift or just a few hundred meters past Cougar Lake. From here double back to the Black Mountain Loop Trail 600 meters back.

CABIN LAKE at 1170 meters is also less than a hectare. After doubling back to the Black Mountain Loop Trail for about 600 meters, climb steadily to one of the summits where you can climb on the rocks to gasp at the sight and perhaps for some air. Continue into a gully and ahead will appear the feature lake about 400 meters from the intersection at Owen Lake. Cabin Lake is a bit deeper and set elegantly within rounded rocks guarding the shoreline. You will first enter on a little gravel beach area which gives you a chance to dive in for a swim. A trail branches around the other end providing access to the large rocks where you can swim again, enjoy a sandwich and some sun.

From here it is a short 220 meters to the viewpoint overlooking some spectacular scenery including Howe Sound and the Baden Powell Trail that takes you back down past the north end of Theagill and back to the main intersection to the lift (about 380 meters). Now you can take the chair lift or hike down, depending on how keen you are.

RECREATION

See previous sections on Cypress Park. The area around the lakes does not have any formal facilities except for the trails which are well-maintained. There are no picnic facilities so everything is very natural and beautiful. It is an area where you can sun, swim, talk to the eagles and really merge with nature.

SEVERAL LAKES are tucked away in the Greater Vancouver watershed, reserved for finer things than recreation. The vast watershed contains many little lakes as well as several larger ones, notably Orchid (1054 meters, four hectares), Peacock (1180 meters, four hectares), Macklin (900 meters, five hectares), Hanging (1110 meters, four hectares) and Enchantment (1030 meters, 24 hectares). The largest is Capilano Lake at 200 hectares at an elevation of 144 meters. It can be viewed from the Cleveland dam at the south end but is also restricted from use. If you want a really spectacular view of the lake try the Grouse Mountain chair lift.

Two others, Dick and Whyte Lakes are set on a bench in the West Vancouver watershed just above West Vancouver, also restricted from access. Whyte Lake is at 325 meters, less than a hectare in size and Dick Lake or *Eagle Lake*, is 9 hectares and an elevation of 390 meters.

BEAVER LAKE and **LOST LAGOON** are two medium-sized bodies of water situated in Stanley Park in the heart of metropolitan Vancouver. Stanley Park is a vast recreational playground of just over 400 hectares, not a particularly large area but packed with facilities. Stanley Park is world-famous, including an incredible list of facilities and features. It has ocean shorelines, an ancient forest, two freshwater lakes, a spawning stream, aquarium, zoo, playgrounds, beaches, picnic and historic sites, meadows, seawall promenade, restaurants and other highlights that service some eight million visitors a year.

Since the park has been expertly described in the book *Vancouver's Famous Stanley Park* by Mike Steele, (1993 Heritage House) it is not my intention to duplicate his tremendous effort. The book covers everything you would ever need to know about the park and is available in the park's gift shops.

BEAVER LAKE is four hectares at an elevation of about 20 meters and is a shallow marshy lake in the middle of the park surrounded by a good trail system. Beaver Lake is dominated by water lilies and marsh grass creating a most spectacular scene when the lilies are in blossom. The lake has also become a bird sanctuary where thousands of waterfowl visit to be fed by strolling visitors.

Finding Beaver Lake Take the Stanley Park Causeway and veer to the right as you leave Georgia Street just as you pass Coal Harbour. This is the Stanley Park turnoff which will take you to the zoo and the one-way road encircling the park. Just as you peel off to the right take the left fork (Pipeline Road two-way traffic) which cuts north across the park and will take you to the closest access trail to the lake. At about .8 kilometers from the intersection you should see a trail sign on the left where you will see the Tisdall Trail, a mere 100 meters from the lake. You can park along the road anywhere in this area. The Beaver Lake Trail circles the lake.

Recreation Beaver Lake has a stream emptying the lake at the north end where you will find a small but nice open gravel area with a bird-feeding dock and some benches where you can rest to observe the birds. Several park benches are positioned strategically along this east shoreline offering good views to the open water. The rest of the lake is not accessible so the trails are set back in the brush away from the swampy shoreline. From here you can connect with the park's trail system and explore at length. Beaver Lake is simply intended for day use and a place to relax with nature.

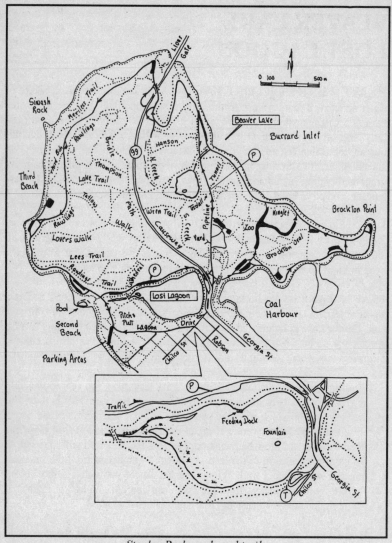

Stanley Park roads and trails

LOST LAGOON is not quite as serene and secluded as its neighbor. It is much larger at around 20 hectares, just at sea level. It was once part of the Coal Harbour sea inundation, but was cut off in the 1940s by the causeway thereby forming a lake. Over the years the lake was converted to fresh water and at one time was even reported to have large trout. Since then the lake has been taken over by waterfowl.

Finding Lost Lagoon is a lot easier than finding a place to park. The difficulty lies in the one-way system of roads (see the map). If you approach from the Vancouver side, get onto Lagoon Drive to get onto the road that cuts across the top of Lost Lagoon. Approach either from Beach Avenue which will force you right, then left onto Lagoon Drive or from Georgia Street taking Denman and cutting right on Robson or Barclay. In this area the streets change like shifting sands as the city attempts to maneuver traffic away from local apartment-dwellers' parking spots. Following Lagoon Drive will take you past the Beach House restaurant and a short two-way traffic section. You will be forced to turn right above Lost Lagoon. There are two long parking lots in this section of road. The other option is to come around the park on the one-way perimeter road to intersect the Lost Lagoon road.

Recreation Lost Lagoon is rather sedate, providing a downtown oasis for the vast population of urban-dwellers living in the concrete city of the West End. With the exception of the east end of the lagoon which borders the causeway, the lake is surrounded by trails, dotted with park benches and laden with gravel view points to feed the birds. As the map shows, these tie into a major network of park trails leading to numerous recreational facilities around the park. Around the lagoon, you can walk, jog, picnic, feed the birds and squirrels or just enjoy nature. There are tennis courts, picnic areas, playgrounds, beaches, flower gardens, restaurants, even lawn bowling, a miniature golf course and cycle paths to enjoy...but the area is *intensely* used!

REGION TWO
NORTH VANCOUVER

THE NORTH VANCOUVER REGION is the second strip of mountainous terrain adjacent to the West Vancouver region. It covers a ten-kilometer wide by 35-kilometer long strip bounded on the east by Indian Arm and on the south by the middle of Burrard Inlet. North Vancouver is the main city covering most of the extreme southern portion. From here wilderness invades just as rapidly from the north as the elevation rises. This particular region is divided into four vast wilderness areas; Lynn Headwaters Regional Park, Seymour Demonstration Forest, Mount Seymour Provincial Park and the Greater Vancouver water supply area. Most of this area is accessible only by hiking. The Seymour River and Lynn Creek are two drainage systems cut deeply into the plateau region of the Coast Mountains where the peaks reach elevations beyond 1300 meters. These areas contain an impressive list of recreational facilities and lakes but, like the neighboring region, the majority of accessible lakes are small ponds that only offer their spectacular sub-alpine terrain settings as recreational features. For this reason the lakes are not of too much interest to a fisherman or boater and unfortunately the larger lakes are hidden away in the restricted areas.

From a recreation standpoint, the whole southern fringe is a playground of private and public facilities, all bordering the city limits. Many smaller parks have been set aside for public use, but the larger places such as Grouse Mountain and Seymour Park are famous for winter sports and summer hiking. The Lynn Headwaters Regional Park offers an extensive trail system and the Seymour Demonstration Forest is a another vast natural playground also offering hiking, biking, educational tours, riding and fishing, all expertly managed to demonstrate how man and nature can coexist. Car access is typically limited to the southern portions so here you have to work up a sweat to get to the lakes.

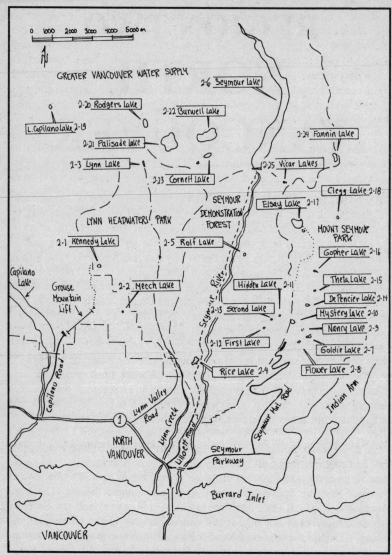

North Vancouver region roads and lakes

ROADS, ACCESS POINTS AND LAKES

Trans-Canada Highway 1 is the southern access route paralleling the coastline along Burrard Inlet traversing along the bottom of the region through North Vancouver. From *Highway 1* there are three key roadways. First, *Capilano Road* will take you through the Capilano River Regional Park, then north past the Cleveland dam at Capilano Lake and to the Grouse Mountain chair lift. This is the easy way of getting to the top of the mountain where you will see **Kennedy Lake (2-1)** and the tiny **Meech Lake (2-2)**. From here you can hike down into Lynn Headwaters Regional Park to see the more remote and tiny **Lynn Lake (2-3)**, accessed through tough hiking trails only. Alternatively, continue along the *Trans-Canada* to take the *Lynn Valley Road* exit into Lynn Headwaters Regional Park then hike into the valley.

The next important road that takes you north off the freeway into the mountains is *Lillooet Road* going along the edge of Lynn Canyon Park directly to the parking lot at the south end of Seymour Demonstration Forest, a short distance from **Rice Lake (2-4)** and **Rolf (Lost) Lake (2-5)**. The road actually continues along Seymour River to **Seymour Lake (2-6)** but this is a watershed area so transportation is limited to bikes and boots.

Finally, the third important route from *Highway 1* is *Mount Seymour Parkway* heading east toward Deep Cove, taking you to *Seymour Mountain Road*. This is a good paved surface reaching close to the top of Mount Seymour Provincial Park where you will find an incredible maze of sub-alpine lakes and mountain trails taking you to a whole series of small lakes including **Goldie Lake (2-7)**, **Flower Lake (2-8)**, **Nancy Lake (2-9)**, **Mystery Lake (2-10)**, **Hidden Lake (2-11)**, **First Lake (2-12)**, **Second Lake (2-13)**, **De Pencier Lake (2-14)**, **Theta Lake (2-15)**, **Gopher Lake (2-16)**, **Elsay Lake (2-17)** and **Clegg Lake (2-18)**.

The rest of the region is covered by the Greater Vancouver water supply area with many small and some larger lakes within this vast isolated watershed, all of them off-limits. They include **Little Capilano (2-19)**, **Rodgers Lake (2-20)**, **Pallisade Lake (2-21)**, **Burwell Lake (2-22)**, **Cornett Lake (2-23)**, **Fannin Lake (2-24)** and **Vicar Lakes (2-25)**

KENNEDY LAKE   2-1
MEECH LAKE   2-2
LYNN LAKE   2-3

LYNN HEADWATERS PARK is now a Regional Park stretching 20 kilometers from the southern entrance at the end of Lynn Valley Road to its most northern extent. The park includes the Lynn Creek drainage basin with its multitude of raging creeks and tributaries flowing into it. It is about 12 kilometers at its widest point, bordering on the Capilano watershed on the west, the Greater Vancouver watershed on the north, the Seymour watershed on the northeast and the Seymour Demonstration Forest on the east. Within its bounds, it also contains the new Kennedy Lake watershed so there are a lot of watersheds here. The park is, without a doubt, rugged with breath-taking views and raging creeks. Much work has gone into opening a trail network in this park but despite the extent, only two tiny lakes; Meech and Lynn, are accessible and these can hardly boast about facilities. The third and largest, Kennedy Lake, is now in another newly formed watershed servicing Grouse Mountain Resort.

From a recreational standpoint these three lakes have little to offer except for the trails, natural settings, and spectacular scenery. The hikes to these lakes are the most impressive feature. Lynn and Meech are tiny ponds and Kennedy Lake is off-limits, so do not expect to have a fun time boating or fishing in this area.

FINDING the LAKES

There are several ways to get to the lakes depending on how long you want to hike. With reference to the Lynn Headwaters Trail map the main access into Lynn Headwaters Park is via the Lynn Creek entrance at the end of Lynn Valley Road. This will take you to the south parking lot and the trail system along Lynn Creek, the route recommended to Lynn Lake. The other way is Capilano Road to the end, taking the Grouse Mountain chair lift to the top of Grouse Mountain. This will get you to Kennedy and Meech Lakes.

KENNEDY LAKE at a lofty elevation of 1015 meters is around four hectares in size just south of Goat Mountain, north of the Grouse Mountain Resort. It recently became part of the Kennedy Lake watershed so access is restricted. The trail system from the Grouse Mountain ski area will allow you to skirt the lake. See the trail map and the following section on trails.

MEECH LAKE set in the little saddle between the peak of Mount Fromme (at 1170 meters) is a tiny pond less than a hectare in size situated just south of the north peak in the saddle called Senate Peak. From the names given to these two features, one would be led to believe there is some deep political significance here.

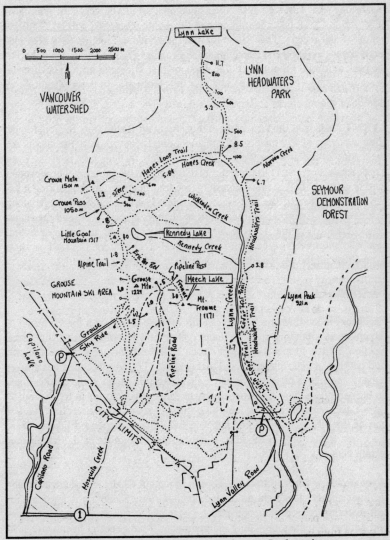

Grouse Mountain and Lynn Headwaters Park trails

I first learned of this little pond from Halvor Lunden, one of the valley's true trailblazers, who graciously showed me the access trails. According to Halvor the lake was named during the great debate about the constitution...obviously an attempt to pay tribute to the larger Meech!

To get to the pond and ponder politics as they did, take Pipeline Road that snakes down the east side of Grouse Mountain. Just as you get to the main turn at Mosquito Creek take the trail up into the divide where you will be at an elevation of 880 meters. Then climb up into the divide to Pipeline Pass (930 meters), about .5 kilometers, cut right on the Fromme Trail to climb straight up to the peak at Mount Fromme (1170 meters) another kilometer away. The distance is not great, only 1.5 kilometers total but the elevation gain is significant. So is the view.

LYNN LAKE is at the very north end of the Lynn Headwaters Regional Park, at an elevation of 790 meters. At just under one hectare in size, the lake is not the feature of the area but the hike most definitely is. This lake is at the Lynn Creek headwaters, an 11.7-kilometer hike from the park entrance. The elevation gain is worst in the last four kilometers (see trail map). From the parking lot at elevation 200 meters, the first eight kilometers is a nice gradual incline along beautiful Lynn Creek. Then things start to change, especially beyond the Hanes Creek Trail (elevation 430) to Grouse Mountain where it deteriorates and climbs to 800 meters at the same time...a great combination! The trail parallels Lynn Creek all the way so you will not be short of scenic pictures.

RECREATION

Facilities No facilities are available at any of these lakes. With the exception of the emergency landing sites in Hanes Valley and Norvan Creek-Lynn Creek junction, all the formal facilities are back at the entrance area where you will find parking, toilets, telephone and picnic tables. The entrance area has a hiker registry and this is highly advisable. Other than this expect some marker signs on the way and a lot of fantastic scenery to enjoy. If you decide to try the trail to Lynn Lake, remember it is a long hike through some rugged terrain. The last part of the hike is difficult and not suggested for inexperienced hikers. There are a few rescue huts in the area, a rather subtle reminder of the treacherous terrain here.

If you decide to come in from the Grouse Mountain Chalet side there are many facilities and services right on the mountain. Grouse Mountain is a private resort featuring rugged mountain peaks, vistas of the valley, skiing, snow rides and endless activities providing entertainment. Many special events are held here including logger sports, chair rides, wildlife shows, wood carving demonstrations, gold panning, theater in the sky, even night skiing. Backcountry hiking, helicopter tours, picnics, even paragliding can be added to the list. The kids are also catered to with playgrounds, playhouses and special events. The restaurant is world-famous and you can even shop for souvenirs. All in all, this is a power-packed recreation area designed for fun...but remember the facilities are not free.

Trails The trail system in the park is really extensive, offering a wide variety of terrain, length and degree of difficulty. Cycles, camping and fires are prohibited. Note that most of the creeks are fast and furious and this is bear country so caution is an important partner. Since this is essentially a day use area (dawn to dusk most of the time) judge the time to get in and out in one day. The trail guide shown will give you the main trails in the park.

Lynn Loop Trail (beside Lynn Creek) is 3.6 kilometers in total length taking one hour to complete. It is a nice easy trail following the creek up to the connector trail (1.8 kilometers) where you can turn around and come back to the parking lot.

Lynn Loop Trail (above Lynn Creek) is 5.7 kilometers long and takes one to two hours. It is an easy trail with some steep sections. You can take the upper trail to the connector, then loop back along the lower creek trail to avoid climbing up the switchbacks.

Lynn Loop Cedar Trail is 7.8 kilometers return. It is an easy 2.5 hour long trail that takes you by some old mill site relics. At 3.8 kilometers near the debris chute and Lynn Headwaters Trail junction, you turn around and head back.

Cedar Mills-Headwaters Loop is 9.5 kilometers taking four hours to return to the parking lot. This follows the creek then returns along the upper Headwaters Trail. It is more difficult than the lower route.

Norvan Creek This is not a trail name but a destination. It is a 15.3-kilometer return trip that will take you six hours. It follows Lynn Creek all the way and is of intermediate hiking difficulty. Norvan Falls will be your signal to turn around. It is a short ten-minute walk from the bridge.

Lynn Lake Trail is 23.4 kilometers return from the main entrance at Lynn Park, so allow the whole day. This trail extends from the Hanes Creek mouth on Lynn Creek (8.5-kilometer mark) to Lynn Lake, another 3.2 kilometers away. The elevation goes from 200 meters at the entrance to 780 meters at the lake but considering the distance this is not too brutal a vertical change. A cautionary note; this section is not well-maintained so conditions can be treacherous and you can easily get lost so *check in at the headquarters before you go.*

Lynn Headwaters to Hanes to Grouse Alpine Area. This is the route from the Lynn entrance up Lynn Creek, along Lynn Headwaters Trail, then along the Hanes Valley Route to Grouse Mountain. The distance is 15.2 kilometers one way to the kiosk. It is a very difficult route, dangerous at times, requiring eight hours one way. *Tell them at headquarters before you go.*

Lynn Peak Trail is 7.2 kilometers return taking three hours. This is a challenging trail with rough, steep sections taking you to the vicinity of Lynn peak (elevation 921 meters).

Dam Mountain Trail is a three-kilometer return trail from the Grouse Mountain alpine kiosk (one kilometer from the skyride). This is a two-hour-return, difficult trail with several rough and steep sections.

Little Goat Mountain Trail is a 3.4-kilometer excursion. The return trip from the kiosk (one kilometer from the skyride) will take three hours. The trail is also steep and rough.

Goat Ridge Trail is a nine-kilometer-return trail. From the kiosk allow six hours. This is also a difficult trail, challenging most fit hikers with several rough steep sections.

Goat Mountain Trail is 5.8 kilometers return from the kiosk and will cost four hours of energy. It is a difficult trail with steep, rough sections.

Crown Mountain Trail is a 7.6-kilometer-return trail. From the kiosk, allow six hours there and back. The trail is difficult with steep rough sections and not regularly patrolled.

Hanes Valley Trail From the kiosk at Grouse hike 3.6 kilometers to Crown Pass where you will pick up the Hanes Valley Trail, another 5.8 kilometers to Lynn Creek. The choice will then be to head *down* to Lynn another 8.2 kilometers (three hours away) or back *up* to Grouse 9.4 kilometers (five hours away). The section just north of Crown Pass is steep and rocky; a very difficult part of the hike so this may influence your plans.

The SEYMOUR DEMONSTRATION FOREST contains the next set of three lakes. This is a 5600 hectare preserved forest originally set aside as the future domestic water supply. The area is currently used to create a natural outdoor exhibit of integrated forest resource management systems open to the public during daylight hours. The idea is to demonstrate how a forest is managed to ensure the resources are used effectively. The key resources include water, wildlife, fisheries, recreation and forests. The unique aspect of this project is that they offer an impressive list of recreational facilities and educational programs to support the concept of effective management. The numerous hiking and biking trails include information panels that describe timber harvesting, reforestation, water management, spacing and thinning, fish and wildlife and recreation restoration. Over 40 kilometers of logging roads network the area, now used for hiking, biking, and horseback riding—a rather unique switch! Two small lakes, Rice and Rolf, are in this reserve and one large lake; Seymour.

FINDING the PARK ENTRANCE

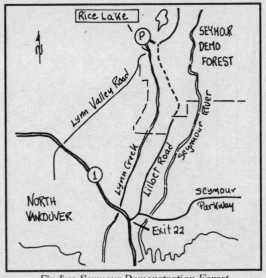

Finding Seymour Demonstration Forest

Access the lake from the Trans-Canada Highway paralleling the north shore of Vancouver. Direct access is from exit 22 which loops you around to give you the choice of proceeding north (Lillooet Road) or east (Seymour Parkway). Zero out and take the inside lane and go north along Lillooet Road. You will be amazed how fast you get into wilderness. The pavement runs out quickly and you hit gravel road and the main gate to the forest at 1.6 kilometers. Continue on the gravel road to reach the forest parking lot and office at 4.6 kilometers. The road continues all the way to the dam at Seymour Lake but is restricted to vehicle traffic although bikes are allowed for part of the way. The park office is in front of you and the parking lot is to the left through the yellow gate.

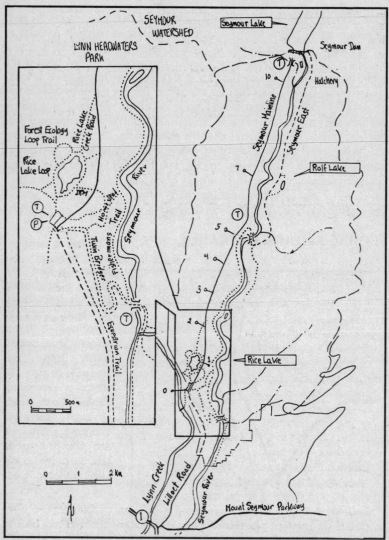

Seymour Demonstration Park trail and road system

RECREATION

Facilities This is a very different place, combining education with recreation, all focused on the management of water, wildlife, fisheries, recreation and forests. In this respect, the area is essentially protected, with no vehicles, campfires, dogs or camping allowed in the park but biking, fishing, hiking and horseback riding are allowed and are the highlights. The facilities are therefore oriented to education and day fun. Good parking facilities are provided at the entrance. There are toilets at four locations, the main entrance, Rice Lake, Mid-Valley and Seymour dam. There is also a salmon hatchery at Seymour dam. Rice Lake also has some unique facilities specially designed for the fisherman. See the detailed map.

Trails In addition to the lakes, it is worth mentioning the extensive trail system, catering to trail bikes, hikers and even horses. There are some 40 kilometers to explore and the office usually has a good supply of trail guide brochures but an extra page is provided here just in case. These trails reach a long way into the forest and are excellent in quality, usually surfaced with gravel or pavement.

> **Integrated Forest Resource Management Loop** (IRM) This is an informative 1.6-kilometer trail so allow 1.5 hours. It focuses on integrated forest management with six interpretive panels. The walk is flat and easy.
> **Forest Ecology Loop Trail** is only 400 meters long but has a good series of interpretive panels on how forest managers study the ecology and determine management treatments long before activities take place. Allow an hour to appreciate the information.
> **Seymour Falls Dam (Mainline)** This is 11 kilometers of paved road with eight designated stops to provide an overview of integrated forest management. On weekends you can only cycle half-way and on other days you can only cycle in to about the two-kilometer mark so it is a long journey but at the end you can get a look at the Seymour dam and a fish hatchery. The cycling arrangement is a bit confusing at times and they seem to change the distance allowed so it is worth asking at the office or telephone the number in the back of the book.
> **Rice Lake Loop** around the lake is 1.6 kilometers taking you in a complete circle around Rice Lake hugging the shore bushes. This flat, easy walk is the one you want if fishing is your game.
> **Equestrian Trail** This is a another loop trail for horses following the main road to the entrance gate then looping around across the river and back to the gate.
> **Twin Bridges Trail** Here is a 2.2-kilometer walk that takes you down to the bridge at the Seymour River paralleling a horse trail.
> **Fisherman's Trail** is 5.5-kilometers and parallels the Seymour River, offering selected fishing areas in season.

Homestead Trail This is a short one-kilometer connector trail between the Twin Bridges and the Fisherman's Trail.

Biking is a feature of the area. Most of the trails are bike trails with good surfaces. A lot of thought has gone into this fairly unique option. If you want to get away from cars and peddle in real fresh air through some magnificent scenery, this is your place.

Fishing Without a doubt another nice feature here is the river fishing—a special treat offering anglers a chance to catch a variety of west coast freshwater game fish...*big* ones! This is a popular sport in both Lynn Creek and Seymour River but strictly controlled so check at the office. The trails following the streams offer good access to numerous deep-green pools and unbelievable scenery. Another fishing feature is in a class of its own; the magic fishing area provided around Rice Lake, a place specially developed to accommodate anglers.

RICE LAKE is a decent size for this area at seven hectares sitting at an elevation of 190 meters at the southern end of the Seymour Demonstration Forest. Set gracefully in a lush forest, the lake was originally created by two dams constructed at opposite ends of a long ditch. The lake looks as if it is actually suspended between the two dams. The flooding process has inundated the surrounding vegetation to create a most peculiar shape. The shore is characteristically marshy with small coves and islands scattered about the perimeter. Not surprising, rough unfriendly brushes guard its shores.

RICE LAKE at a GLANCE		
ACTIVITIES	**FISHING, TRAILS, BIKING, EDUCATION**	
LAKE STATS	Elevation & Size	: 190 meters, seven hectares
	Lake Setting	: Seymour Demonstration Forest
ACCESS	Vehicle Type	: car, plus one-kilometer walk
	Nearest Highway	: 4.6 kilometers to Highway 1
FACILITIES	Type & Class	: organized, focus on day use
	Camping	: not allowed
	Boat Launch	: not allowed
FISHING	Fish Stocked	: not required
	Size Reports	: rainbows to 30 cm, tales of two kgs
	Restrictions	: no flotation devices
		: GVRD fishing permit

Believe it or not, this little lake was created to provide a water supply to the early North Vancouver residents. A few little streams trickle in on the sides so there is some water movement, certainly enough to harbor fish life.

FINDING RICE LAKE

To get to Rice Lake start from the Seymour Demonstration Forest parking lot. If you haven't read the previous section on how to find this parking lot, backtrack a few pages to *Finding the Park Entrance*. Information boards and the trailhead to the lake, a short one-kilometer walk are at the north end of the lot. The lake is only ten minutes of level walking on good gravel walkways. At the second fork the trail goes around the lake and the right fork offers the best lake access, leading across the south end dam. This trail takes you to an elaborate dock network and several open areas where you can cast a line. There are other conspicuous foot-trails that will take you to the lake's edge, but the best access to the lake is the dock and the dams at the ends.

RECREATION

Facilities at the lake are particularly focused on fishing. The dock is specially designed for fishermen with wooden boardwalks poking out in different directions, offering a way to reach the deeper sections. The Rice Lake trail surrounds the lake and is about 1.5 kilometers long. The lake itself has a lonesome picnic table, a few garbage cans and a toilet, but the feature is indeed the fishing dock. The lake is designed for day use only, so don't get too excited about rising at dawn to catch those big fish!

Fishing in the lake is not as easy if you want to try the west shoreline. The detailed lake map shows the deepest section is a mere five meters, with the deeper holes in hard-to-access places. A deeper channel runs the length of the lake—obviously the original manmade ditch. The west side is shallow and marshy, particularly where the inundated coves poke into the heavy vegetation. The brush is thick but a few footpaths have been worn to lake's edge. An open area can be found at the north end where the lake drains into the Seymour River. Here you can cast out easily. However the best location is the elaborate dock system on the east side—reaching into the open water just far enough to make you perform an outstanding cast. Another popular spot is on the rocks at the southwest end where you push your way through a short footpath through the bushes. This is always a hard spot to get to unless you are at the gate at whistle time but as you can see from the depth contours the water is deeper here quite close to shore, obviously a good spot for those *huge* lunkers to hide.

Another obvious spot is at the south end where the open trail allows you to cast into the deeper channel (again you need a good arm). There is another hole between the two little islands just opposite the dock. Take the little footpath off the main trail to ford the little water channel to the island. The path leads to the lakeside open area.

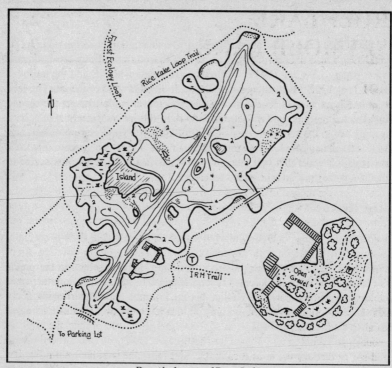

Detailed map of Rice Lake

The stocking program began in 1990, with the fisheries placing rainbow catch-ables into the lake in subsequent years. The total number is unknown.

ROLF LAKE   2-5
SEYMOUR LAKE   2-6

ROLF LAKE also known as *Lost Lake* is situated in the Seymour Demonstration Forest. If you need information on this forest and how to get there, read the detailed description for Rice Lake (2-4) in the previous section. Rolf is a tiny lake of around two hectares sitting in the bush at an elevation of 230 meters. Not publicized much, the lake has remained hidden and obscure, probably the reason it was called *lost*. In discussing this lake with forest management, they suggested they would prefer to keep the little lake in a natural state and that there were no real plans to develop it like its neighbor, Rice Lake. The lake is not deep and is mostly inundated with marsh and brush. There appears to be fish in the lake and circulation is via the small stream from Mount Seymour, but fishing is difficult. The management also discourage fishing in the lake.

With reference to the Demonstration Forest Trail maps presented in the previous section, access to the lake is via the Seymour Mainline Road from the south parking lot. At just past the five-kilometer mark take the southern trail to the old spur four bridge, cross the bridge and turn left onto the Seymour East Road parallel to the Seymour River on the east side. From the bridge the walk is about three kilometers on a good trail to the Lost Lake footpath, rather obscure and not marked so watch for it carefully. Since the lake is a short 500 meters in from the Seymour East trail, you can afford to try a few alternatives to find it. The bush trail will get you lead into the dense thickets within 100 meters of the lake, then you are on your own to find the shore. Now almost overgrown, the trail is not maintained. There is no trail around the lake so shore access is difficult. The lake and its surrounding environment is therefore primarily of ecological interest.

SEYMOUR LAKE is a large manmade lake of 89 hectares at an elevation of 495 meters. This beautiful lake is held back by the Seymour dam reaching six kilometers back into the rarely seen Seymour Valley. This area has been restricted since the late 1920s when the dam was built. In 1987 it was decided that the public would be allowed partial access to view the area so you can now take an 11-kilometer bike trip to view the dam.

SEYMOUR PARK LAKES include a long list of lakes high up in the sub-alpine terrain near Seymour Mountain. Although an impressive list, the recreational value of the lakes is limited in summer but it does offer impressive hiking trails and unforgettable scenes of meadows. Seymour Park itself provides a long and impressive list of winter recreational facilities including 3508 hectares of semi-wilderness established as a park in 1936. Within its bounds are some very high peaks such as Mount Seymour at 1453 meters, Mount Elsay at 1418 meters and Mount Bishop at 1508 meters. Due to its vertical range the park contains an incredible variety of sub-alpine forests and meadows with some of the higher areas yielding many colorful flowers in the short summer.

There are several lakes in this area but the majority should be classified as ponds. Elsay is the largest but requires a considerable effort to get to it. Its waters and those of De Pencier, Gopher and Goldie drain eastward to Indian Arm while the other lakes feed the Seymour River basin. The park is extremely rugged and the trails can be dangerous, particularly if you plan to visit the northern lakes. In the south, near the ski area most of the lakes are accessible within easy walking distance.

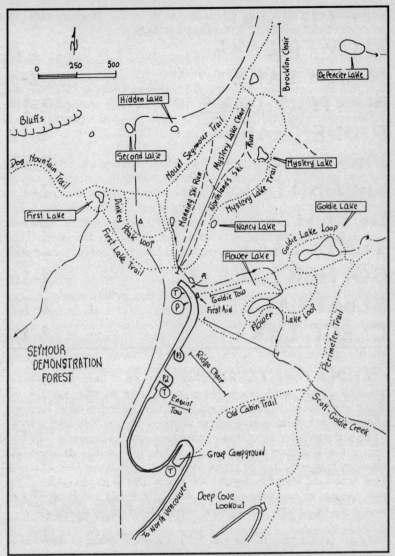

Lower Seymour Park roads and trails

FINDING SEYMOUR PARK

To get to the lakes drive from Highway 1, exit 22 onto Seymour Parkway toward Deep Cove until you hit Seymour Mountain Road and turn left. It is well marked and leads through the gate at the foot of Seymour Mountain where you begin your ascent toward the ski area and parking lot.

The road is paved, snaking its way 12 kilometers to the parking lot near the summit. From here you can access an extensive trail and ski network. It is an easy walk through impressive sub-alpine coniferous forests to little lakes and lookouts that will give you spectacular views of the valley and mountains. The following description will take you on a tour to the lower lakes first. Refer to the Lower Seymour Park roads and trails map.

GOLDIE LAKE is set carefully at 950 meters, about one kilometer from the Seymour parking lot. In this case you actually drop down in elevation from the parking lot. The trail measures a total distance of two kilometers, taking 60 minutes round trip, with minimal elevation change. This includes the **Goldie Loop Trail** a self-guiding interpretive trail around the lake. The main trail starts at the first aid building and winds past the Goldie rope-tow area to Goldie Lake. This trail also connects with the Flower Lake Trail and the top end of the Perimeter Trail system.

Goldie is an interesting lake, deeper and larger than its little, swampy counterparts. Rocks flank the east end where the stream leaves the lake through a small beach. The west end is much different with a flat marshy meadowland typical of sub-alpine vegetation. There are little open gravel areas littered with boulders on the northwest and south shores, providing a picturesque setting for a picnic. There are no formal facilities here except the trail, described below.

Goldie Lake Loop Trail an interpretive trail explaining the dynamics of a sub-alpine hemlock forest is the feature here. At an elevation of 950 meters life constantly struggles against the forces of winter for eight to nine months of the year. Over 300 centimeters of rain falls to create acidic conditions which would seem hostile to plant and animal life yet the area abounds with lush green life. The interpretive trail explains how this has evolved:

1. **Breakdown** The dead tree is a casualty of the perpetual struggle and now helps to ensure the survival of others such as ants, beetles and grubs, all enticing woodpeckers and other wildlife to feed and grow. The trunk will eventually fall and rot to support new seedlings.

2. **Snow Creep** Most trees on the slope are bent from the pressure of the snow moving down the slope. They must either bend or be swept away. As they age, they get stronger and resist the weight but still display the marks of the struggle.

3. **Why Needles?** The narrow needles of the conifers have less surface area than leaves making them less susceptible to water evaporation forced by

winds and sun. This leaves more water for the tree to use for food allowing such trees to thrive in drier areas.

4. Acid-Loving Plants In areas of high rain and snowfall most nutrients are washed away, leaving an acidic soil. Plants of the heather family have special chemical magnets for attracting and converting the remaining nutrients in the soil into useful materials and thrive in these areas as a result.

5. You Help Me—I'll help you The cycle of survival between conifer seeds and animals such as birds and squirrels is explained at this spot. They do not consume all the seeds and shake many of them loose to 'whirl' to the ground where the cycle begins as a seedling.

6. Battlefield This is a stark illustration of how young trees crowd closely together in a fierce battle for survival. Some outgrow others, winning the battle for light, water and nutrients surviving to claim the resources.

7. Nurse Logs This discusses the fallen trees the acid-loving plants can grow on. The rotting wood of the nurse log provides nutrients and holds water like a sponge, allowing the recycling process to prevail.

8. Sowing Seeds The topic here is the wild berry packets. These seeds are fruits that attract animals who eat them. The eaten seeds are 'prepared' by the digestive tract as the juices break down the seed coating and pass them with a dropping, deposited in a rich nutrient coating, ready to begin growing.

9. Preparing the Way The lake is slowly filling in to lose its present look. The edge of the lake has different rings of plants with different shades of green. Each shade requires a different environment, such as, moving from wet to dry, lilies, sedge and willows. As each grows and dies, the ground becomes drier allowing the drier plants to encroach on lakeshore. The process of succession will eventually fill in the lake.

10. The Beginning The struggle for survival is based on the ability to cope with harsh climates and poor soil. The plants have found ways to adapt and recycle nutrients in unique ways that have allowed them to continue for centuries.

FLOWER LAKE is a pond less than a hectare in size sitting at an elevation of around 950 meters. It is appropriately named since it is completely filled with water lilies. Set graciously within a forest of tall timbers on one side and open heather meadows on the other, the lake is well worth a visit just to see the picture. It is an extremely pretty body of water and the trail is a very pleasant walk. The **Flower Loop Trail** is 1.5 kilometers long, taking 45 minutes one way. It is an easy walk with a moderate elevation drop. The Flower Loop trail starts at about 500 meters from the parking lot, along the Goldie Lake Trail. It leads through the sub-alpine bog around the lake and then north towards the Goldie Lake Loop Trail. There are several other trails in this area so you may want to walk around and explore the many ponds and prolific bird life.

NANCY LAKE at 1070 meters in elevation, is less than a hectare in size. It is a small pond about 500 meters away from the lot, found by taking the Mystery Lake Trail from the head of the main parking lot.

MYSTERY LAKE is also at around 1150 meters, but a bit larger, about a hectare in size. The Mystery Lake Trail will take you directly to it starting at the north end of the main parking lot. The length is 1.5 kilometers, requiring a hike time of 45 minutes. From the lot, the elevation gain will be around 100 meters so this is a moderate workout, just enough to warm up in preparation for a cool swim. Mystery Lake is very pretty, set in a rocky outcrop with rounded flat rocks that slip into the clear water all around the perimeter. This is an excellent place to stop for a picnic or swim in spite of the lack of facilities.

HIDDEN LAKE is at an elevation of 1100 meters and less than a hectare in size. This little pond is found off the main Mount Seymour Trail. By *off* I mean there is no formal trail, that's why it's *hidden* so you have to hunt for it. Look for it to the right of the top of the Manning ski run about a 15-minute hike uphill from the parking lot.

FIRST LAKE is around 1020 meters in elevation and tiny at less than a hectare in size. This one actually sits in the fringe of the Vancouver watershed. The hiking distance to it is one kilometer from the parking lot, or about 20 to 30 minutes. The First Lake Trail slopes gently from the north end of the parking lot through the sub-alpine vegetation to the lake. It intersects the loop trail around the lake that has a mere 60-meter elevation change—enough to give you a thirst.

SECOND LAKE is also at around 1100 meters and less than a hectare in size. It is actually situated on the west side of the divide inside the Vancouver watershed. No official trail leads to it but I am sure you can find the footpath.

De PENCIER LAKE is situated at around 1020 meters and about a hectare in size. There appears to be no trail to it but the best way you find it would be to head into the bush past Brockton lift. From the lift, it is only about 500 meters away but you will drop down into a basin. The De Pencier Bluff to the south should be avoided because it is steep and dangerous, so although the distance is short, the time needed to get to this lake is not.

THETA LAKE is a tiny pond at 900 meters and less than a hectare set down in a small basin east of the peak of Mount Seymour. Since the main trail cuts through here at around 1000 meters it is not far from the pond. You may even see it from the main trail but the terrain is steep and dangerous so *caution is advised*.

GOPHER LAKE sits at 790 meters and is about one hectare in size with no formal access to it so you are on your own. This area is on the east side of Mount Seymour where the vegetation is lush and the terrain is *steep, dangerous and isolated.*

ELSAY LAKE is set down in the valley behind Mount Elsay in the northern end of Seymour Park. At 765 meters in elevation this is a long way down from the peak which sits at 1422 meters. The lake is the largest in the park at 20 hectares, well worth a visit if you are in good shape and well experienced. To get to this lake requires seven kilometers of hiking *each way* or ten hours *return.* The elevation change is 500 meters because you go up, then down, to get there. If you start at the parking lot you will be at 1050 meters then climb up to the Mount Seymour junction 2.5 kilometers away to reach an elevation of 1200 meters. From here the lake is at 765 meters in elevation. The trail continues from the junction down into the bowl, splitting just before First Pump Peak. The trail is well-developed until a point northwest of Gopher Lake where it narrows and is marked with flashers and tape. A small backcountry shelter is found at the end. The lake was stocked with fish years ago but it obviously does not need any help from fisheries. The lake is set lower in the valley and is fairly marshy, so don't forget your mosquito repellent. Note that this is a very difficult trail taking you into isolated rugged country. *Many people have been lost here* so it is not for the inexperienced. The fog in this area can cover you almost instantly, to the point where you cannot see a few meters ahead so beware.

CLEGG LAKE is at an elevation of 1190 meters, another high elevation pond less than a hectare in size. It can be found on the east side of Mount Bishop if you are a trail scout. There is no trail into it so this is as remote as you can imagine.

RECREATION

Facilities None of these lakes have facilities. The trails are typically the best sign of any formal development. With the exception of the backcountry shelter at the end of the Elsay Lake Trail, there is nothing except for natural beauty and the stomped clearings that act as natural camp sites created by other enthusiastic explorers. There are places to camp at Elsay but nothing is formally developed. The Seymour area, however, is focused on winter activities so you will find this a great place for skiing and winter sports. There is ample parking with several rope tows. There are four lifts, various ski slopes and runs with a variety of steepness. A cafeteria is available as well as a first aid building, ski equipment rental and a ski school. There is even a snowshoe interpretive program offered in season.

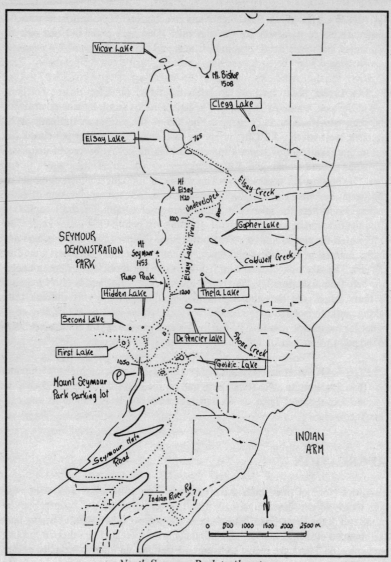

North Seymour Park trail system

Trails In addition to the trails mentioned in the section on finding the lakes, there are many major trails in the area, as shown on the North Seymour Park map:

Old Buck Logging Road is a moderate hike of 2.3 kilometers taking 45 minutes one way to Baden Powell or 5.5 kilometers and two hours one way to the Perimeter Trail. Note a 670-meter change in elevation! The trailhead is located near the park entrance across the road from the gatehouse. From here the trail winds its way up to the beginning of the Perimeter Trail following the grade of the old logging road.

Old Buck Access is an easy one-kilometer hike taking 30 minutes one way. The trail starts at the Vancouver lookout parking lot and terminates at the junction with the Old Buck Logging Road Trail.

Horse Trail A 2.5 kilometer loop trail used mostly by bikers, this is an old logging road.

The Mushroom parking lot is one for the curious. It is 750 meters long taking a mere 15 minutes one way with minimal elevation change. The trail begins just across the road from the Vancouver lookout parking lot and is an easy hike to the historical site.

Baden Powell was a BC Centennial project initiated in 1967 by the Boy Scouts and Girl Guides. Completed in 1971, the trail connects Deep Cove with Eagle Ridge Drive near Horseshoe Bay, about 43 kilometers long. About five kilometers of it is in the park, accessed from the Baden Powell picnic area and parking lot along the main road at the park entrance. One section leads west to the Mushroom Trail junction. This is 1.7 kilometers long and takes 40 minutes with an elevation change of 130 meters. The other section leads east to Deep Cove. It is 3.2 kilometers long taking an hour. The elevation change is 275 meters, giving a moderately difficult hike.

Perimeter Trail is a moderate hike 1.5 kilometers long taking 45 minutes one way with an elevation change of 240 meters. It begins at the Deep Cove lookout and ends at the Goldie Lake access trail junction.

Old Cabin Trail is only 430 meters taking 20 minutes one way. There is a 25-meter elevation change. This is an easy connector trail running from parking lot 1 to the Perimeter Trail junction.

Dinky Peak is 750 meters long, taking 15 minutes one way, with minimal elevation change. A short trail starts 250 meters along the main Mount Seymour Trail and leads to the peak of Dinky Bluff, providing spectacular views of the valley.

First Lake Loop-Dog Mountain are moderate hikes which can be combined as follows:

- to First Lake is one kilometer, 30 minutes, elevation change minimal.
- from First Lake to Dog Mountain is two kilometers, 40 minutes, minimal elevation change.
- from First Lake to complete the loop is three kilometers, 45 minutes, 60 meters elevation change.

The main trail begins northwest of the chair lift and climbs gently through dense sub-alpine forest to First Lake and the trail junction for Dog Mountain or Mount Seymour. From this junction follow the trial west to Dog Mountain for a spectacular view of Vancouver and the Seymour River valley or follow the trail north from the junction to Mount Seymour and eventually loop around back down to the parking lot.

Mount Seymour Trail is four kilometers long and takes 2.5 hours one way. The elevation gain is 450 meters and the hike is classified as moderate to difficult. The trail starts at the north end of the top parking lot, traversing Brockton Point and First and Second Pump peaks.

Mystery Lake Trail is 1.5 kilometers long and takes 45 minutes one way. The elevation change is 100 meters. This is a moderate hike with the trail beginning at the north end of parking lot 4. It parallels the chair lift right-of-way to the lake.

Elsay Lake is tough at seven kilometers, five hours one way. This is a difficult trail for experts only. The 500 meters elevation change is *down* from the upper height of 1200 meters which you get to from the parking lot (at 1050 meters). The rugged trail begins on the main Mount Seymour Trail and follows it until the trail divides just before First Pump peak. The trail is good until a point northwest of Gopher Lake where it narrows but it should be marked with tape where you can lose the trail very easily since it gets extremely obscure. A backcountry shelter is provided here.

Winter Sports The park has extensive winter recreational facilities. This is a main feature for this park in the winter. The ski tows are shown on the map. See the section on facilities.

GREATER VANCOUVER WATER SUPPLY It is worthwhile to mention a set of lakes situated in the Vancouver water supply area, not for their recreational value but just to note that they *are restricted*, even though they are close to residential areas. The Vancouver water supply comes from several vast drainage basins mainly the upper Capilano and Seymour basins that drain into the Capilano and Seymour lakes, both dammed. Vast and rugged, this portion of the Coast Mountains are essentially *off-limits* to one and all.

REGION THREE

BURNABY

THE BURNABY REGION The next region moves us south of the West and North Vancouver regions away from the northern mountains into the densely populated area along the Fraser River. The region of interest is a 20 by 30 kilometer area covering the rolling flatlands of the river delta. The city of Burnaby is at the northwest end of this strip with several lakes close by. On the north the region is bounded by the Fraser River with the cities of Vancouver and Richmond to the west. The US border is on the south and the municipality of Burnaby/New Westminster is on the north. The area is very heavily populated with only a small number of lakes but these have been carefully preserved to provide some unique recreational options, even in the mainstream of city life.

The terrain is mostly flat compared to the northern mountains. Burnaby is the region between the north arm of the Fraser River and Burrard Inlet to the north between Boundary Road and Port Mann. Three small lakes are within this area and have been carefully reserved from intense development, featuring a wide range of superb recreational facilities. Due to the population density in this region and the small size of the lakes, they have received some special attention including special restrictions to protect the ecosystems, especially with regard to fishing. Although the fishing is rather tame to most anglers, these lakes provide surprising opportunities for the whole family. This is where junior can be taught to fish while the rest of the family enjoys the facilities.

To the south, near the city of Langley, there are another three lakes tucked away in the flatlands of the river delta. Not quite as heavily populated, this area is essentially a mixture of flat farmland and new subdivisions created from the eastward march of Vancouver's overflow population. These lakes are small and not quite as popular as their northern counterparts but nevertheless offer some diverse recreational options.

ROADS, ACCESS POINTS AND LAKES

There are five lakes in the Burnaby and Langley region, all in populated areas. With reference to the regional map, *Highway 1* is the main roadway cutting through the region but, because the lakes are accessible from just about any direction, you can make your own entry path. The first lake is found west of the freeway near the Sunnyhill area just on the outskirts of Vancouver.

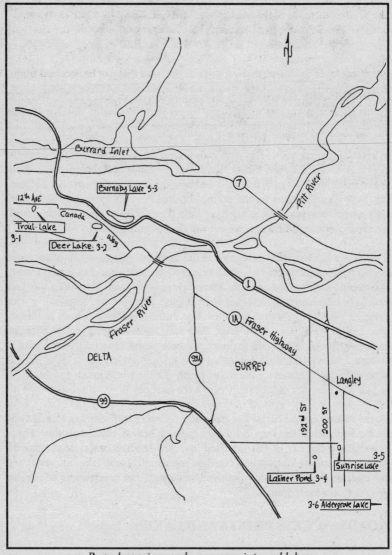

Burnaby region roads, access points and lakes

The key roadway is *12th Avenue* where it changes to *Grandview Highway* between *Victoria Drive* and *Nanaimo Street*. This area contains the little **Trout**

Lake (3-1) in John Hendry Park. Traveling east on the freeway get onto *Canada Way* which will get you to **Deer Lake (3-2),** found in a good-sized forested area of the Oakalla Park site and Century Park in Burnaby. Just north of Trout Lake, on the other side of the freeway, you will find **Burnaby Lake (3-3)** in the Burnaby Lake Regional Park accessed via *Kensington Avenue* on the west or *Winston Street* on the north.

Three more lakes are found in the south Langley area that can be accessed from *200th Street* off Highway 1. The first is **Latimer Pond (3-4)** nicely hidden off *28th Avenue* in south Surrey, while its private neighbor **Sunrise Lake (3-5)**, surrounded by *28th Avenue, 204th Street, 208 Street* and *32nd Avenue*, is ringed with private residential development. Finally, just east of Langley off *8th Avenue*, past *272nd Street* is a unique Greater Vancouver Regional District-developed park called the Aldergrove Lake Regional Park containing the tiny **Aldergrove Lake (3-6)**.

TROUT LAKE

TROUT LAKE is the first lake on the westerly tour. It is truly a city lake situated in John Hendry Park right on the eastern edge of Vancouver. Quite small at four hectares and at an elevation of 53 meters, the lake sits glistening in a flat, open, well-maintained park area relatively free of vegetation. The park boundary is made up of city streets and residential development completely surrounds the lake.

TROUT LAKE at a GLANCE

ACTIVITIES	FISHING, WALKING, PICNICKING, PLAYGROUND, RECREATION CENTER	
LAKE STATS	Elevation & Size	: 53 meters, four hectares
	Lake Setting	: John Hendry Park
ACCESS	Vehicle Type	: car
	Nearest Highway	: city streets
FACILITIES	Type & Class	: developed for day use
	Camping	: not allowed
	Boat Launch	: not allowed
FISHING	Fish Stocked	: 2000
	Size Reports	: small 20-25 cm trout
	Restrictions	: no boats, no swimming, age limit

This small urban lake has been subjected to intense urban pressures to use the recreational facilities, many of which have changed significantly over the years. As it now stands, the lake's ecosystem seems to be in a delicate environmental balance. As pretty as it looks, the lake is slowly being polluted as poor water circulation and intense use place the environment in jeopardy. The weeds and the shoreline accumulation of mud are slowly invading more and more of the lake's water area.

Over recent years, fishing, light boating and even swimming have had to be increasingly restricted in attempts to preserve a balance between nature and the community. Nevertheless, the lake is a refreshing little oasis in the middle of city life.

FINDING the LAKE

This lake is readily accessible, with city streets surrounding the entire park. John Hendry Park is surrounded by 12th Avenue/Grandview Highway on the north, 19th Avenue on the south, Garden Drive on the east and Victoria Drive on the west. With 12th Avenue as a starting point, there are three main parking lots.

If you are driving east along 12th Avenue, you would pass Victoria Drive where a right turn would get you to the large *west* parking lot at the recreation center between 15th and 19th Avenues.

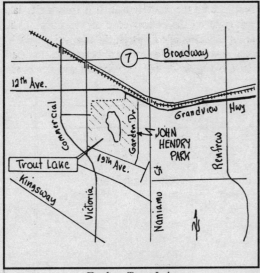

Finding Trout Lake

If you continued along 12th, just after the jog past Victoria as it changes to Grandview Highway, you would turn right on Templeton and find a second *north* parking lot off 13th Avenue bordering the park.

The *south* parking lot is found by turning off Grandview Highway onto Garden Drive, then following it to 19th Avenue. This street borders the south end. The main parking is found by continuing along 19th, then tuning right and entering the driveway into the park just opposite Lakewood. This lot is near the little beach area, picnic and concession.

RECREATION

Facilities at the lake include the usual city park conveniences such as picnic tables, parking lots, playgrounds, tennis courts, washrooms, a concession and trails. In addition there is a small sandy beach area with a few logs and real sand although swimming is not allowed because the swampy water does not meet standards. There is a dock at the north end used for seasonal fishing. The recreation center with an ice arena is found at the southwest corner and a walking and jogging trail surrounds the lake.

Fishing The lake is stocked faithfully every year by fisheries and is designed to keep a delicate balance. Since 1986, the lake has been stocked with catchables in an attempt to maintain it as a fishery. Historically, this has been a successful project, giving the locals an excellent urban fishing hole but the lake is so small and shallow it has slowly succumbed to invading shoreline weeds and mud. Fisheries has been careful to not overpopulate the waters and equally careful to not allow excessive fishing. As a result local regulations change rapidly so it is advisable to check these before you are embarrassed.

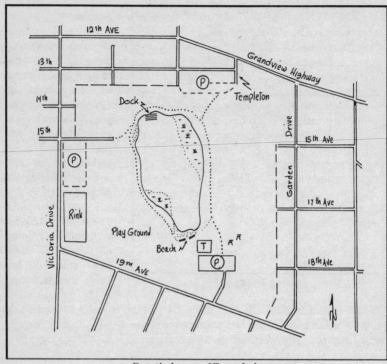

Detailed map of Trout Lake

The lake also contains crappies and catfish as well as trout, so this is most definitely the place to teach your youngster to fish. The dock provides an excellent place where a line can be freely cast into the water. Reports indicate that the trout tend to be small. An age restriction is in effect most of the time and no floating devices are allowed on the lake. In fact it may even be possible to see a 'no fishing' sign, so check first.

FISH STOCKED	YEAR	TYPE	NUMBER
Rainbow & Cutthroat	1986	catchables	200
Rainbow	1987	catchables	200
Rainbow & Cutthroat	1988	catchables	350
Rainbow	1989	catchables	900
Rainbow & Cutthroat	1990	catchables	320

DEER LAKE is another lake set in the middle of suburbia but this one is quite unique. Much larger than its little neighbor Trout, this area combines a power-packed list of recreational items with a decent-sized chunk of natural forest. When you first see this lake, you won't believe that a lake measuring 30 hectares and such a large natural wilderness area actually exists within Burnaby. Deer Lake sits low in the valley at an elevation of 20 meters, in the Deer Lake Municipal Park. It also borders on the Oakalla Park so the two areas combine to make up a good chunk of protected wilderness. An interesting feature is that this lake is easily classified as the best fishing hole in the city.

From a recreational standpoint the lake and its surrounding area offers several unique alternatives. The lake itself offers boating, fishing and swimming but there are also several cultural treats where you can stroll through gardens and go to a restaurant. You can visit a recreated village, ride a miniature train and even use the park for a garden wedding.

FINDING the LAKE

Getting to the lake can be a bit tricky depending on where you are coming from and what you want to do so take a good look at the detailed lake map before you go. Typically the best access route is via Canada Way.

Finding Deer Lake

If you want to put your boat into the water, you will need to go to the east parking lot, also the main recreation area. Take Canada Way to Burris Street, then turn onto Buckingham Street. Turn left at the end of Buckingham onto Sperling Avenue. Note that it is necessary to come around this way because Sperling is a one-way street going toward Canada Way so you cannot enter directly from the latter. Only the last block at Canada Way is two way. You will see the east end of the lake and the large parking lot just a short drive south on Sperling (see detailed map).

If you want some privacy, would like to picnic, just walk or fish in the weeds offshore, the parking lot off Royal Oak Avenue is the best bet. It is about 840 meters through the bushes to the picnic area at the west end of the lake so don't even think about hauling a big lunch or a boat!

If you have cultural inclinations, park over near the art gallery off Deer Lake Avenue in Century Park. From here you have access to the theater and the trails around the lake. If you want to dine first head for the parking lot near the Hart House Restaurant overlooking the lake. From here you also have access to the museum just across the road featuring a recreated village.

DEER LAKE at a GLANCE

ACTIVITIES	FISHING, BOATING, HIKING, PICNICKING, CULTURE, NATURE	
LAKE STATS	Elevation & Size	: 20 meters, 30 hectares
	Lake Setting	: Deer Lake Municipal Park
ACCESS	Vehicle Type	: car
	Nearest Highway	: surrounded by city streets
FACILITIES	Type & Class	: developed
	Camping	: not allowed
	Boat Launch	: yes
FISHING	Fish Stocked	: 70,000
	Size Reports	: rainbows to 35 centimeters
	Restrictions	: no powerboats, possible age limit

RECREATION

Facilities at the lake are quite impressive, offering something for everyone. The east entrance has the beach area, dock, boat launch and washroom facilities. A nice picnic area is also set in the willows overlooking the dock. The parking lot is a good size and you have access to the trails. This is also where the canoe club hangs out and you will usually find canoe rentals. There is a picnic site on the west end of the lake but it requires a walk from the parking lot on Royal Oak Avenue.

Culture is a rather unique bonus for this lake. If this is your desire, park near the art gallery off Deer Lake Avenue in Century Park. This is the best place to get access to a myriad of cultural (and culinary) offerings and Cowan Theater is over there as well. If you want to dine first, then wear the calories off, head for the parking lot near the Hart House restaurant overlooking the lake. The museum, with a recreated village, is just across the road. The cultural conveniences are all nicely distributed in a forested area, with strict attention paid to molesting nature as little as possible.

Trails The trails around the lake are worth mentioning under a separate heading simply because of their extent. These are very good walking trails, taking you through lush swamps and tall timbers in a wide variety of vegetation. Due to the size of Oakalla Park on the southwest end, you can actually get away from the roar of city traffic and find natural tranquillity within easy walking distance. The trails are shown on the map, some being quite a walk so distances are marked. These take you several kilometers into the woods carefully skirting private residential buildings. There are two picnic areas on the more isolated west end of the lake. The hike around the lake is about five kilometers and will take a few hours.

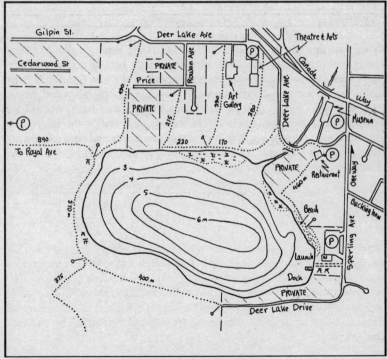

Detailed map of Deer Lake

Boating The lake also offers a nice setting for the 'quiet boater'. There are not many places in Burnaby to satisfy canoe lovers, so this is a rare find. Nicely protected and surrounded by forest, the lake is a haven for inconspicuous aquatic life and it is large enough to allow you to paddle quietly for hours in an interesting natural area. In fact, the canoe club trains here. The best access is at the parking lot and beach area at the east end of the lake where there is a small boat launch and dock beside the concession building.

Fishing The lake has been stocked faithfully since 1986 with rather large quantities of rainbow as you can see from the stocking tables. This program has helped to maintain this lake as an excellent urban fishing hole for the whole family.

FISH STOCKED	YEAR	TYPE	NUMBER
Rainbow	1986	yearlings	5600
Rainbow	1986-1988	yearlings	11200/yr.
Rainbow	1989	yearlings	22400
Rainbow	1990	catchables	230
Rainbow	1990	yearlings	25000

To maintain this lake as a good fishing hole no power boats are allowed. Shore fishing is not easy since the lake is surrounded with a lot of marsh vegetation and is quite shallow at the edges. The southern shore drops to five meters fairly rapidly but the access is difficult since this shoreline is steep, bushy and private residences line a part of it. If you are hiking the perimeter trails, you will see the odd beaten-open spot where ardent anglers have sought the illusive big fish. A canoe is the best bet. Plop it in at the launch area and head straight out along the south shoreline. The deeper section of the lake is right down the middle, reaching just six meters.

BURNABY LAKE is a complete change of pace compared to its neighbor Deer Lake. Also in Burnaby, set amidst the frantic pace of the traffic just north of Highway 1, the lake is a virtual oasis that guarantees relaxation. The size of the lake seems to be a bit of a mystery depending on who measured it and when it was measured. The main channel is about five hectares but it is unfortunately shrinking year by year, slowly losing the battle for shoreline.

The lake is part of the 300-hectare Burnaby Lake Regional Park. It was originally much larger but over the years the lake has silted up and marsh vegetation has slowly moved the shoreline. At the current time, a narrow channel of just around two meters in depth runs most of the two-kilometer length. This has become a natural waterway for rowing teams. The lake water is delicately held back by a small dam at the east end where the Brunette River flows out to the Fraser. Since the area is made up of an unusual natural marshland, the Greater Vancouver Regional District has gone to considerable effort to protect it along with the prolific wildlife using the area. They have developed over ten kilometers of superb trails as well as many nature-oriented recreational facilities around the lake. Due to the marsh dominant habitat, the lake provides a marvelous, easily accessible unique environment for anyone interested in relaxing with nature—especially among the birds.

BURNABY LAKE at a GLANCE

ACTIVITIES	ROWING, CANOEING, TRAILS, EQUESTRIAN, NATURE, RECREATION CENTER	
LAKE STATS	Elevation & Size	: 14 meters, 5 to 10 hectares
	Lake Setting	: Burnaby Lake Regional Park
ACCESS	Vehicle Type	: car
	Nearest Highway	: surrounded by city streets
FACILITIES	Type & Class	: developed
	Camping	: not allowed
	Boat Launch	: yes, for canoe and rowing team
FISHING	Fish Stocked	: natural
	Size Reports	: to 25 centimeters
	Restrictions	: no power boats

FINDING the LAKE

The Regional park is right beside Highway 1 in Burnaby. Bounded by the highway on the south, Sperling Avenue on the west and Winston Street on the north, the lake is still a hidden oasis. There are several access points depending on what you want to do.

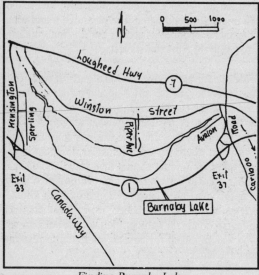

Finding Burnaby Lake

As a rough guide; recreation center on the west, equestrian on the east and nature on the north.

Access the west end of the lake from Highway 1 traveling east. where you can take Kensington Avenue North (exit 33) to Sprott Street and turn right. This will take you to Sperling Avenue and the Burnaby Sports Complex. Following south on Sperling will take you to Roberts Street which leads to parking and the rowing pavilion. The Wildlife Rescue Center is along Glencarin, at the south trailhead. For access to the north, your best bet is to drive along Winston Street to Piper, which heads south into the park. The east end of the lake is accessed by continuing on Winston, then turning right on Caribou Road. Parking is provided farther down on Avalon Avenue.

RECREATION

Facilities at the lake are extremely varied. The west end, off Sperling Avenue, is well-endowed, with a complete sports complex, play fields, swimming pool and ice rink. Just below the sports complex is a large structure overlooking the lake which caters to the rowing club where you will find a large parking lot, a training center and a grandstand overlooking the water. Continuing south along Sperling to Glencarin Drive, you can visit the Wildlife Rescue Center. Here the Wildlife Rescue Association has a wild animal rehabilitation facility where you will find a self-guided wildlife habitat garden which will tell you how to design wildlife-friendly backyards.

The north shore of the lake, accessible from Winston Street to Piper Avenue caters to the nature-lovers where you will find parking, picnicking, interpretive trails, washrooms, a spit/walkway projecting into the lake, a bird watching tower and even a nature house with special information on the area. There are also several short interpretive loop trails throughout the marshy shore on this side.

The east end of the lake, accessible through the Avalon Avenue entrance is different again, focusing the recreational facilities toward equestrian activities. Here you will find the Burnaby Equestrian Center, parking, unloading areas, washrooms, picnic areas and a network of riding trails. The equestrian trails also connect to the other numerous nature trails around the lake.

Equestrian The Burnaby Equestrian Center is operated by the Burnaby Horsemen's Association administered by Burnaby Parks and Recreation. It is an excellent facility, situated at the east end of the lake where access is specially designed for trailers. The area is nicely laid out, offering access to the 2.7-kilometer Freeway Trail and the .8-kilometer Avalon Trail. These are designed specifically for horseback riding, following the south shoreline where foot traffic is minimal. Since the foot-trail parallels the horse trail, there is usually no need to worry about nature-loving pedestrians who may prefer the horse trail and obstruct your horse's gallop. Nevertheless, remember you *share* the trails with hikers so don't get your horse too steamed up!

Nature The natural aspects of this marsh habitat are a rather special feature of the area. This is a place where you can conduct nature studies involving birds, flowers, vegetation and a myriad of natural marshland life. Not surprisingly, the natural waterways have convinced an incredible population of ducks and geese to stay permanently. A nature house is open through the summer, offering a chance to see several displays describing the lake's animal and plant life complete with terrariums with live specimens. A viewing tower is also provided from which you can observe a wide array of wildlife and a great view of the area. The Wildlife Rescue Association has a wild animal rehabilitation facility on the south shore where you will find a self-guided wildlife habitat garden which will tell you how to design wildlife-friendly backyards.

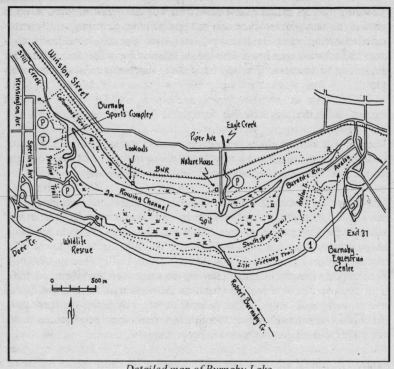

Detailed map of Burnaby Lake

Trails The trail system in the area is extensive, covering over ten kilometers. These are level, soft surfaces excellent for strolling and even jogging. To walk the complete loop trail system around the lake will require about 2.5 hours, taking you through an incredible variety of natural plant and animal life. The distances are as follows:

From the **Nature House**, walking west, take the north shore Cottonwood Trail (2.6 kilometers) that leads to Pavilion Trail (2.5 kilometers) where Glencarin Drive takes you to the southern Southshore Trail (2.4 kilometers) to the Avalon Trail (.8 kilometers) and along Brunette Headwaters Trail (1.8) back to the nature house.

The **Piper Mill, Conifer Loop, Cascara Loop** and the **Spruce Loop** trails are between 500 to 1000 meters long, specially created to let you saunter slowly through various types of vegetation.

The **horse trails** are also available for a walk, offering another four kilometers of trails, but these may have a few larger animals on the pathway and may not be so relaxing.

Canoeing Another unique feature of the area is the lake itself, an incredible and amazing aquatic world that can only be appreciated by skimming quietly across the shimmering waters in a canoe. If you want a peaceful interlude with a marsh wonderland, place your canoe in the water at Piper Spit and spend a day exploring the lakeshore. The lake is shallow, dominated by marsh and only viewed well from a canoe and every meter of the shore is different. Since the marsh edges are an important feeding and nesting area for wildlife you must respect the fact that they were there first.

Fishing in Burnaby Lake is discouraged by the Greater Vancouver Regional District. Since this is a delicate nature reserve, you may feel a bit guilty walking in with your new graphite fishing rod! Since most of the lake has been taken over by vegetation and mud, you can find better areas to fish elsewhere, like Deer Lake but, if you would like to fish for frogs or have the courage to walk between the naturalists to insist on trying, the fisheries lists this lake as fair game at the time of this writing. It would still be best to check with local authorities if you are going to fish the lake.

Burnaby Lake is a maximum of three meters deep along the rowing channel. This is all that is left of the lake. But even that appears to be filling in fast as the lush vegetation slowly encroaches on the channel. Reports suggest rainbows are stocked and cutthroat are also present, along with many other species. Since there are five streams entering and exiting the lake, there is certainly ample fresh water and marsh life to encourage fish to stay. The fish are reportedly small at 25 centimeters.

LATIMER POND   3-4

LATIMER POND also known as *Surrey Pit* is situated in the southern part of the valley between Langley and Surrey and is a whole new experience. The unique feature here is the well-kept secret fishing and swimming hole created from an old gravel pit. At six hectares, the lake is a good size and entirely manmade. For some reason, this little oasis has escaped being shown on even the most detailed map. The interesting aspect of this lake is that it has been virtually filled with trout and is not visible from the road. With the garbage dump to the south, one would hardly believe such a pretty spot is really in the vicinity, a mere 70 meters from the road.

LATIMER POND at a GLANCE

ACTIVITIES	FISHING, BOATING, TRAILS, PICNICS, BEACH	
LAKE STATS	Elevation & Size	: 45 meters, six hectares
	Lake Setting	: Latimer Park
ACCESS	Vehicle Type	: car
	Nearest Highway	: surrounded by streets
FACILITIES	Type & Class	: natural
	Camping	: no rules posted
	Boat Launch	: on sandy beach
FISHING	Fish Stocked	: 53,000
	Size Reports	: rainbows to 30 centimeters
	Restrictions	: no power boats

The lake is fairly shallow, shaped like a square, covering most of a Surrey block. It was called Surrey Pit but, because it is now in Latimer Park, it has taken on a more refined name. This lake is one of the most heavily fished lakes in the valley. When the gravel pit was abandoned it filled with water and a fringe of deciduous trees grew on the surrounding gravel to hide the lake from view. Set beside the flat wooded area of the Latimer Park forest there appears to be no streams feeding it, creating a bit of a mystery about how this lake maintains its fishing status. This small area has nevertheless developed into a neat little oasis for the locals. Since there are not many lakes in the region, this well hidden, forested, completely protected one is a treat! Even though there are no facilities, you can let the kids play, have a barbecue, swim, canoe and fish, all at the same time.

FINDING the LAKE

This is easy if you know there is a lake here. Access is via paved road since it is in a residential area. Coming from the north or south 192nd Street will get you there. Latimer Park is set between 192nd Street on the west to about 194th on the east, with main access along 28th Avenue. At first you will not see the lake as you drive by. Perhaps this is an attempt by the locals to keep it secret. Even when you park along the shoulder on 28th Avenue you won't believe there is a lake in here. If

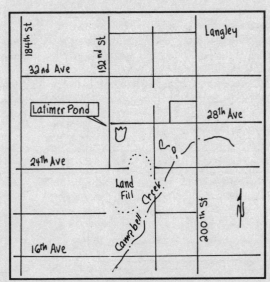

Finding Latimer Pond

you stop on a weekend the anglers carrying fishing rods in and out of the bushes should help you find it and there are several beaten paths leaving the shoulder along 28th. As you walk in you will enter a flat gravel area where the cottonwoods give way to willows and a magic picture of the lake's northern shore—just a short 100 meters from the road.

RECREATION

Facilities at the lake are all natural—nothing has been developed—this very functional facility has just evolved. The uniqueness of the setting and the natural surroundings offer a great recreational facility. A pathway has been literally beaten, rather than developed, around the lake, paralleling the lakeshore through the trees. All the way around, the trail breaks into little open gravel areas free of vegetation, where you can place a chair and cast your line. The north side of the lake contains several natural sandy beach areas where the locals sun, swim and perhaps launch a canoe or rubber raft. The other three sides are thickly wooded with little trails poking into the thickets in various directions away from the lake. The east side of the lake is dominated by conifers and thick forested terrain, with its own set of walking trails through Latimer Forest.

95

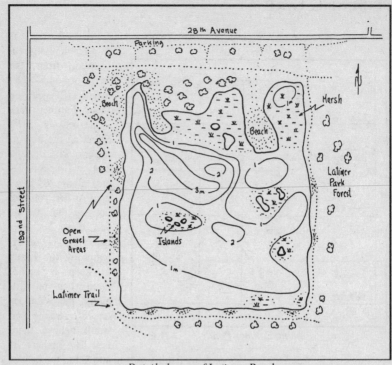

Detailed map of Latimer Pond

Horse and walking trails also network the area to the south but apparently not even these were developed—everything just appears to have evolved naturally—all that was done was to add water, fish and call it Latimer Park...quite an interesting evolution from a once-noisy industrial site!

Swimming Obviously a favorite swimming hole, the lake has clean water and several sandy areas where the shoreline slips gracefully into the clear water. Most of the best beach area is on the north shore where a few gravel bars poke out, creating an excellent spot to drop a chair or towel, place a picnic basket and watch the kids swim. The area is not extensive so can't absorb large numbers of people, probably another reason the area is a bit of a secret.

Canoeing Without a doubt, this little lake is a great place to drop a floating device. It is easy to carry a canoe into the water from 28th Avenue, only a short 100 meters of flat walking. If you carry it through the bikinis and plop it in at the beach you can paddle quietly through the little islands and marshes, casually trolling a fly or just enjoying the natural beauty.

Fishing is another obvious highlight of the lake. Rainbows have been stocked heavily, but cutthroat are also present—a bit of a peculiarity since the lake appears to have no streams entering or leaving it. The stocking table is shown below and obviously fisheries means business when it comes to rainbows in this little lake.

FISH STOCKED	YEARS	TYPE	NUMBER
Rainbow	1986	catchables	14600
Rainbow	1987	catchables	8400
Rainbow	1988	catchables	6100
Rainbow	1989	catchables	8300
Rainbow	1990	catchables	6000

Over 50,000 catchables is an impressive number of rainbows for a lake this size. Fish are reportedly small at 25 centimeters, but 30-centimeter fish are also pulled out. Looking at the map, the lake has quite a lot of marsh area and is quite shallow. The deeper area is north of the little island, with a three-meter-deep cove reaching into the northwest beach area making it a good place to launch your boat. Most fishing is done from shore but requires a fair cast to get into two-meter water so expect smaller fish along the shore.

SUNRISE LAKE

SUNRISE LAKE is another manmade phenomenon in the south Langley area. This lake, unlike its neighbor at Latimer, is completely private and is a fair size, stretching from 204th to 207th Streets between 32nd and 28th Avenues, almost four square Langley blocks! Essentially square in shape, the lake appears to have originally been formed from a large gravel pit that was naturally filled with water. The big difference here is that this lake was not protected by being included in a park; it is more of a commercial-residential oddity.

The inventive developers who owned this lake set about building some rather spectacular homes around the perimeter. The result has created quite an exclusive neighborhood of impressive homes, all backing onto the lake. Their private back yards slope gradually to the shore. A unique setting indeed, this creates a dilemma for those who would like public access to the lake. Sorry, this is one you can only look at unless you know someone in the neighborhood!

FINDING the LAKE

It is easy enough to find this lake but access to the shore is a whole different matter. I thought I should avoid describing how to get to it except that it is such a unique area that it is worth seeing if you have the chance. If you've ever dreamed of fishing off your back yard outside your dream home, take a drive and have a look at this place. The lake is completely surrounded by large beautiful homes along 204th, 208th, 32nd and 28th, all of which have lake frontage. The more spectacular ones are

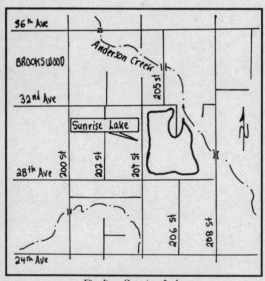

Finding Sunrise Lake

on the east shore where a small bay projects into a very exclusive area. There is no way to the lakeshore except by trespassing through private property. If you drive along 32nd Avenue and down 206th, you can get a good view of the lake (at least you could in 1993) but a fence prevents access. You can at least ponder and dream a bit while watching the locals fishing in their back yards.

RECREATION

Facilities at the lake are superb but private, so there is little to say about it from a public recreation standpoint. There are no public facilities and there are probably none planned. Fishing information is essentially an unknown but there is no doubt fish are in this lake since risers can be seen actively surfacing in the cool of the evening.

ALDERGROVE LAKE is a small lake of less than a hectare at about 50 meters above sea level preserved in a beautiful spot tucked away between the farmlands of the area directly south of Aldergrove. The lake sits in the Aldergrove Lake Regional Park, developed by the Greater Vancouver Regional District. Located in the central valley in the farm belt on the Langley/Matsqui border, the park contains 250 hectares of lowland forest and rolling uplands. Throughout the length of the park the meandering Pepin Brook flows quietly. The park is an interesting place, alternating between groves of lowland deciduous trees and grasses. Not a large park, it nevertheless offers a surprising array of day use activities including swimming, walking, riding, picnicking and beaches.

The park borders several farm properties to the south, presently leased pending park development. Although these are closed to the public now there are plans to extend the trail system into the pastures and even the barns of the adjoining farms. This would create a rather unique recreational system, integrating farm life into park facilities.

FINDING the LAKE

The main entrance to the park is from 8th Avenue. To get to this spot five kilometers south of Aldergrove, take 8th Avenue from the east or from the west take a jog south from 16th Avenue at 272nd Street. From the north, highway 13 south is the best bet since it has a freeway exit back at Highway 1. In this area the roads have a tendency to dead-end so plan your traverse carefully or you will drive around looking at farmer's fields all day. Traveling south on highway 13, you

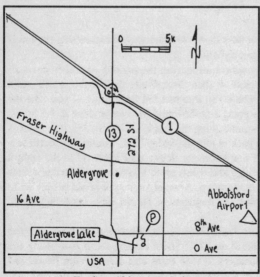

Finding Aldergrove Lake

can turn left onto 8th Avenue and drive to 272nd Street. The main entrance is a short distance from 272nd Street off 8th Avenue with ample parking inside the park.

If you are bringing your horse here, the *equestrian entrance* is on 272nd Street and not via the main gate. Continue down 272nd and the entrance is on the left.

RECREATION

Facilities The park has an impressive system of well-designed and integrated facilities to support walking, hiking, horseback riding, picnicking, swimming, beach activities, group picnicking, viewing of farming activities and wildlife observation. In support of these activities you will also find parking lots, a picnic shelter, playing fields, flush toilets, change rooms, walking trails, a group activity area, picnic tables and hibachi stands, even drinking water and an equestrian center.

Equestrian The equestrian facility is a major feature of this area. Facilities for horse trailer parking, unloading and hitching rails are just off the entrance on 272nd Street but parking is very limited. The main trailhead leads from here through about six kilometers of interesting marked riding trails through groves and fields that are also used by pedestrians,

Trails The trails in the park are not extensive but are well-maintained, easy walking and interesting, taking you through a variety of unique lowland vegetation.

Sedge Trail is just a short (less than a kilometer) trail connecting the information area and the Sedge playfield.

Pepin Brook Trail is the main trail leaving the parking area then paralleling the brook for 500 meters. It then turns south, then curves north again back towards the brook where you intersect the horse trail. If you take the horse trail back, it is easy going and the round trip can be done in 1.5 hours. Alternatively, you can continue along the brook, taking the left fork to cross the bridge and then loop back to join the Sedge Trail, circling the north section of the park. A short one kilometer doggy trail leads off to the right a short distance past the bridge and winds up to 8th Avenue where dog events sometimes take place in the meadow. Another short trail heads steeply up to another meadow containing the remnants of an old cabin, and then to 8th Avenue.

Hunt Bridge Equestrian Trail involves six kilometers of trails starting from the equestrian trailhead on 272nd Street cutting south paralleling the park boundary for .8 kilometers. It then turns east across Pepin Brook and the Hunt Bridge to parallel the south boundary all the way to the east side and the 'big rock' (a house-sized boulder left by the glaciers). From here you have two choices. You can backtrack about 700 meters to the intersection and take the Pepin Brook Trail back to the main facilities. Note that Pepin is not a horse trail. Alternatively, you can continue left past the big rock and out onto the road. Turn left just past the gravel pit onto the Rock 'n' Horse Trail that picks up here to join the Pepin Brook Trail just south of the bridge. This makes a nice loop walk.

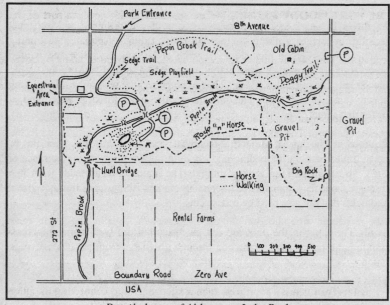

Detailed map of Aldergrove Lake Park

Swimming and Beach If you had to classify this lake you would call it a 'country swimming pool', an odd place created by dumping tons and tons of sand around the perimeter and bottom of the lake. It sits suspended above the rest of the terrain completely surrounded by sandy beach. The water is circulated and clean. It is a bit odd to see the culverts poking above the sand but nevertheless this place has its rather unique appeal for granny and the kids. If you want to see what this lake originally looked like there are a few smaller swamps left in the area. Swimming season typically runs from Victoria Day to Labor Day. This lake is very small but has a nice beach area and the picnic area and main washroom facilities are all near the lake. Don't expect to find anything like Spanish Banks here and you won't be disappointed!

102

REGION FOUR
PORT MOODY

THE PORT MOODY REGION We are now back to the northern part of the Fraser Valley. The region of interest covers a ten- by 35-kilometer strip. Its southern extent includes Port Moody, a heavily populated residential area at the head of the Port Moody Inlet. Our region extends mostly north and a bit south of Port Moody, thereby including the populated rolling hills area of the south and the rugged unpopulated mountainous areas to the north. As a result, there is quite a variation in terrain, population density and lake size. Eastern Port Moody is the main focal point since it provides access to several wilderness lakes to the north The lakes are smaller in the south and typically found in the local parks within the heavily populated urban areas. So you have a fantastic variation of lakes, settings and recreational features within a relatively small region. Much of the area is wilderness with the majority of it Crown forest—a strip along the east side of Indian Arm. The Greater Vancouver watershed is beside the Crown strip, extending eastward. Below is Belcarra Park, Buntzen Lake recreation area and Port Moody Conservation Reserve, the larger areas allocated to recreation. Back in the suburbs, Mundy and Como Lake Parks both contain small lakes.

ROADS, ACCESS POINTS AND LAKES

The *Barnett Highway (route 7A)* is the main roadway through this region and continues in an eastward direction along the south shore of the ocean inlet skirting Burnaby Mountain. It continues to the city of Port Moody where it changes to the *Lougheed Highway (route 7)*. Just at the end of the Port Moody inlet *Ioco Road* allows access into the north and leads to *Bedwell Bay Road* and *Sunnyside Road* taking you into Belcarra Park to **Sasamat Lake (4-1)**, then to Buntzen Lake recreation area and **Buntzen Lake (4-2)** itself.

From the Buntzen Lake recreation area, it is possible to hike up to a series of small lakes on Eagle Mountain accessed from the parking lot at the south beach area of Buntzen Lake. Not an easy hike, the climb will take you up Buntzen Creek well into the Port Moody Conservation Reserve, where a series of small lakes are perched along the west side of Eagle Ridge. From the south, **Cypress Lake (4-3)** is the first and largest.

The north trails get you to **Wren Lake (4-4)**, **Sisken Lake (4-5)**, **Robin Lake (4-6)**, **Chicadee Lake (4-7)**, **Demelza Lake (4-8)**, **St. Mary's Lake (4-9)**, **Mac Lake (4-10)**, **Jay Lake (4-11)**, **Jessica Lake (4-12)** and **Lindsay Lake (4-13)**, all tiny ponds scattered throughout Eagle Ridge.

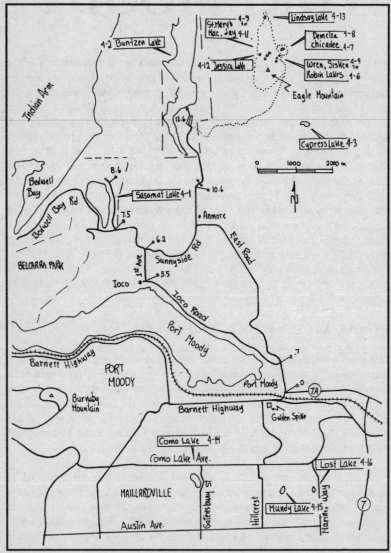

Port Moody region roads, access points and lakes

Two parks are situated right on the top of Port Moody Hill on the south side of *Highway 7A* accessed by getting to *Como Lake Drive* (or *Austin* if you are coming from the south) via *Mariner*. This will take you to **Como Lake (4-14)** in the tiny Como Lake Park. **Mundy Lake (4-15)** and its little neighbor **Lost Lake (4-16)** are found in the large Mundy Park, just to the east.

SASAMAT LAKE or *Deer Lake* is located in the heavily forested area of Belcarra Regional Park resting on a peninsula between the inlet at Port Moody and the waters of Indian Arm on the way to Bedwell Bay. Covering 690 hectares of natural beauty, Belcarra Park contains a host of recreational highlights including swimming, hiking, a freshwater lake, trout fishing, trails, three archeological sites, fantastic scenery and even nine kilometers of ocean shoreline for crabbing or swimming.

SASAMAT LAKE at a GLANCE

ACTIVITIES	FISHING, BOATING, HIKING, SWIMMING, DIVING, PICNICKING	
LAKE STATS	Elevation & Size	: 70 meters, 45 hectares
	Lake Setting	: Belcarra Regional Park
ACCESS	Vehicle Type	: car
	Nearest Highway	: 8.7 kilometers from Highway 7A
FACILITIES	Type & Class	: developed
	Camping	: not allowed, day use only
	Boat Launch	: on beach
FISHING	Fish Stocked	: 13,100
	Size Reports	: cutthroats to 45 centimeters
	Restrictions	: no power boats, electric Oct.-Apr.

Within a short 8.5 kilometers from Highway 7A, you can drive through the urban sprawl of Port Moody into the lush, timbered hills behind Ioco, quite a contrast to the intense industrialization in the harbor and plant at Ioco. Sasamat Lake sits on the eastern side of the park while Belcarra Park borders Burrard Inlet and Indian Arm on the western side. Here the Belcarra Picnic Area provides a whole new set of ocean-oriented recreational facilities. The combination of salt and freshwater recreation facilities is quite unusual.

At 45 hectares, Sasamat is a nice-sized lake offering enough water to get away from the crowds. The lake is easy to get to at only 70 meters and a must if you have never seen it. The lake's best recreational features are at the well-developed northern beach area but this is also a great place to fish, boat and swim.

FINDING the LAKE

Access the lake via paved road from our trailhead at the Lougheed Highway (7A) and Ioco Road. If you zero out the odometer at this intersection, you will turn on Ioco Road and proceed north through a busy area across Guildford Drive at .4 kilometers. At the next intersection you must turn left to continue on Ioco Road (.8 kilometers), a bit tricky since this intersection is always frantic with traffic so prepare ahead of time by taking the inside lane.

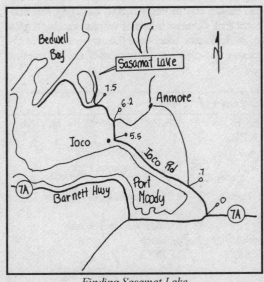

Finding Sasamat Lake

Once on Ioco Road traffic slows down a bit and as you drive along the coastline through Pleasantside and into Sunnyside, you can drool over the homes overlooking the ocean. At 5.5 kilometers turn right up 1st Avenue, which is also Sunnyside Road. The church and the school will mark the intersection. From here, drive north on Sunnyside Road where, at 6.2 kilometers, you will turn left onto Bedwell Bay Road. Sunnyside will continue to the right, taking you to the fantastic site called Buntzen Lake. At 7.5 kilometers turn right into Belcarra Park, a paved road that takes you another 1.1 kilometers to the main parking lot at White Pine beach. The continuation of Bedwell Bay Road will take you to the western section of Belcarra Picnic Area on the ocean.

RECREATION

Facilities at Sasamat Lake are quite well-developed and the northern White Pine area is extremely well organized. The parking lot is tiered since it is set on a hill overlooking the two beaches at the northeast end of the lake. The lot is obviously designed for volume, probably because this lake has the best freshwater beaches in the area.

The White Pine beach area offers washrooms, a concession in summer, access to trails around the lake, white sand beaches and a fantastic setting. A floating bridge that doubles as a trail and a fishing dock is on the south end of the lake, a special feature. On the northwest, the Sasamat Outdoor Center is accessed from the Bedwell Bay Road. The Association of Neighborhood Houses of Vancouver operates summer camp programs here for children and families in July and August.

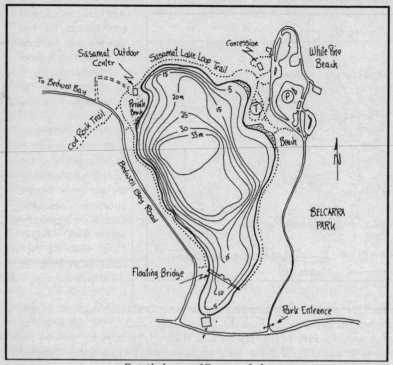

Detailed map of Sasamat Lake

At the Belcarra Picnic Area in the western section of Belcarra Park there is a different set of facilities. This is a well-developed picnic area with beaches, picnic tables, a wharf, washrooms, concession in summer and several trails. There are two picnic shelters with seating for 110 people and with two electric barbecues nearby. Here you can go crab fishing, swimming, boating, scuba diving, picnicking, fishing, hiking and even have a look at some archeological sites along Belcarra's shoreline.

Beaches White Pine Beach has two picturesque bays with real sand. There are washroom facilities, drop-off points along the parking lots and even a pavilion where you can bring your own food for a group barbecue in the summer. As there is no formal boat launch, the two beaches can be used to launch a canoe. The walkways are a short distance to the lake's edge.

Trails around Belcarra Park

Diving An interesting twist at Belcarra is that this is one of the few places advertising diving as a feature attraction. Sasamat Lake is the freshwater option and Whiskey Cove, near the Belcarra picnic area is the saltwater option.

Trails There are several in the area. Sasamat Loop Trail is the main one around the lake. The park extends from the Sasamat Lake area to Burrard Inlet and Indian Arm, so drive to the western side at the Belcarra picnic area on the ocean at the end of Bedwell Bay Road where you will find some new facilities, including three other trails (see the map of the area).

Sasamat Lake Loop Trail is a rough but navigable walking trail surrounding the lake, providing a nice walk through the tall timbers lining most of it. Another unique facility at the south end is a 200-meter floating bridge creating a link between the trails at opposite shores and an incredible place to fish. This bridge has guard rails and opens to two good-sized docks right in the middle of the lake.

Cod Rock Trail (under construction) is a connector trail being created to link the Sasamat Lake Loop Trail to the Admiralty Point Trail. This trail will extend south of the outdoor center, crossing Bedwell Bay road. I am including a small inset map to show the trails, even though they are currently not connected to the lake.

Bedwell Bay Trail takes you to the tidal mud flats on Bedwell Bay. The round trip takes about an hour from the picnic site.

Jug Island Beach Trail takes you down to a quiet, cozy little ocean beach. It has a steep slope, taking two hours round trip from the picnic site.

Admiralty Point Trail follows the shoreline and takes you along the coastline forest to some pocket beaches and finally to Burns Point, about two hours return from the picnic site.

Fishing Cutthroat and rainbow are the dominant fish, although other species are also present. Stocking is a fairly serious matter here as shown in the table below.

FISH STOCKED	YEAR	TYPE	NUMBER
Rainbow	1985-1987	yearlings	1300/yr.
Rainbow	1988	catchables	3000
Rainbow	1989	catchables	4500
Rainbow	1990	catchables	3000

For those without a boat, the 200-meter floating bridge at the south end provides an incredible fishing spot. Two docks are attached to the floating bridge at about the 12-meter depth where the lake channel spills out through the creek. The west side of the bridge is accessible from Bedwell Road, just about .4 kilometers from the intersection at the south end of the lake. The left fork goes down to the BC Hydro powerhouse, while the right fork continues as Bedwell Bay Road. Just about .4 kilometers from this fork it is possible to pull off beside the road where a short trail of about 40 meters takes you down into the tall trees at the lakeshore where you can get onto the bridge.

For those with a boat, the deeper section is in the middle of the lake where a large hole takes you to 33 meters. The western shoreline plunges straight down quickly and consistently almost along the entire length, while the opposite shore has a wide bench (see the map). The lake has a few restrictions which may change so check before you try your boat. No power boats are allowed from May to September, but electric motors may be used in the winter (October to April). There may also be a parking restriction along Bedwell Bay Road, so heed the signs!

BUNTZEN LAKE

BUNTZEN LAKE is a marvelous deep-water lake set in the tree-clad hills above Indian Arm at an elevation of 123 meters. The lake is about five kilometers long, squeezed between Buntzen and Eagle Ridges. The Buntzen Lake recreation area is a BC Hydro-managed site that forms an integral part of the local reservoir system. At 182 hectares, the lake is large enough to support a fair number of people. It is long and thin with a well developed trail system, making it easy to leave the popular south end and find isolation very quickly.

BUNTZEN LAKE at a GLANCE		
ACTIVITIES	BOATING, FISHING, HIKING, RIDING, PICNICKING, SWIMMING	
LAKE STATS	Elevation & Size	: 123 meters, 182 hectares
	Lake Setting	: Buntzen Lake recreation area
ACCESS	Vehicle Type	: car
	Nearest Highway	: 12.5 kilometers to Highway 7A
FACILITIES	Type & Class	: well developed
	Camping	: not permitted
	Boat Launch	: good gravel
FISHING	Fish Stocked	: 75,000
	Size Reports	: rainbows to 30 centimeters
	Restrictions	: no motors

In 1903 the Buntzen Lake hydroelectric project, designed to provide the first power to Vancouver, was put into production by the Vancouver Power Company so it has some interesting history.

The Buntzen Lake system is just one part of the overall project. Water was first raised in the upper Coquitlam Lake to a point where it could flow into a tunnel 3.6 kilometers long under Eagle Mountain into Buntzen Lake. This tunnel reaches a depth of 1.2 kilometers at one point, finally emptying into the north end of Buntzen Lake. It then flows out of the south end of the lake down through a penstock tunnel to Indian Arm where Buntzen Lake Powerhouse 1 was constructed in 1903 followed by Buntzen Lake Powerhouse 2 in 1914, both operated remotely from the control facility on Burnaby Mountain.

The lake and its surrounding area is a well-planned day use recreational site with excellent facilities and trails. When you first see the lake from the picnic area at the south beach, you will hold your breath momentarily for this has to be one of the most beautiful lakes in the Fraser Valley. Its shoreline is rocky but carpeted with lush green conifers. The incredibly picturesque mountains in the distance contrast the lake's dark, deep clear green waters, forming a postcard picture.

FINDING the LAKE

Access the lake from Barnett Highway 7A onto the Ioco exit to Ioco Road. If you zero out the odometer at this intersection, you will turn on Ioco Road and proceed north across Guildford Drive at .35 kilometers. At the next intersection you must turn left to continue on Ioco Road (.75 kilometers). At 5.5 kilometers, turn right up 1st Avenue, which is actually Sunnyside Road.

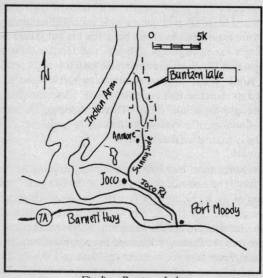

Finding Buntzen Lake

The church and the school will mark the intersection. From here you will drive north on Sunnyside Road where, at 6.15 kilometers, you take the right fork through the little area of Anmore. Finally at 10.5 kilometers you will reach the entrance to the trailer park (left) and the corner store with canoe rentals. The gate to Buntzen is to the right at 10.6 kilometers and the closed gate guarding access to the north end of the lake is at 12.3 kilometers. Turn left here and three parking strips are just to your right. This is the end of the road unless you want to launch a boat. Then, go left to the launch and the main beach picnic area is dead ahead.

Alternatively, you could have followed Ioco Road from Barnett Highway, gone up Heritage Mountain Boulevard, turned right on Parkside Drive, left on Water Street, gone straight through on East Road, then right on Sunnyside to take you to the gate.

RECREATION

Facilities at the lake are extremely well-organized and -maintained. From the main entrance gate, you will first encounter the equestrian staging area then the main triple parking lot near the south beach and picnic area. This is the main recreation site, sloping gradually into the lake waters, a perfect setting containing a large grassy playground and picnic area. There is a well-positioned boat launch and dock at the end of a circular paved road, making it easy to launch a cartop or canoe. The large picnic area is set elegantly in the tall trees sloping nicely to the south beach area. Washrooms and ample parking are also found here. Several developed viewpoints along an extensive trail system and various equestrian trails surround the lake. Several interpretive trails are also carved expertly into the area. The north beach area is another well-developed and less-populated picnic site.

Hiking The main Buntzen Lake area is particularly well-endowed with good-quality trails for both man and horse offering quite a wide variety of terrain and scenery. Most of the trails are maintained by Hydro but a few are not. There are nine trails in total offering a varied degree of difficulty and terrain. Buntzen Lake Trail is the most popular at 12 kilometers around the lake if you cut across the suspension bridge at North Beach. It offers breathtaking scenery and lush vegetation that hugs the lake's shoreline for most of its length. Elevation gain is virtually nil at about 70 meters, so the hike is easy. There are several spectacular viewpoints and many short footpaths to shore for fishing along the way. The pedestrian trails around the lake are described below.

Buntzen Lake Trail requires about four hours to complete, forming a complete loop around the lake. The *east* side portion starts at the Buntzen Creek bridge at the north end of the picnic area. It is a bit over three kilometers and takes 1.5 hours to get to North Beach. The *west* leg starts at the south end of the first parking lot then crosses the south arm of Buntzen Lake via the floating bridge. Between the floating bridge and the pumphouse the trail follows Pumphouse Road. From here you can take the Buntzen Lake Trail to the suspension bridge at the north end and cross over to North Beach. The distance is about six kilometers so allow 2.5 hours. At the north end of the lake, the trail follows the Powerhouse road from the Coquitlam tunnel outfall until it turns south along the west side of the lake. There are viewpoints along the trail and several access trails to the lakeshore so allow extra time to dilly-dally.

Viewpoint Trail is a short hiking trail that forms part of the Buntzen Lake Trail. From the South Beach area follow the east side, walking the Buntzen Lake Trail north for about a kilometer then cut left to the viewpoint which will take a mere ten minutes to get to the wooden view deck. You can skirt the dock and get out onto the rocks here—a popular fishing spot.

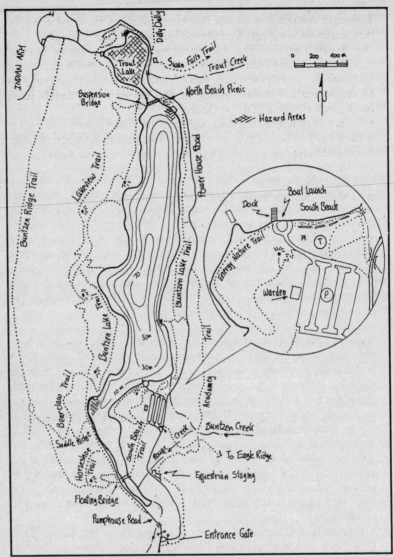

Detailed map of Buntzen Lake and trail system

Energy Nature Trail is a self-guided nature trail, one kilometer long, looping around the heavily treed knoll just south of the boat launch. It follows the shore of Buntzen Lake for a short distance before returning through the forest to the south beach picnic site. This trail features a variety of forest landscapes and views of the lake. Interpretive displays are found along the way describing how plants, animals and man acquire their energy.

Dog Bypass Trail is another hiking trail appropriately named for its function. Dogs are allowed on this one *if they are on a leash*. This is a connector trail providing access between the parking area and Buntzen Lake Trail. It is for visitors and their leashed canines, but dogs are not permitted in the south beach picnic area from May 1 to October 1.

Entrance Trail is another hiking trail accessed from the south parking lot. It takes you 1.5 kilometers south along the lake panhandle. If you arrive at the main entrance on foot or by bus, follow the Pumphouse Road for one kilometer to the floating bridge. Cross the bridge and follow the Buntzen Lake Trail to the main picnic area.

Diez Vistas-Buntzen Ridge Trails take you from the end of the Equestrian Trail loop, high along the ridge overlooking Indian Arm, all the way to the north Hydro access road. From here you can loop back along the Lakeview Trail or take the west side Buntzen Lake Trail. This is a significant journey so allow a full day. This particular ridge trail is **not** maintained by Hydro so you should be familiar with the trail routes and be able to deal with variable terrain conditions. From the south end at the footbridge, an elevation of 123 meters, the trail climbs to 560 meters elevation at the crest, then follows the ridge north to drop slowly to an elevation of 200 meters at the north end. From the footbridge the trail is about eight kilometers to the north end of the lake then another seven kilometers back, so this is not an easy hike.

Dilly Dally and Eagle Ridge Trails (see the trail map in the next section on Cypress Lake (4-3)). This is a rather long trail loop that carries on from the Powerline Road just past the North Beach area. The trail takes you north past Buntzen Bay (on Indian Arm) to Croker Lookout, (for 3.5 kilometers) then straight up the ridge to Dilly Dally Pass (another 3.1 kilometers) to skirt the Port Coquitlam Conservation Area, back to the Swan Falls trail junction (2.2 kilometers) where it plunges back down to the north beach area. Alternatively, you can continue to Eagle Peak past Eagle Mountain then descend (and I mean *descend*—1000 meters!) the Eagle Ridge Trail along Buntzen Creek to the main parking lot at the south end of Buntzen Lake. This is another 11.4 kilometers from the Swan Falls junction. This is a *long* trail totaling 25 kilometers and requires a full day. Since this trail system leads to a series of small lakes on the ridge, it is described in more detail in the next section under Cypress Lake.

Equestrian There are five equestrian trails in the area that can also be used for hiking. They are quite extensive, accessible either from the main gate or from the equestrian staging area about a kilometer in from the entrance gate, just over half-way between the entrance and the South Beach site if you need to bring in a trailer. Equestrian rest areas are located near Rouge and Trout creeks.

Academy Trail extends from the Alpine Riding Academy near the main entrance gate to the north end of Buntzen Lake paralleling the main entrance road, Rouge Creek and a transmission line before joining the Powerhouse Road.

Lake View Trail has steep portions, traversing the eastern slopes of Buntzen Ridge on the west side of the lake. Access via Powerhouse Road at the north where it connects with Academy Trail and at the main entrance gate (via Pumphouse Road) where it connects with the south end of Academy Trail. Portions are steep and rough, particularly at the north end, so riders and horses should be experienced.

Bear Claw, Saddle Ridge, Horseshoe Trails are short loop trails accessible from the main Lake View Trail. For hikers, Horseshoe and Saddle Ridge trails connect to Diez Vistas and Buntzen Lake Trails.

Biking Another small but unique feature is the inclusion of biking in the recreation roster. The trail starts at the entrance gate and follows along Pumphouse Road going across the floating bridge north on the South Beach Trail, across the top of the parking lot to Powerhouse Road. This gets you all the way to the North Beach picnic area—the end of the line for bikes. This may not seem like much but it covers just over five kilometers of super terrain.

Boating A major highlight of the Buntzen Lake area is the superb boating. Being set between two ridges, the lake is a long thin protected body of water nestled against an impressive shoreline of rolling rocks, cliffs and lush forest offering many interesting little bays and coves perfect for canoeing. The lake deepens quickly so the waters are cool, clear and green, giving you many rocks along the shore to sun on, dive or fish from. The shoreline is long and variable so you can easily spend all day exploring or fishing.. The area is well organized for small boat lovers, providing an excellent launch facility with a canoe rental back at the entrance gate. Power boats are not permitted so you will not be disturbed by buzzing motors.

Fishing in the lake is another highlight but only from a non-power boat or from the lakeshore as power boats are not allowed on the lake and this is a day use facility only. Although there are many spots where you can reach the water's edge, the south end boat launch is really the only convenient place to launch. A word of caution...if you are planning on swimming or boating be extremely careful about certain areas. The water flow in and out of the lake is activated by remote control, changing the water levels and movements without warning, causing sudden unpredictable, strong and dangerous surface and underwater currents. *There are certain areas which should therefore be avoided near the outflow near the north beach picnic area and the pump intake area at the north end of the lake, from North Beach. Beware of the tempting little channel lead-*

ing past the North Beach picnic area. It is best to keep out of there and another intake at the south end of the lake which is also hazardous (see map).

There are a variety of fish types and sizes in the lake including cutthroats, rainbows and kokanee. An aggressive stocking program has been in place since 1986, as the stocking table shown below indicates:

FISH STOCKED	YEAR	TYPE	NUMBER
Cutthroat	1986 to 1990	yearlings	15000/yr.

BC Hydro has their own fisheries program researching habitat and recently placing experimental spawning facilities on the lake. The Buntzen Lake Trail follows most of the lake's shoreline with numerous side trails leading down to the rocks on the shore. The lake is in a deep gorge so the water deepens rapidly from shore offering many excellent fishing areas. As noted on the map, the lake goes to 70 meters in depth within 200 meters from shore. Just at the South Beach area in the little bay the water dives to 50 meters almost immediately.

THIS GROUP of LAKES is perched high up on Eagle Ridge in the Port Moody conservation reserve. Appropriately named, Eagle Ridge is high up, reaching elevations of 1200 meters. From this ridge you can see spectacular views in almost every direction but the effort required is exceptional. The ridge forms the divide between the Buntzen Lake recreation area and the Port Coquitlam conservation reserve better known as the Coquitlam watershed. The Eagle Ridge Trail follows this thrust of rock northward for several kilometers. Clusters of tiny lakes trapped in the sub-alpine outcrops of the ridge dot this trail. Most are less than a hectare in size so the recreational value is not in the use of the water but in the hiking. The views and the peaceful isolation also make up for lake sizes. There are more than 11 lakes on the ridge but some are unnamed so they have not been included.

FINDING THE LAKES

The lakes are most 'easily' accessed from the Buntzen Lake parking lot. To find the parking lot take Barnett Highway 7A onto the Ioco exit to Ioco Road. Proceed north across Guildford Drive and turn left onto Ioco Road. At 5.5 kilometers turn right up 1st Avenue, then right at 6.2 kilometers, through Anmore, right into the Buntzen Lake recreation area entrance at 10.6 kilometers and finally park at the Buntzen Lake parking lot. Now it is time to get the packsack and boots.

Be aware that this visit requires a vigorous hike up Buntzen Creek from an elevation of 130 meters to the first major plateau area at 800 meters. From here one can trudge north to five little lakes just north of Eagle Mountain (1050 meters) or south to an old logged area around Cypress Lake (790 meters). The area around Cypress Lake is quite a contrast to the northerly route simply because the messy logging practice around the lake has left its scar on this once-pristine lake. The trail to the lakes is described under 'trails' covered below.

RECREATION

The major attraction in this area is the set of hiking trails and the fantastic scenery from Eagle Ridge. The trail system takes you from the parking lot at 130 meters to some incredible viewpoints at 1200 meters that will make your camera come alive. If you decide to make the trek make sure you are in good shape, start early and be well-prepared. It is possible to make the whole *23 kilometer* loop in one day but just in case check in at the ranger station by the Buntzen parking lot (for day use only) and let them know where you are heading.

Facilities With the exception of the organized facilities at Buntzen (see previous section on Buntzen Lake) there is nothing but a trail and views to remind you that civilization still exists. Once you leave the paved parking lot and climb onto the ridge there are many open alpine meadows where overnighters have decided to take in some of the freshest night air in the valley but that's it, no formal facilities...only nature at its best.

Trails Thanks to Halvor Lunden, a grand old gentleman, a good hiking trail has been cut right from the parking lot up to Eagle Mountain and along the ridge all the way to Dilly Dally Pass. From here one can drop down to Croker Lookout, come back south along the Dilly Dally Trail then all the way to the dam at the north end of Buntzen Lake. From here you can reach Buntzen Lake Trail taking you back to the parking lot. Note that this is a grand total of 23 kilometers! You will also climb to over 1200 meters in elevation and then drop back down to an elevation of 130 meters...not your average walk in the park! Note that these are tough hiking trails guaranteed to strain even the best athletes. They are rough in places with rocks and windfalls making it more difficult. If you try this trail system, be prepared. The trails are described below.

Eagle Ridge Trail has not officially been named the *Lunden Trail* but considering the effort and dedication this man has expended on the area, I would consider that naming it after him would be the least anyone could do.

119

Even after retirement he still maintains the trail system. The trail starts off the Powerhouse Road at the gate across from the south parking lot, at an elevation of about 130 meters.

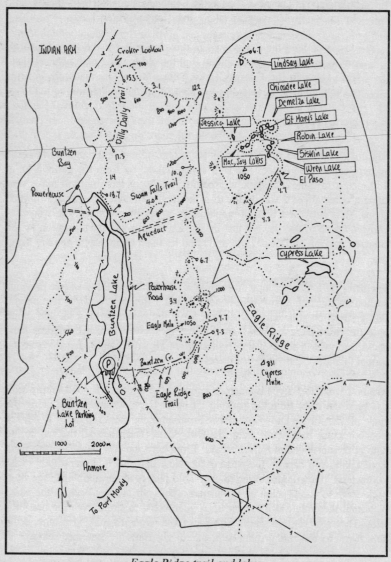

Eagle Ridge trail and lakes

From here it begins its gradual ascent, slowly curving around to approach Buntzen Creek. From here you begin a steady grind as you parallel the creek all the way to the first viewpoint, Polytrichum Lookout (640 meters and 2.8 kilometers). The next view is at Longview Lookout (810 meters and 3.7 kilometers) where you can take a diversion to Cypress Lake.

Just at around the Longview Lookout you will see the logged area to the southeast where it is possible to find the old logging road network that will take you into the **Cypress Lake** plateau area. The roads are growing in rapidly and Mr. Lunden has not made a formal joining to the road system, preferring to keep the rather ugly logged area away from the untouched north area. You are on your own, but there are several unnamed lakes (ponds) in the area, as shown on the map. Finding Cypress is a challenge, since there are no roads right to the lake.

Back at Eagle Ridge Trail, from Longview the next decision is at 4.7 kilometers (elevation 890 meters) where you can cross the creek to take a spectacular loop around Eagle Mountain. This is a 3.4 kilometer trail that cuts back southwest then heads north to the main trail at Lindsay Lake which continues straight through to take you to a smaller right loop trail around a chain of little lakes (see the inset map).

Wren Lake is first, then you loop to **Sisken**, **Robin** and the longer **Chicadee Lake**. The trail curls around **Demelza Lake**, then cuts back to the north tip of Chicadee to intersect the main trail again. The inner left loop curls around **St. Mary's**, **Mac** and **Jay Lakes** and **Jessica Lake** is just west of Jay, close to the bypass trail around Eagle Mountain. This is the place you want to spend some time. The lakes are small but they sparkle in a wondrous sub-alpine setting, making this a most relaxing place to sit and ponder. The trails continue, converging at **Lindsay Lake** (6.7 kilometers) via the east side trail and an elevation of 1150 meters. From here the trail continues along the ridge to the next spectacle at Eagle Peak (Mount Beautiful) where you get views both east and west. The elevation is 1280 meters, distance is now 9.5 kilometers. At exactly ten kilometers (1105 meters elevation) you encounter the left branch of Swan Falls Trail to Buntzen Lake. Eagle Ridge Trail continues to Dilly Dally Pass (12.2 kilometers and 1050 meters).

Dilly Dally Trail connects the north end of Eagle Ridge Trail with the road at the north end of Buntzen Lake. If you continued on the Eagle Ridge Trail (from Dilly Dally Pass at elevation 1050 meters and 12.2 kilometers along the Eagle Ridge Trail) you would drop to Croker Lookout at an elevation of 225 meters in 3.1 kilometers. There is a short side trail here to the lookout over Indian Arm. From here (15.3 kilometers, 225 meters) you would proceed south to the short trail to Buntzen Bay (17.3 kilometers, 115 meters).

Continuing south you would hit the Powerhouse Road (18.7 kilometers, 115 meters elevation). From here it is easy sailing to the south parking lot, making a total of 23 kilometers.

Swan Falls Trail connects Eagle Ridge Trail and Powerline Road plunging four kilometers down the mountain to the north end of Buntzen Lake. This is a *steep* trail. From the bottom elevation of 125 meters you will climb to 1105 meters at the top, with hardly a break.

Fishing With the exception of Cypress Lake which was stocked in the early 80s, the lakes are too small to support fish. Cypress Lake, at four hectares is deep enough to possibly support fish so may be well worth a try. The lake is cluttered with logging debris so be prepared for a rough tangle with brambles and bushes.

COMO LAKE

COMO LAKE known as *Welcome Lake* is a little jewel sitting quietly at an elevation of 150 meters atop the hill in Maillardville. Carefully preserved by the community of Como Lake, it is situated in Como Lake Park surrounded by residential homes. The lake is five hectares in size, contained in a municipal park hardly much larger than that but it is still large enough to offer the local residents an interesting array of recreational conveniences. It is not hard to see the lake and park play an important part in the activities of the surrounding community. In fact, if you visit the lake, you may even feel like a foreigner as you watch the locals relax and frolic in this community playland.

FINDING the LAKE

Finding this lake is an easy matter since you can drive right to the lakeside parking lot. The main roadway skirting the lake is north-south Gatensbury Street intersecting Austin, Foster or Como Lake Avenue. Each of these will get you to Gatensbury. If you are traveling north, Gatensbury will take a jog to the right as you cross Foster Avenue. The lake will be glistening on your left side a short distance farther. Just as you see the lake, you will also see the entrance to the parking lot at the south end. This parking lot was not designed for a lot of

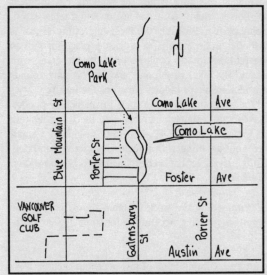

Finding Como Lake

visitors, so you may need to continue through to the one at the north end off Gatensbury, just opposite Regan Street.

On the other side of the lake all the east-west streets dead-end on the park boundary so forget parking there. Private residences skirt this west side, so you may want to respect their territory. From the parking lots, you can access the walking/jogging trail that surrounds the lake.

COMO LAKE at a GLANCE

ACTIVITIES	PICNICKING, FISHING, WALKING, PLAYGROUND	
LAKE STATS	Elevation & Size	: 150 meters, five hectares
	Lake Setting	: Como Lake Park
ACCESS	Vehicle Type	: car
	Nearest Highway	: surrounded by streets
FACILITIES	Type & Class	: developed
	Camping	: not allowed, day use
	Boat Launch	: canoe
FISHING	Fish Stocked	: 30,000
	Size Reports	: small trout
	Restrictions	: no motors, are restriction

RECREATION

Facilities at the lake are modest but well designed and convenient considering the available space. The feature at this park is just the relaxing environment that hits you when you enter. This is where you can slow down and relax, stroll, picnic and watch the kids play or fish. Probably the most interesting aspect is the degree of stocking by fisheries in an attempt to provide a place for kids to fish. The park contains two parking lots at opposite ends, picnic areas with benches, a jogging track around the lake, washrooms and several playgrounds on the west side. There is even a Kinsmen's kiddies park. For the leisurely types park benches placed around the lake offer romantic spots to smooch or ponder. For the junior anglers, two excellent U-shaped docks jut into the water making great platforms from which the kids can fish. It is possible to launch a small flotation device into the lake…but anything with a motor is strictly prohibited. Due to the size of the lake, it is inevitable that *no* boats will soon be allowed on the lake, so please check before you try.

Fishing information is well summed by the stocking table shown below. You will see that the program is quite aggressive, accounting for some 30,000 catchable fish since 1986.

The lake is very shallow, with a maximum depth of just over four meters. Nevertheless, the lake has some interesting fishing features, with two docks to fish from, a rocky area to cast from and marshes near the exit stream. This is a popular area to learn fly fishing since there is not a lot of vegetation to interfere with your casting and this is a popular spot for fly fishing courses. Like some of the other lakes in the area, there is an age restriction simply because it is a small lake with an intense recreation demand on it.

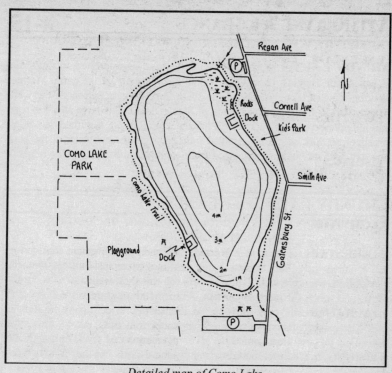

Detailed map of Como Lake

FISH STOCKED	YEAR	TYPE	NUMBER
Rainbow	1986	catchables	7500
Rainbow	1987	catchables	6000
Cutthroat	1988	catchables	200
Rainbow	1988	catchables	6500
Rainbow	1989	catchables	8200
Rainbow	1990	catchables	1000

MUNDY LAKE 4-15

MUNDY LAKE is situated in Mundy Park, a large forested area atop the hill in Austin Heights. Bounded by Como Lake Avenue on the north, Mariner Way on the east, King Albert on the south and Hillcrest/Wilson on the west, Mundy Park is Port Moody's version of Stanley Park. This large area has been carefully preserved to include a large area of natural forest, disturbed only by an excellent network of well-maintained trails. Around the perimeter of the park you will find various well-developed facilities to accommodate a wide range of sports activities and recreation needs.

MUNDY LAKE at a GLANCE

ACTIVITIES	TRAILS, PICNICKING, FISHING, RECREATION CENTER, PLAYGROUNDS	
LAKE STATS	Elevation & Size	: 122 meters, one hectare
	Lake Setting	: Mundy Municipal Park
ACCESS	Vehicle Type	: car plus short walk
	Nearest Highway	: surrounded by streets
FACILITIES	Type & Class	: developed
	Camping	: not permitted
	Boat Launch	: not allowed
FISHING	Fish Stocked	: natural
	Size Reports	: small cutthroat
	Restrictions	: no boats

Central to the park is an undisturbed forest containing the larger Mundy Lake, less than a hectare in size and well preserved in a natural setting. Lost Lake is on the eastern side, not quite as well protected from the outside world. The park has been organized to cover a wide range of recreational needs, the highlights of which are the superb trails, the playgrounds and the natural forest containing the lakes.

FINDING the LAKE

Mundy Park is bounded by Como Lake Avenue on the north, Mariner Way on the east, Austin Avenue on the south and Hillcrest on the west. Although there are several access points into the trail system, (see the trail map), access to Mundy Lake is best accomplished by getting on to Austin, then turning north onto Hillcrest. Just before the jog in the road at Foster, take a right turn into the park where you will enter a parking lot and the swimming pool area. Keep going if you want to get to the lake. Since it is situated in the center of the park continue on the roadway behind the pool complex, heading down to a second parking lot. Drive to the far end where you will see a sign at the trail. It is a short walk of about 15 minutes from here to the lake.

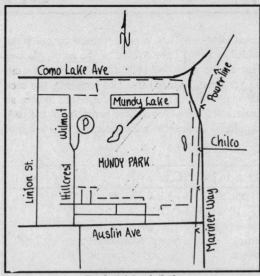

Finding Mundy Lake

Walk in from here on the blue trail, turn right still on blue at the junction. The trail will then curve to the left on a slight downhill grade, keep left onto the yellow trail at the junction. It is just a short walk to the south end of the lake where you will find a landing. There is a dock half-way up the lake, accessed by following the yellow trail that parallels the shore. If you feel up to it, you can hike along the maze of trails to get to Lost Lake, the little neighbor, but it is easier accessed from Mariner if you are driving (see the next section Lost Lake 4-16).

RECREATION

Facilities Most of the formal facilities are scattered along the west side of Mundy park, offering extensive open grassed areas, parking lots and swimming pool. There are washrooms, picnic areas and a multitude of playgrounds for different field sports but the more impressive highlight is the system of trails that networks the park providing access to the two lakes. At Mundy Lake, the facilities are sparse, with two small docks and circumference foot-trails.

Trails The trail system is shown on the map. These are extremely good hog fuel (wood chips, bark and sawdust) trails, making them a dream to stroll on and the soft footing makes them great for jogging. The area is relatively flat, requiring little effort—a place where you can walk quietly and enjoy the forest. Since the flat areas are also swampy, the use of the bark mulch elevates the trail above the mud so this is an excellent way to walk right through marsh that would otherwise be impossible to walk in. Each of the trails is identified by a color and each is thusly marked. Four main trail systems criss-cross the park, as shown on the map, varying from 5.7 kilometers to 1.4 kilometers.

127

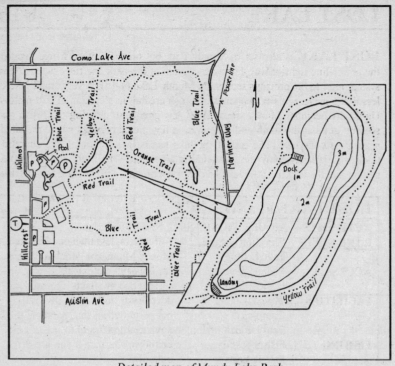

Detailed map of Mundy Lake Park

Yellow Trail is a short 1.4 kilometers originating at Como Lake Avenue. It drops south to Mundy Lake and circles it.

Orange Trail is 1.9 kilometers cutting diagonally across the park, originating at the school ground in the northwest corner of the park.

Red Trail is a north-south trail that cuts through the middle of the park, with a branch to the main playground. It is 1.6 kilometers, starting at the end of Hickey Drive (aptly named I'm sure!) and Como Lake Avenue.

Blue Trail This one allows you to take a complete loop around the park, 5.7 kilometers in length. Several perimeter access points are provided.

Fishing As an interesting feature, little Mundy Lake is a popular fishing hole for the younger set. Surprisingly, the lake has small trout so obviously the few tiny streams are enough to create water circulation. There is a landing at the south end to cast from and a dock half-way up the west side of the lake. You can cast off the dock into two meters of water. The rest of the lake is heavily-brushed making a cast into the deeper water difficult. The lake is only three meters in the deepest section so you will be fishing for smaller fish. No formal stocking program is in progress.

128

LOST LAKE is also set in Mundy Park but on the eastern fringe, against the power-line right-of-way. For a description of the park and the extensive trail system refer to the previous section on Mundy Lake (4-15). A very small lake of less that a hectare, it sits in a swampy brush area at an elevation of 130 meters. Unlike its neighbor Mundy, some effort has gone into clearing the brush and seeding grass at the south end. There are a few picnic benches where the small stream exits the lake. The rest of the lake has been left natural, the shoreline thick with brush so only the west side is accessible. The highlight is the trail system and the way the little lake has been left alone...a great place for a picnic.

LOST LAKE at a GLANCE

ACTIVITIES	TRAILS, PICNICKING, NATURE	
LAKE STATS	Elevation & Size	: 130 meters, less than one hectare
	Lake Setting	: Mundy Municipal Park
ACCESS	Vehicle Type	: car plus 400 meter walk
	Nearest Highway	: surrounded by streets
FACILITIES	Type & Class	: developed
	Camping	: not permitted
	Boat Launch	: not permitted
FISHING	Fish Stocked	: unknown
	Size Reports	: unknown
	Restrictions	: no boats

FINDING the LAKE

Lost Lake is best accessed from Mariner Way on the east side of Mundy Park. Refer to the trail map for Mundy Park in the previous section if you decide to come in from a different direction. The quickest access is the orange trail system but it is not obvious where this starts if you are coming from Mariner Way. There is shoulder area to park on at Chilco Street and a footpath that crosses the rather ugly-looking Hydro power-line right-of-way—sort of obscures your perception of a nice, natural park!

The footpath cuts across the open Hydro field, allowing you to enter the open grassed area at the south end of Lost Lake, also the access to the Orange Trail. There is another parking area to the north, with access to the Blue Trail but it is a ten-minute walk to the lake.

RECREATION

Facilities The lake is definitely not developed for heavy volume. There are a few picnic tables, an open gravel area with a lone park bench for lovers and a grassed area that allows the kids to play. The south creek trickles through the grassy playfield, making it a nice quiet place to watch the ducks, stop for rest, or have a picnic.

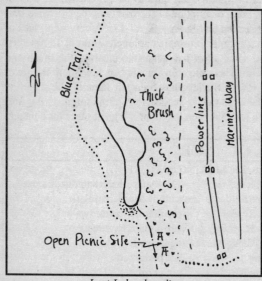

Lost Lake shoreline

Trails Lost Lake borders Mundy park, providing access to the vast network of trails inside the area. These are quite extensive and are detailed in the previous section on Mundy Lake (4-15) and are not repeated here.

REGION FIVE
PORT COQUITLAM

THE PORT COQUITLAM REGION consists of a ten- by 40-kilometer strip of land projecting north of the Fraser River from the city of Port Coquitlam which marks the southerly extent of the region, a heavily populated suburban area that gives way to wilderness very rapidly as you proceed north. Laterally, the area covers the mountainous region between Indian Arm and the vast valley of the Pitt River and Pitt Lake. Within the southern portion, the towns of Pitt Meadows and Port Coquitlam make up the two communities, containing virtually all the population. As far as the terrain is concerned, the mountains rise rapidly from the valley floor to reach rugged wilderness within a short five kilometers of the city limits. From the lower valley at Port Coquitlam the mountains climb steeply to elevations in excess of 1500 meters. Due to this dramatic climb the congestion and urban intensity evident along the highway to the south gives way to absolute isolation in a very short distance and you get into totally undeveloped, difficult-to-access wilderness very rapidly.

The lakes in the region are scattered in three major areas; the Crown forest reserve, the Vancouver/Port Coquitlam watershed and Burke Mountain Park. From a recreational standpoint, much of the region is simply undeveloped and the lakes are fairly difficult to get to. With the exception of a lake mid-city in Port Coquitlam, none have any developed facilities. Typically you are in for a good hike, a great opportunity to do some primitive camping and some unbelievable scenery.

ROADS, ACCESS POINTS AND LAKES

The main access through the region is *Lougheed Highway (7)* coming from the south turning easterly as it meets *Highway 7A (Barnett Highway)*. Two access points are noted, taking you to wilderness areas rapidly within eight kilometers north of the highway.

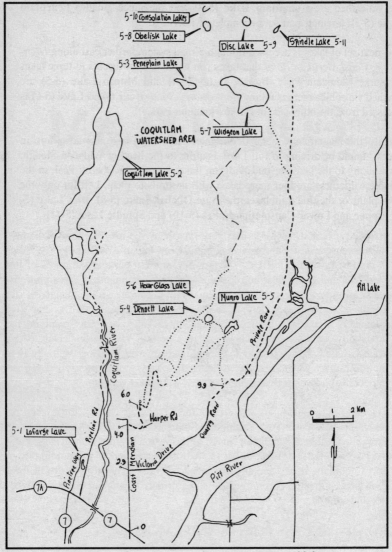

5-10 Consolation Lakes
5-8 Obelisk Lake
Disc Lake 5-9
Spindle Lake 5-11
5-3 Peneplain Lake
COQUITLAM WATERSHED AREA
5-7 Widgeon Lake
Coquitlam Lake 5-2
5-6 Hour-Glass Lake
Munro Lake 5-5
5-4 Denoett Lake
Pitt Lake
Coquitlam River
Private Road
6.0
9.9
Harper Rd
5-1 Lafarge Lake
Pipeline Rd
4.0
Quarry Road
Coast Meridian
Victoria Drive
2.9
Pitt River
Pinetree Way
7A
7
7
0
0 1 2 Km

Port Coquitlam region roads, access points and lakes

The first access is from the intersection of *Highway 7* and *Pinetree Way*. From here, a short 1.9 kilometers will get you to the manmade **Lafarge Lake (5-1)** or Coquitlam Pit, right in the middle of the city congestion. Continuing on *Pinetree Way* which gives way to *Pipeline Road* you follow the Coquitlam River to the edge of the Coquitlam watershed where access is restricted. Also found in the watershed are **Coquitlam Lake (5-2)** and the much smaller **Peneplain Lake (5-3),** a remote pair set in complete wilderness.

The next set of lakes is accessed through a road system farther east along *Highway 7, Coast Meridian Road* that takes you north to allow access to three lakes in Burke Mountain Park. **Dennett Lake (5-4)** and **Munro Lake (5-5)** are reached via some vigorous hiking from *Quarry Road.* **Hour Glass Lake (5-6)** is accessed from the other side of Burke Mountain Park.

Finally, the magnificent, isolated **Widgeon Lake (5-7)** is a new adventure in access, found by driving to Pitt Lake, boating to the head of Widgeon Slough, then hiking to the lake. Beyond Widgeon Lake, far up near Obelisk Peak in the remote wilderness are four more lakes with no trails to them. Left for only the float plane or the true trailblazer, these are **Obelisk Lake (5-8)**, **Disc Lake (5-9)**, **Upper** and **Lower Consolation Lakes (5-10)** and **Spindle Lake (5-11)**.

LAFARGE LAKE or *Coquitlam Pit* is another manmade lake situated in the residential area of Port Coquitlam, just a bit north of the Coquitlam shopping center. At five hectares, the lake is a reasonable size, a nice fate for an old gravel pit and sits low in the valley at an elevation of 45 meters, nestled in the small Lafarge Park. This park contains the Town Center Stadium on the north end and Lafarge Lake at the south end.

Once a large pit operated by Lafarge Cement, the pit was abandoned and flooded, leaving a scarce bit of vegetation along the southern and eastern shores. One of the unusual features is the development of a fantastic fishing spot from this peculiar gravel hole. It is indeed an oddity to see fishermen sitting quietly on the bank, casting floats into the glistening water...right in the hustle of city life! Due to its proximity to urban life this is a very popular spot for locals to take a relaxing stroll around the lake or even a quiet float in a canoe. The area is small, however and not able to support a large volume of visitors.

FINDING the LAKE

The lake is found in Lafarge Park between Pinetree Way and Pipeline Road, two main streets in Port Coquitlam. The easiest access to the lake is from the junction of Highway 7 (Lougheed Highway) and Highway 7A (Barnett Highway). Pinetree Way goes north from the intersection, passing right through the middle of the Coquitlam shopping area. If you use the intersection as the trailhead and stay on Pinetree Way, you will get out of the congestion reasonably fast. At a mere 1.4 kilometers get ready to pull off to the right. Much to your surprise you will see a pretty

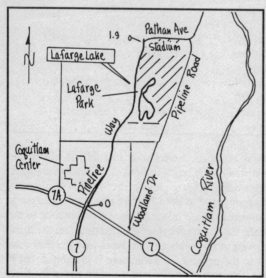

Finding Lafarge Lake

134

little lake on your right, glistening calmly beyond the open grassy area. You can park along here if you wish since this is the closest access point to the lake.

Alternatively, you can continue and turn into the town center stadium parking area at 1.7 kilometers. This is the formal parking lot used by overflow visitors. The parking lot curls around to the right and a walking trail is easily accessible from the end of the parking lot where it is just a short jaunt to the north end of the lake where you can walk all the way around.

RECREATION

Facilities With the exception of the town center stadium, the facilities around the lake are fairly basic. Another delight is the way the angling facilities have been developed. A fair amount of thought has gone into making this little lake a good fishing hole. The park is not large and the north half of it is dedicated to the stadium and parking facilities while the south half is mostly natural. The west side has some informal trials littered with the flurry of kids on their bikes. If you want some peace, follow the paved trail along the west side of the lake where a level walkway has been designed for anglers...quite an unusual 'fishway'.

LAFARGE LAKE at a GLANCE

ACTIVITIES	FISHING, WALKING, CANOEING, STADIUM	
LAKE STATS	Elevation & Size	: 45 meters, five hectares
	Lake Setting	: Lafarge Lake Park
ACCESS	Vehicle Type	: car
	Nearest Highway	: 1.4 kilometers to Highway 7
FACILITIES	Type & Class	: developed
	Camping	: not permitted
	Boat Launch	: not formal, use gravel beach
FISHING	Fish Stocked	: 43,000
	Size Reports	: rainbows to 35 centimeters
	Restrictions	: no power boats

This is a level paved roadway about six meters wide that follows almost the entire shoreline. There is a strip of sandy beach in front of it a few meters wide. With nothing to obstruct your cast (except a passing stroller) this is a perfect arrangement for casting into open water. A little T-dock projects into the lake at about midway. An upper pathway parallels this fishwalk, curving around to the south end of the lake where the trail continues along the shoreline into the trees, emerging at the exit stream weir at the southeast end. From here the trail continues around the lake back to the parking lot. Swimming is prohibited, but if you want to launch your canoe, the best place is just at the north end at the head of the fishway. There is a little open sand-gravel area where it would be reasonably simple to launch the vessel.

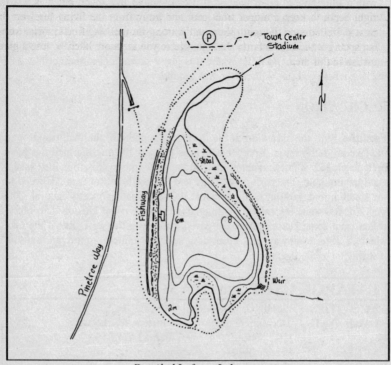

Detailed Lafarge Lake map

Fishing includes rainbow and catfish, quite a combination. The stocking table is shown below:

FISH STOCKED	YEAR	TYPE	NUMBER
Rainbow	1986	catchables	10000
Rainbow	1987	catchables	8300
Rainbow	1988	catchables	6400
Rainbow	1989	catchables	8700
Rainbow	1990	catchables	9000

For a lake this size, there are plenty of places to cast and this is a lot of fish ready for the frying pan. The fishway is positioned along the deeper section of the lake where it drops quickly to six meters. If you have a canoe or a rubber float, you can get out into the middle but it doesn't get much deeper than six meters. The opposite southeast shore is also open for casting and accessible from the perimeter trail where the water also plunges to a staggering 6 meters with a little hole at eight meters. It doesn't sound like much but it is just the right depth to keep a bigger trout cool and away from the flying lures on the west shore! Around the south shore in the trees you will also find favorite worn-out spots but the lake is fairly shallow here so you are more likely to lure a giant catfish in this area.

COQUITLAM LAKE   5-2
PENEPLAIN LAKE   5-3

COQUITLAM LAKE at 1100 hectares is the largest lake in the region. A large lake set in the Coquitlam Conservation Reserve (part of the Greater Vancouver water supply area) it is about 11 kilometers from Highway 7 at the end of Pipeline Road. Unfortunately, a gate at eight kilometers, some rather stern-looking guards and an *unfriendly* Doberman are sure to stop your venture into the area. The lake is low down at an elevation of 154 meters and as it is the key source of water it is off-limits for recreation.

PENEPLAIN LAKE is another smaller lake of 23 hectares also set in the Coquitlam Conservation Reserve but in a truly remote wilderness area. This lake sits at an elevation of 990 meters, high up on the east ridge overlooking the north end of Coquitlam Lake, just south of Peneplain Peak. This lake is apparently a real jewel, set in an untouched U-shaped valley below the towering backdrop of Peneplain Peak (1702 meters) but it is now rarely seen by human eyes.

MUNRO LAKE   5-4
DENNETT LAKE   5-5
HOUR GLASS LAKE   5-6

MUNRO and DENNETT LAKES are found high up south of Burke Mountain in Burke Mountain Park. Munro Lake is nine hectares in size, resting at an elevation of 830 meters, perched on a wide bench overlooking the Pitt River marsh. Munro's blue waters glisten, reflecting green and rocky slopes along the shoreline. Its neighbor, Dennett Lake is another one kilometer northwest, higher up at an elevation of 950 meters, eight hectares in size. Tall rocky cliffs form a picturesque backdrop to this deep, circular lake. For years these lakes were on private properties with limited access but they have now become part of Burke Mountain Park. Due to their proximity to each other it is easy to visit both lakes, making this a nice day hike or overnight visit, particularly if you like natural surroundings but beware that the ruggedness of Burke Mountain and the steepness of the trails will surely test your stamina.

FINDING the LAKES

Burke Mountain Park can be accessed from two sides by car up to the foot of the mountain (see the trail map) but from there you have no escape from a strenuous hike. There are two ways of getting here, one on either side of the mountain. In either case, take the Coast Meridian Road off Highway 7 in Port Coquitlam and set your odometer to zero as you turn left (north) on Meridian. Proceed 1.3 kilometers across Prairie Road. Once at 2.9 kilometers make a choice whether it is the grueling shorter *east* route or the less-grueling but longer *west* route.

The **west** entry is from the old access road at the end of Harper Road where you park on the shoulder just before the gun club but you will walk from the gate over six kilometers and climb from 320 meters to 830 meters to get to Munro. See Burke Ridge and Village trails described below if this is your choice. If you're wondering about the difference, the east route is four kilometers long and 730 meters vertical to Munro.

The **east** entry is off Quarry Road, the shortest but perhaps more strenuous route where you take Coast Meridian Road off Highway 7 in Port Coquitlam. Set your odometer to zero as you turn left onto Meridian, then right onto Victoria Drive at 2.9 kilometers. Follow Victoria straight through until 4.2 kilometers where you turn left onto Victoria Drive (yes you *are* at the intersection of Victoria

Drive and Victoria Drive!). Follow the upper Victoria Drive until 6.2 kilometers where you cross the bridge, pass Gilly's Trail and get onto Quarry Road.

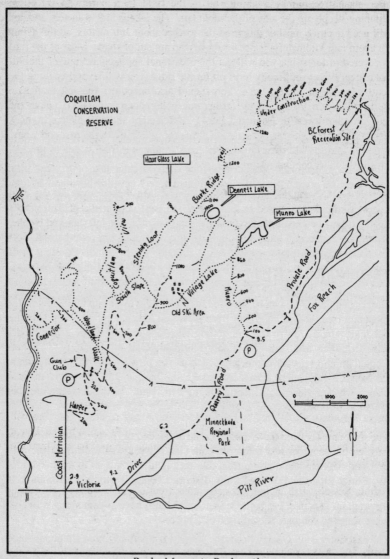

Burke Mountain Park trails

On Quarry, you will cross over MacIntyre Creek at 8.4 kilometers, Diener Creek at 9.1 kilometers then, at 9.5 kilometers, you will see a very rough pull-off loop on the left, the east trailhead to Munro Lake. There is an old logging road that comes down the hill near the Burke Mountain Park sign and intersects the trail after about five minutes, taking you to the right in a northwest direction, climbing steeply up the side of the mountain. The lake is at 830 meters and you will need to climb most of this from the road at about 100 meters, so this climb (of about four kilometers) is not for those who are out of shape. Most of the trail is covered in forest but you will get the occasional spectacular view of the Pitt Lake area. When you finally level off on the ridge, you will be approaching the southwest end of Munro Lake. You should also encounter the left branch to Burke Mountain Village. A bit farther you will encounter another trail to the left going northwest to Dennett Lake (1.2 kilometers and 130 meters higher). You will now parallel the old footpath along the lakeshore to the east end where you will find the old dam on Munro Creek (and some fresh water to drink!). This is the most popular resting spot.

HOUR GLASS LAKE is a small odd-shaped lake tucked away on the west side of Burke Ridge, found by parking at the west gate at the end of Harper Road. Follow the gravel road to the wide dirt road off to the left, marked by blue and orange markers. Follow this until the fork then take the right branch. Follow the orange markers across the Hydro cut and into the woods. Continue until a wide, level trail heads right. After passing a large sawdust pile on the right, look for an old road with a gate across it, the South Slope Trail which leads to the **Sterling Loop Trail** (see trail descriptions below), a new trail that connects the South Slope Trail with the Burke Ridge Trail, bypassing Hour Glass Lake. Get on the South Slope Trail, then midway take the left branch and you will parallel the ridge, passing Hour Glass Lake and cutting back on Burke Ridge.

RECREATION

Facilities at these lakes are essentially non-existent. These lakes are high on Burke Mountain set in very isolated wilderness so any facilities you find will have been left by the last overnighters. Camping at Munro is best by the dam at the Munro Creek exit, in a natural setting. At Dennett you may have to hunt out your own special place.

Fishing Resident fish includes eastern brook trout of catchable size. No stocking program is active, but both Dennett and Munro have stream systems to circulate water so you may be surprised by a big one!

Trails The Burke Mountain Park trail system has just recently been expanded by the Burke Mountain Naturalists. Historically, this area has had several uses including private residences, skiing and logging providing a network of old roads that can now be used as an extensive system for hikers. Already mentioned, the two parking spots are on Harper Road and Quarry Road, depending on how challenging a hike you want. The trails are long and arduous but rewarding. All are color-coded and tagged, but there is no guarantee that the animals have left them there.

Burke Ridge Trail (red) is 20 kilometers round trip with an elevation gain of 880 meters requiring six to eight hours. Walk up the gravel road to the old ski village (2.5 hours) then head off to the left of a collapsed woodshed. Note a blue tag on the right to Dennett Lake. You will climb continuously to meet the ridge at about 1100 meters. This is an extremely difficult trail where clouds, wind, rain and fog can spoil things quickly.

Burke Ridge Summit (orange/pink) is a continuation of the Burke Ridge Trail and it will get you to the Burke Summit and beyond, reaching 1200 meters along the ridge. It will take you *20 hours* to return to the gate. The current trail is being extended into Widgeon Bowl so you will have to watch your distance or you may walk farther than you expect.

Village Trail (yellow) is reached by the gravel road to the cabin area turn-off. This trail is 15 kilometers round trip, elevation gain of 680 meters and takes six to eight hours. Beyond the cabins the trail crosses bog meadows and heads for Munro Lake. The lower trail parallels the shore to the east end and the old dam. The trail past the west end of the lake (pink/green) leads to Dennett and back to the main route to the cabins.

Coquitlam Lake View Trail (orange) Round trip is 9.5 kilometers, taking four to six hours. The elevation gain is 680 meters. Follow the gravel road to the wide dirt road off to the left marked by blue and orange. Follow this to the fork then take the right fork. Follow the orange markers across the Hydro cut and into the woods. The trail winds and climbs to an eventual opening high above Coquitlam Lake.

South Slope Trail (red) is an 18-kilometer, six- to seven-hour round-trip trail that gains 880 meters in elevation. Follow the gravel road to the wide dirt road off to the left marked by blue and orange. Follow this until the fork then take the right fork. Follow the orange markers across the Hydro cut and into the woods. Continue until a wide, level trail heads right. After passing a large sawdust pile on the right, look for an old road with a gate across it. Follow this to reach the Burke Ridge Trail by the old ski village.

Woodland Walk Trail (blue) is an easy seven-kilometer round-trip taking three to five hours and the elevation gain is a mere 200 meters. Follow the gravel road to the wide dirt road off to the left with blue and orange markers. Follow this until the next fork then take the left branch. You will start on the old road then go through the forest to the Hydro cut after which it goes into the woods. Numerous loop trails offer alternative pathways. These woods contain some massive stumps and windfalls to remind you of the old forest.

Sterling Loop Trail (orange) is a new trail that connects the South Slope Trail with Burke Ridge Trail, bypassing Hour Glass Lake. Get on the South

Slope Trail then, at about midway, take the left branch and you will parallel the ridge, finally passing Hour Glass Lake and cutting back on Burke Ridge Trail. Allow about six hours for this hike.

Munro-Dennett Loop Trail (red) This trail starts from Quarry Road and climbs sharply up the ridge, taking in both lakes. The elevation gain is 830 meters and will require five to six hours for a round-trip of ten kilometers.

WIDGEON LAKE Visiting this lake is probably one of the most incredible wilderness experiences possible in the valley. An unusually isolated place considering its proximity to Port Coquitlam, the valley demands that its visitors be in reasonable shape. The task of getting there involves a bit of a safari. The lake itself is nestled high up, west of Pitt Lake at an elevation of 770 meters, deep in the Widgeon Valley. On Crown land outside of the adjoining watershed, the lake is fair game to the fit adventurer who wants to see some of the most spectacular virgin country in the valley. At 773 hectares, this lake is big, deep and incredibly beautiful. The crystal clear waters plunge to depths of 120 meters in the middle and the lake is ringed with equally steep shorelines thrusting upward, the north and west ridges reaching 1200 to 1400 meters in elevation. Add to this a lush cloak of forest, craggy cliffs and crystal streams and you have a most spectacular place to camp, like nowhere else on earth. Unfortunately, this place is not for everyone to see for the trek to the lake includes close to five kilometers by canoe, then an eight-kilometer hike to 770 meters elevation. The trip is quite a challenge but, at the end of it are rewards that a fisherman, hiker or naturalist will remember for a long time.

FINDING the LAKE

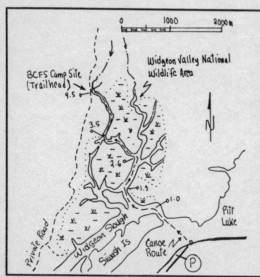

Navigating Widgeon Slough

To visit this lake be well prepared. As a side note you may wonder, if you have looked at some maps, why Quarry Road on the north side of Widgeon Slough is not mentioned here as the access route. This road has a gate across it at about 12 kilometers from Highway 7 so vehicle access is prohibited. Several private residences also block the access farther up so you have no choice but to get in from the other side of Pitt River.

The trek will start by first finding Pitt Lake, plopping a boat into Grant Narrows, paddling about five kilometers to the outlet of Widgeon Creek, leaving your canoe at the BCFS recreation site, then hiking eight kilometers to the lake.

First, find Grant Narrows Regional Park (see also Pitt Lake 6-1). The best access is via Highway 7 to Dewdney Trunk Road as you cross the Pitt River Bridge (first light). If you are new to this area set your odometer to zero here. Turn left and follow Dewdney Trunk to the stop sign and turn left onto Harris Road (at 2.3 kilometers). Continue north along Harris until 5.3 kilometers and then turn right on McNeil. Follow this road through the rural area to intersect Neaves at 9.0 kilometers and turn left (Neaves is the same as 208th Street and becomes Rannie after McNeil). Now it is straight north on Rannie to its end on Pitt Lake. You will eventually take a curve right and encounter the parking lot at 17.5 kilometers. The boat launch area is at 17.7 kilometers. As you come up onto the dike, you will see the south end of Pitt Lake and Grant Narrows. You can rent a canoe here in the summer.

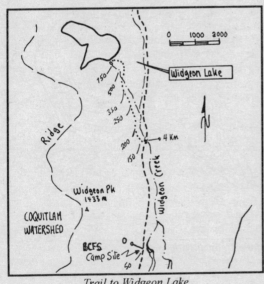

Trail to Widgeon Lake

Next, to get to the campsite at the head of Widgeon Creek take your boat northwest to the little opening across the Pitt River (Grant Narrows) from the boat launch area. From here paddle across into the east end of Widgeon Slough (one kilometer), then follow the eastern shore to the main split in the slough (2.6 kilometers). Follow the left branch and continue to the split (3.5 kilometers), then follow the right channel north for another kilometer through the Widgeon Valley National Wildlife Area to the head of the slough which will change to running water. Typically, this will cost you an hour. The forest service has developed a primitive but free campsite here. You will have to leave your canoe and start your eight-kilometer trek to Widgeon Lake.

Now get onto the old road and head north from the campsite. The first four kilometers is reasonably flat, following the old road and taking you from about 40 meters to 150 meters in elevation, then, past the lower falls, you will encounter the left branch just before you cross the bridge to Widgeon where things begin to change. From here it is another four kilometers and the pace changes as you start to gain elevation. The grand finale is in the last section which tests how well your quads have warmed up. You will cross the creek and curl around to finally emerge at the south end of the lake...and it will all be worth it!

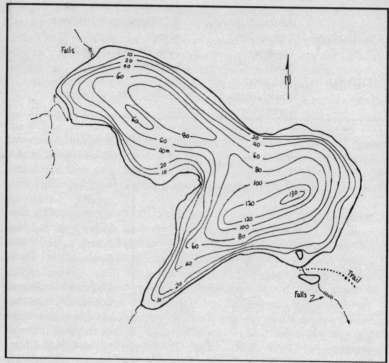

Detailed map of Widgeon Lake

RECREATION

Facilities at the lake are natural. That is, with the exception of the open areas left by overnight visitors, there are no formal organized facilities developed here. The BCFS campsite at the head of Widgeon Marsh is the closest formal facility but this is not a hindrance since there are several areas where prior campers have helped to develop natural open spots. The open sites are probably better placed, more picturesque and functional than any developed park facilities but you have fresh water and tree cover so what else do you need? After all, this is remote wilderness; a magic place where you can really get away and become one with nature.

WIDGEON LAKE at a GLANCE		
ACTIVITIES	HIKING, CAMPING, FISHING, CANOEING	
LAKE STATS	Elevation & Size	: 770 meters, 773 hectares
	Lake Setting	: Buntzen Valley, Crown Forest
ACCESS	Vehicle Type	: car, 4.5 kilometers by canoe, plus eight-kilometer hike
	Nearest Highway	: 30.2 kilometers to Highway 7
FACILITIES	Type & Class	: natural
	Camping	: in natural forest settings
	Boat Launch	: forget it
FISHING	Fish Stocked	: 20,000
	Size Reports	: rainbows to two kilograms
	Restrictions	: none

Hiking The Widgeon area is slowly being absorbed into the Greater Vancouver Regional District parks system so it is becoming more and more protected and accessible. The Burke Mountain Naturalists have made a significant contribution to its preservation and development, adding several new trails in the area.

Widgeon Lake Trail is the main trail described earlier, going from the forest service camp to the south end of Widgeon Lake. Probably the most impressive section is the upper falls where the creek forms a pond, then plunges down the rocks into the valley. The trail is eight kilometers one way and will take you about four hours (one way).

Widgeon Bowl Lookout Trail starts right across from the canoe landing at the forest service campsite. This trail is designed for Olympic athletes and mountain goats, taking you up to about 700 meters in a short two kilometers and gives you a spectacular view of Pitt Lake. The trail is planned for extension to the Widgeon Bowl Lookout (1200 meters) and on to Burke Ridge Trail (see Burke Ridge Trail under Munro, Dennett Lakes in the previous section).

Widgeon Valley Trail—as an alternative to the Widgeon Lake Trail, it is possible to continue up the main branch of Widgeon Creek deep into the valley. Starting from the bridge past Widgeon Lake Trail, it (including a new section) continues for another six kilometers with little elevation gain so is a good easy walk. A new extension is planned from the end of this trail to reach into the next valley at DeBeck Creek. The proposed trail is shown.

Fishing The lake is stocked with rainbows—fisheries report sizes of *two kilograms!* The stocking table is shown below:

FISH STOCKED	YEAR	TYPE	NUMBER
Rainbow	1987	fry	10000
Rainbow	1990	fry	10000

This is a deep lake reaching 140 meters in the middle and will convince you there are monsters living here. The shoreline is tough and there have been no boats up here. If you have the stamina, a belly-boat will get you into the water and those deep coves that only exist in angler's heaven!

THESE LAKES sit in a very remote section of the virtually untouched De-Beck valley west of the head of Pitt Lake. If you have ever heard the old Indian legend of *Slumac* and the lost gold mine, you will understand how remote this area is. A cluster of untouched lakes hides in this valley, varying from a very high 1325 meters (upper Consolation Lake) to Spindle Lake at 780 meters. There is no existing trail system into this area, at least any that I am aware of. The proposed DeBeck Creek extension from Widgeon Valley will certainly change this in the future. In the meantime this is a chance to visit a seldom-seen group of lakes surprisingly close to civilization.

In fact, up here in this remote plateau area there are a whole set of unnamed lakes, all within a four-kilometer radius, hidden in this secret DeBeck valley on the dark side of the Obelisk ridge with no *easy* access. They are included here for those who *really* like to get away from it all. Just take your compass, your packsack (including your survival kit), even your climbing spurs, some real bush experience and a map...*always* a map!

FINDING the VALLEY

Looking at the map of Widgeon and DeBeck valleys, these lakes are in a true wilderness area, some even in the permanent snow line. I have chosen to lay out the 100-meter contours of the area to give you a better picture of the dramatic elevation changes. The creeks and snow lines are also shown for reference. If you are contemplating this adventure, I suggest getting the 1:50000 Pitt River (92G/10) and Port Coquitlam (92G/7) Energy Mines and Resources topographical maps—and a *good* compass. There is really no set way I am aware of to get to these lakes short of flying, in which case the upper Consolation Lake would be the best bet, approaching it from the northeast after flying up DeBeck Creek. The north end of the lake is open, dropping rapidly to the lower lake which is about 1.3 kilometers long so you should be able to take a float plane in. From this lake you can work the area, dropping down to the others. I will admit I have not been here myself so I cannot offer specific information based on experience. *I can only tell you what I know so please be aware that you are essentially unguided and on your own.*

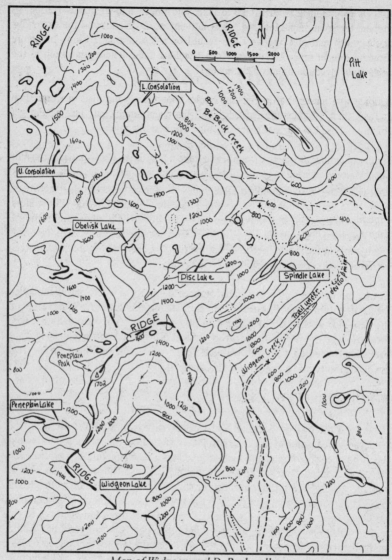

Map of Widgeon and DeBeck valleys

The other alternative would be to head for Obelisk or Disc Lake by continuing north from Widgeon Lake. The difficulty starts when you climb over the north ridge (1600 meters elevation) if you head due north from the north end of Widgeon Lake (770 meters). This requires a 'goat climb' of 830 meters vertically, then a decline of 450 meters to Obelisk. The horizontal distance, as the eagle flies, is 3.4 kilometers from lake to lake, but almost half of that is vertical so prepare for some rock-climbing. Alternatively, a traverse around the east ridge at the south end of Widgeon Lake would be a less-dramatic climb but more dramatic (about seven kilometers) to get to Disc Lake where you climb to the ridge at an elevation of only 1200 meters!

Another alternative is to phone the Burke Mountain Naturalists in Coquitlam and ask them whether the DeBeck Trail has been completed. This would get you to the Disc Lake area where you could climb to the others.

Finally, the other alternative would be to take a boat up to DeBeck Creek on Pitt Lake where there used to be a trail following the south side of DeBeck Creek for about three kilometers, getting you to 400 meters in elevation. This road is across Pitt from Cactus Point. There are several summer homes and a lot of mineral claims near the mouth of the creek possibly barring access. From here climb up the creek, taking the first tributary (2.5 kilometers) to Spindle Lake (1.8 kilometers), the second tributary (another one kilometer) to Disc Lake (1.5 kilometers) and the next tributary (another .5 kilometers) to the Consolation chain (four kilometers). Good luck!

CONSOLATION LAKE (Upper) is the larger of the set of Consolation Lakes at 52 hectares. It sits at an elevation of 1325 meters, below the Obelisk Ridge that rises to 1720 meters. The lake is long and narrow, 1.3 kilometers by 400 meters in an area that sees snow most of the year.

CONSOLATION LAKE (Lower) is the smaller lake at 28 hectares and lower, at 1142 meters. It is about 400 meters by 700 meters with several small streams including the one from the upper lake. There is a small divide to the southeast where six unnamed lakes can be found draining east into DeBeck Creek, then Pitt Lake.

OBELISK LAKE is also a fair size at 20 hectares nestled beneath the towering Obelisk Peak just about 1000 meters south of Upper Consolation Lake. At an elevation of 1150 meters it is in sub-alpine terrain, a short 700 meters long.

DISC LAKE is 25 hectares in size at an elevation of 870 meters and 600 meters in diameter. The creeks that join the Disc and Obelisk would represent the most likely way to get between the two despite the rather abrupt drop of 280 meters in 1.4 kilometers.

SPINDLE LAKE is a small thin lake of only four hectares squeezed between the walls of the Spindle Creek ravine. Theoretically, the most likely path would be from Disc Lake traversing east for 600 meters to a small unnamed lake, then turning southwest for another 700 meters. The lake is at about 780 meters so this would not be a serious drop from Disc Lake. The lake is only about 400 by 100 meters.

RECREATION

As far as recreation is concerned, these lakes would certainly represent the ultimate adventure for the true wilderness explorer. This area is virtually untouched with the exception of prospectors and explorers and you *will* see signs of them on the lakeshores. There are no facilities, no trails other than those made by wildlife (including prospectors) and *no help!*

REGION SIX
MAPLE RIDGE

THE MAPLE RIDGE REGION is a strip of terrain ten kilometers wide and 45 kilometers long. This is the strip that you would encounter when you travel east along Highway 7 as you cross the Pitt River, enter the Pitt Meadows district municipality and head toward the Maple Ridge municipality. The strip is bounded by the Fraser River to the south, extending north into the far reaches of Golden Ears Park. Pitt Meadows district municipality borders the west while the Mission municipality borders the east. Within this region, the southern portion along the river is populated, with the towns of Pitt Meadows, Haney and Maple Ridge containing the majority population where you have a mix of rural and urban development localized to the foothills. From here the rolling terrain gives way quickly to wilderness and rugged mountains with two major valleys cutting through the mountains in a northeast direction, forming massive drainage basins reaching deep into the wilderness.

To the north, several large areas have been reserved for public use. The area of interest includes the vast mountain ranges between the two large Pitt and Alouette lake systems. Between these two large lakes is a massive mountain range which includes the UBC Research Forest and Golden Ears Provincial Park reaching upward of 1700 meters. In these hills is a set of lakes and some park facilities as varied as they are spectacular. These two massive wilderness areas are the focus for recreation. Quite a contrast to the western regions, this is really the first place traveling east where you have fully developed camping facilities on any lakes. From a recreational standpoint, this particular area has everything you could ask for, all within easy access. The list covers everything: spectacular hiking, fishing, boating, camping and horseback riding.

ROADS, ACCESS POINTS AND LAKES

With reference to the regional map, the main roadway through the region is *Lougheed Highway (7)* and its northern branch, the *Dewdney Trunk Road* running east-west along the foot of the mountains providing the key access points to three lake systems. Starting from the west, the first major one is **Pitt Lake (6-1)**, a massive lake accessible only at the south end. The best access route is via *Dewdney Trunk Road* just after crossing the Pitt River Bridge, along *Harris Road, McNeil* and *Neaves* to the lake 17.7 kilometers north. In the same area, you can hike up the mountain overlooking the south end of the lake to visit the tiny **Cranberry Lake (6-2)**.

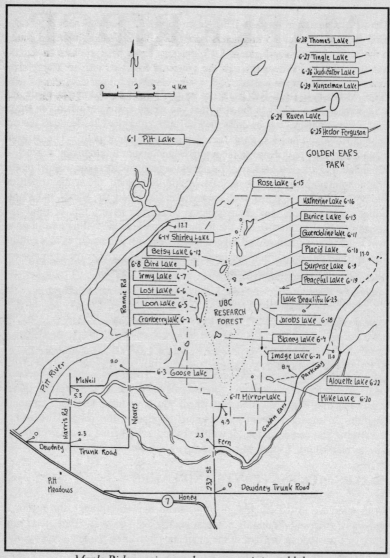

Maple Ridge region roads, access points and lakes

Farther east, back on Dewdney Trunk Road past the town of Haney there are several smaller mountain lakes reached primarily by hiking. The important ac-

154

cess point and trailhead is at *232nd Street* and *Dewdney Trunk Road*. This provides access into the UBC Research Forest Reserve and the south end of the massive Golden Ears Provincial Park.

The first excursion is into the UBC Reserve via *232nd Street*. From the Trailhead you would travel 3.5 kilometers north, take *Silver Valley Road* and come to the research station and gate at 4.9 kilometers. From here you hike an extensive and vast trail system through the protected forest to visit an impressive number of lakes. On the western trail system, about 16 kilometers (return) will let you see the larger **Goose Lake (6-3)**, **Blaney Lake (6-4)** and **Loon Lake (6-5)** as well as their tiny neighbors **Lost Lake (6-6)** and the little pond, **Irmy Lake (6-7)**. Following the central trail system extending over ten kilometers (one way) into virgin wilderness, you can get to another set of lakes called **Bird Lake (6-8)**, **Surprise Lake (6-9)**, **Placid Lake (6-10)**, **Gwendoline Lake (6-11)**, **Betsy Lake (6-12)**, **Eunice Lake 6-13)**, **Shirley Lake (6-14)**, **Rose Lake (6-15)** and **Katherine Lake (6-16)**. On the east side of the reserve you can find two more, **Mirror Lake (6-17)** and **Jacobs (Marion) Lake (6-18)**. The last one, **Peaceful Lake (6-19)** sits on the border of the reserve, essentially inaccessible.

The other system of lakes is accessed along *232nd Street* which leads to *Fern Road* just as it crosses the Alouette River. It then proceeds east into Golden Ears Park where you can drive to **Mike Lake (6-20)**, then hike to **Mirror Lake (6-17)** and **Image Lake (6-21)**. Driving farther into the park leads you to the popular **Alouette Lake (6-22)** from which you climb high into the park to visit **Lake Beautiful (6-23)**. Finally, the last set of lakes is accessible by float plane. These are **Raven Lake (6-24)**, **Hector Ferguson Lake (6-25)**, **Judicator Lake (6-26)**, **Tingle Lake (6-27)**, **Thomas Lake (6-28)** and **Kunzelman Lake (6-29)**.

PITT LAKE is massive, covering 5380 hectares, reaching from the southern farmland at Pitt Polder to a distance 24 kilometers north into some of the most rugged, remote wilderness in the valley. Fed by the mighty Pitt River, which has its headwaters in the ice fields of Garibaldi Park, the river picks up scores of raging tributaries over a length of 40 kilometers before it empties into the lake and finally into the Fraser River. The huge valley formed by the Pitt is indeed a spectacle if you care to take your boat into it. Due to the rugged terrain, there is no road system around this lake and only the south end has direct access. There are logging roads at the remote north end but a boat trip is required as the rugged 50 kilometers of spectacular shoreline is only accessible by boat.

PITT LAKE at a GLANCE

ACTIVITIES	BOATING, FISHING, TRAILS, NATURE	
LAKE STATS	Elevation & Size	: 50 meters, 5380 hectares
	Lake Setting	: Grant Narrows Park, Crown forest
ACCESS	Vehicle Type	: car
	Nearest Highway	: 17.7 kilometers to Highway 7
FACILITIES	Type & Class	: developed
	Camping	: remote natural sites
	Boat Launch	: good gravel
FISHING	Fish Stocked	: natural, not required
	Size Reports	: 30-centimeter rainbows up to two kgs
	Restrictions	: none

Over the years, the lake has had a progressive development of summer cabins in some of the secret little coves and bays, but essentially the lake, despite its proximity to urban development, is undeveloped. A logging road system at the north end of the lake has scarred some of the pristine wilderness but the majority of water is remote. Multitudes of good-sized streams enter Pitt Lake with many coves, even islands, presenting a boater with a variety of interesting shorelines to explore but the lake can also be rough and dangerous. Harsh winds gather momentum from the northern glaciers and whistle down the valley, creating boating nightmares for the unprepared. There is shelter at Christian Cove marina when the water kicks up. It's just about the only shelter available.

At the south end of the lake, which is easily accessible, massive areas of marsh have formed in the area called Pitt Polder. As a side note "Polder" refers to an area of low-lying land, especially in the Netherlands, that has been reclaimed from a body of water and is protected by dikes. Here you will find an impressive network of dikes keeps the Pitt waters from flooding the area, also allowing hiking access deep into some of the unusual marshes. This is a place where naturalists can watch an incredible variety of bird life in their private and unique ecosystem.

FINDING the LAKE

Despite its size, there is only one tiny access area to Pitt Lake, at the south end where the Pitt River continues its flow through Grant Narrows into the Fraser River. The road is paved all the way to the lake. To get to the south end turn off

Finding Pitt Lake

Highway 7 onto the Dewdney Trunk Road just as you cross the Pitt River bridge (first traffic light). Zero the odometer and turn left here to follow Dewdney Trunk to the stop sign and turn left onto Harris Road (at 2.3 kilometers). Continue north until you reach 5.3 kilometers then turn right on McNeil. Follow this road through the rural area to intersect Neaves at 9.0 kilometers and turn left. (Neaves is the same as 208th Street and it becomes Rannie Road past McNeil). Now you travel straight north along Rannie for quite a stretch. You will eventually curve right to parallel the river dike and encounter the new parking lot at 17.5 kilometers at Grant Narrows Park. The boat launch is found a bit farther at 17.7 kilometers. As you drive onto the dike, you will see the south end of Pitt Lake.

RECREATION

Facilities Despite the lake's surface area and its lengthy shoreline perimeter, there are really very few developed recreational facilities on the lake. With the exception of the south end which has been converted into the Grant Narrows Regional Park, facilities on the main lake are either private or accessed only by boat and those accessed by boat have had no help from the parks board but the south end has recently been upgraded to provide some reasonable facilities for the boater.

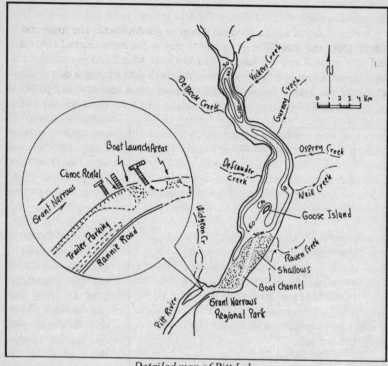

Detailed map of Pitt Lake

There is a good gravel/sand boat launch with a dock, paved parking lot and a boat rental facility here. The launch is good enough for a cruiser but you will need to leave your trailer along the newly created parking lot you passed on the way in. The area is used heavily in the summer so it can be a very busy place. Since the road is a dead end, traffic snarls during mid-summer are common. There are several summer cabins on the lake so the launch is used to service weekenders as well as summer fun traffic.

Boating The area is a favorite place for nature lovers and canoeists. Just across Grant Narrows it is possible to paddle a canoe to Widgeon Slough behind Siwash Island (see the map). The northern area is protected, part of the Widgeon Valley National Wildlife Reserve, a nesting area for many species of marsh birds. The Widgeon Slough area is a maze of waterways with slow-moving water meandering its way from Widgeon Creek where you can paddle quietly to

158

observe the marsh habitat or stop for a picnic. On many parts of the shoreline you will find short spurts of sandy beach where a swim or a bit of fishing can be a pleasant diversion.

Pitt Lake is a whole different matter. The lake is large and it can be as hostile as it is beautiful so you need a good-sized boat to get anywhere. The south end is heavily silted and shallow so be careful to stay in the main channel (see map) until you get well into the lake, almost to Goose Island and pay attention to water depths. Grant Narrows flows along the south dike forming a deeper channel. At the end, against the mountain, the channel turns northeast, first paralleling the rock cliffs then heading out to mid-lake. The sides of the lake are silted, muddy and laden with submerged debris including 'deadheads' (partially-submerged logs). Although the channel is marked with buoys, the best tactic is to take a heading straight for Goose Island eight kilometers away. Once you get close to Goose Island the lake deepens rapidly to 60 meters. You should not really enter Pitt Lake without an up-to-date nautical chart. Use the 'red-right-returning' rule and keep the red buoys to starboard on the way up and to port on the way down, never straying outside the markers.

Once on the main lake you will enter a whole new world. The lake opens to deep green waters and plunging shorelines where you will find deep placid coves, crashing streams and a marvelous variety of estuaries. In many sections you will find inviting smooth rocks where you can beach the boat and take a sun break. In this area you can fish, swim, water ski or just cruise. Be aware that many of the best coves are private so you're on your own for facilities. If you decide to park along shore remember this is wilderness and bears, cougars and biting flies live here.

Fishing The lake has a direct link with major waterways allowing all types of fish so there is no need for a stocking program. Pitt Lake is a hard lake to fish because of its size, but typically the deeper bays, larger stream estuaries and dark, deeper cliff areas are the better bets for both dolly varden and trout.

Nature Trails The massive marsh area to the south of Pitt Lake is shown in the map. This marsh is protected from flooding by an extensive network of dikes and backup dikes (in the event of primary dike failure). As a result, an impressive list of bird species have nested here over the years. Not surprisingly, the dike system is a natural walking or viewing area. In addition, new features such as viewing towers have been strategically placed on the dikes with viewing platforms along the ridge—a favorite place to view eagles.

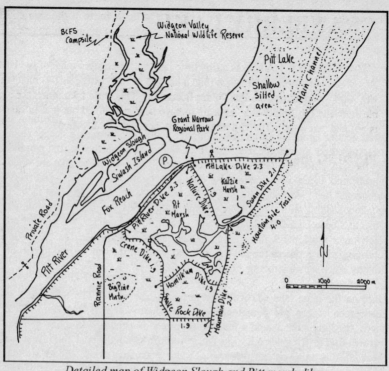

Detailed map of Widgeon Slough and Pitt marsh dikes

The Dikes are extensive, all flat and easy walking. With reference to the map, following are the distances:

Pitt Lake Dike is 2.3 kilometers	**Pitt River Dike** is 2.3 kilometers
Swan Dike is 2.1 kilometers	**Homilk'um Dike** is 1.9 kilometers
Mountain Dike is 2.3 kilometers	**Snake Rock Dike** is 1.9 kilometers
Nature Dike is 1.9 kilometers	**Crane Dike** is 1.9 kilometers
Mountainside Trail is four kilometers with a climb of 160 meters	

You can choose your combination of dikes to form a trek through the marsh. Several viewing platforms and bird lookouts are provided at strategic locations. Each dike is around two kilometers long so if you are timing your walk, a stroll will take 20 minutes per kilometer while a steady walk will take ten minutes per kilometer. The mountainside trails are a different matter. They start out looking gradual and inviting but they give way to steep, rough, brutal pathways higher up so use 20 minutes per kilometer as a reasonable estimate. The excellent viewing platforms at the end are well worth the effort.

CRANBERRY LAKE is a tiny little lake on the western edge of the UBC Research Forest Reserve. It is less than a hectare in size, sitting at 140 meters in elevation, overlooking the Pitt Polder floodplain. This little lake, once accessible from the Pitt Polder side, appears to have been privatized but just in case it is not and you want to find out more about it, here are the directions.

FINDING the LAKE

Turn off of Highway 7 onto Dewdney Trunk just as you cross the Pitt River bridge at the first traffic light. Zero the odometer and turn left here to follow

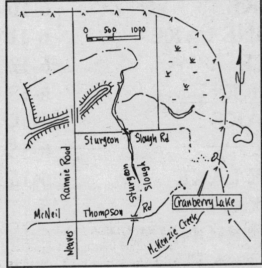

Dewdney Trunk to the stop sign and turn left onto Harris Road (at 2.3 kilometers). Continue north along Harris Road until you reach 5.3 kilometers then turn right on McNeil. Follow this road through the rural area to intersect Neaves at 9.0 kilometers and continue straight through on Thompson Road. It turns northwest as you approach the mountain. Just as you begin the climb up the hill the road splits

Finding Cranberry Lake

and changes to gravel. Two signs indicate you are approaching private property. I suspect this lake is now on private land. There was a trail through here, a mere 600 meters to the lake but I suspect the road is now the trail and it leads to a private estate. The other access route may be from the north along Sturgeon Slough Road.

The lake appears to have been privatized so it is an unknown as to what is around it. Basically just a large pond, this is the headwaters of McKenzie Creek.

The UBC RESEARCH FOREST contains an unbelievable number of lakes. The above lakes are all grouped together because they all fall into a special class since they all belong to the vast UBC Research Forest, strictly protected by UBC. From a recreational standpoint, there are two types who will love this area...the nature-lover and the hiker. This vast area is preserved specially for this but first a bit of history.

Bordering on the Golden Ears Provincial Park, the forest covers an area of 5157 hectares. Its earlier history began in 1868 when settlers lost control of a fire, devastating some 1200 hectares of forest. Many of the dominant trees have now

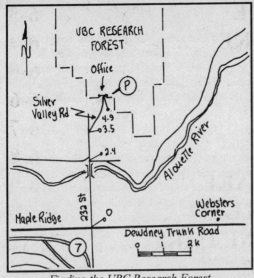
Finding the UBC Research Forest

reclaimed the area as 110-year-old second growth. Logging began in the 1920s, slowly gaining momentum over the following years. Aggressive logging of some 2800 hectares of virgin timber continued until another forest-fire raged through the area and destroyed most of the operations. This destruction and the effects of the Great Depression in 1931 provided the final blow to logging in the area. Ownership reverted to the Crown who officially granted the forest to UBC in 1949 so a dedicated area could be created for research and education in the promising new science of forest management.

Today the forest is a wonderland of natural science and beauty carefully preserved by the UBC Faculty of Forestry who take their obligations seriously. The area is about four kilometers wide and 11 kilometers long, reaching far into the northern wilderness bordering Golden Ears Park. This area includes just about every type of terrain and vegetation found in the lower coastal region including areas where the timber is over 100 years old. Every year, students conduct research and hold educational sessions in the reserve, gaining international recognition in fields such as ecology, biology, climatology, hydrology and genetics. The forest provides a natural laboratory and training ground for the BC Forest Service, BCIT and several regional colleges, as well as elementary and high school students.

There are seven larger lakes on this vast reserve, ranging from six hectares (Goose) to 45 hectares (Loon) and 10 smaller lakes typically less than a hectare in size. None of these lakes can be used for any recreational purpose other than hiking, viewing and research. For casual visitors the reserve is strictly for day use. Virtually hundreds of projects are carried out on a continuous basis, so visitors need to tread lightly and abide by the rule of not disturbing *anything*.

FINDING the RESERVE

The UBC Research Forest is shaped like a thin wedge with the access gate at the south end. To get to the gate just north of Haney, take Dewdney Trunk Road east out of Haney then turn left onto 232nd Street. The paved road carries on north for 3.5 kilometers where it splits. Take the right branch (Silver Valley Road). The office and parking lot are at the end of the road at 4.9 kilometers.

RECREATION

Facilities When you first enter the reserve you will notice an immediate air of organization, thinking that perhaps you have entered someone's private estate. The truth is the reserve is very organized and very well-endowed with facilities, but not entirely for the public. Obviously, a lot of research goes on here so the roads, camps, trails and buildings are for the studious types. When visiting, remember you are a visitor so you can exercise your eyes, brain and legs but that's it. From the parking lot at the south end it is possible to access a vast network of trails, old roads and footpaths.

The area contains 17 lakes, all in their natural state. Other than the trails and the student camp at Loon Lake, there is little sign of man's assault on nature. The area is for day use only, dawn to dusk, with strict attention paid to closing the gates. The rules are fairly straight forward, there is *no:*

camping	*fires*	*fishing*	*bicycles*
dogs	*horses*	*collecting*	*wandering*

That is a long list and they mean it. Fishing is prohibited in this area so I have not provided information on angling or water depths, although I *know* there are probably *monsters* in the lake. It would only serve to frustrate any ardent angler who dreams about untouched waters. You'll just have to let those giant trout be. Try Mike Lake right next to the reserve if you really feel cheated.

Trails As you can see, the reserve is riddled with a network of roads and trails. All of these are shown on a free map sheet available at the parking lot. In addition, the office has a color brochure of the lower trails for a dollar. Since the money helps with their costs I have not reproduced it here and the color is useful since the trails are marked by colors. In addition, the brochure describes in vivid detail all of the important aspects of the ecosystem and some history with reference to the distance markers posted along the trails so please purchase a booklet—it is worthwhile. In the event the place is closed, there are four trail systems in the lower area (1.8 kilometers north of the office) marked in red, yellow, green or blue. Each color indicates the trail length and the average walking time. These are the suggested distances and times:

Red Trail	1.4 kilometers	allow one hour
Yellow Trail	3.2 kilometers	allow two hours
Green Trail	2.4 kilometers	allow 1.5 hours
Blue Trail	6.5 kilometers	allow three hours

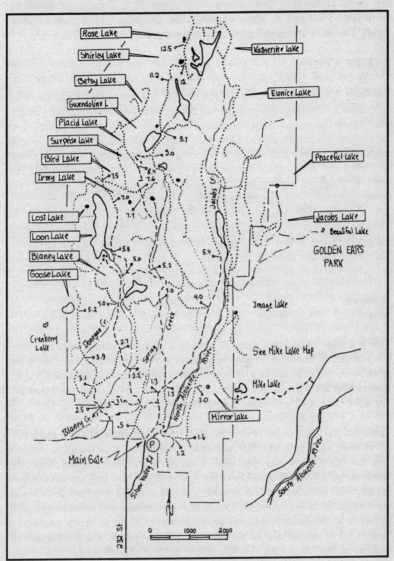

Detailed map of the UBC Research Forest

165

I am including a detailed trail map of the whole reserve. Note that only the lower 1.8 kilometers (north of the office) is covered by the UBC brochure. The reserve actually reaches 12 'eagle' kilometers north of the office. The spectacular North Alouette River cuts through the lower southeast corner and the area is riddled with fresh mountain streams. These lakes are available to the public on a restricted basis and do not have public facilities of any kind, so the recreational value is in hiking and appreciation of nature.

As a consequence, I have presented all the lakes together as a group. In this reserve put your worldly goods away and truly get in touch with nature. Just remember that the most northerly lake (Katherine) is 13 kilometers (one way) from the main gate so you must be a strong hiker to get there and back during the day.

Looking at the trail map you will note the lakes are accessed by following a different combination of roads, trails and footpaths networking the area. For this reason I have attempted to distinguish between an old road, a trail and a footpath since they all vary in quality. There are 17 lakes to visit but remember the travel length and *always* tell someone where you are heading. From the parking lot at about 140 meters in elevation, you will typically gain elevation gradually as you trek north. The distances however, are significant...and all those indicated here are *one way*.

GOOSE LAKE is six hectares in size and it sits at an elevation of 140 meters. on the extreme west side of the reserve. From the parking lot of the same elevation you will take several different trails and old roads descending to 80 meters at the Blaney Creek bridge then ascending slowly to the lake, 5.2 kilometers from the lot.

BLANEY LAKE is eight hectares in size and sits at 335 meters. It is best accessed from the main road system and is found just over four kilometers north of the parking lot.

LOON LAKE at 45 hectares is the largest lake in the reserve, sitting at 350 meters. From the parking lot, the south tip of the lake is at 5.8 kilometers, a fair distance but easy going. Loon Lake also has buildings acting as the student camp but the facilities are off-limits to casual visitors.

LOST LAKE sits behind Loon Lake at 350 meters. It is less than a hectare in size and is just essentially a pond, part of the Loon Lake system. To get close to it you come southwest around the top of Loon Lake off the main trail at 7.5 kilometers from the lot. The branch takes you another kilometer to within 300 meters of the pond. From here access is not guaranteed.

IRMY LAKE is also less than a hectare in size, feeding into the east side of Loon Lake through a small stream. This lake has no trail to it so the best tactic is to climb up the creek running into the north end of Loon. Ask at the office for permission to do this. The distance is about seven kilometers to the creek and the climb from the trail is about 90 meters to the lake elevation of 470 meters.

BIRD LAKE is 465 meters high, a short 500 meters east of Irmy Lake in the same plateau area. It is also a tiny pond inaccessible from any formal trail. The best route is from the main road to Gwendoline Lake, a distance of about 7.4 kilometers from the office. The pond is only 300 meters from the main road.

GWENDOLINE LAKE is ten hectares and sits at 550 meters. It is nine kilometers from the parking lot. Follow the main north road through the middle of the reserve.

SURPRISE LAKE is another little pond less than a hectare in size at 555 meters. This lake is tiny and just partially accessible by taking the south trail system from Gwendoline Lake (nine kilometers from the parking lot). A fork cuts around the pond just 500 meters south of the branch.

PLACID LAKE is at 503 meters, 1.5 hectares in size. It is also accessible from the south trail branch close to Gwendoline Lake, only 300 meters south of the main trail. The distance from the parking lot is 9.5 kilometers.

BETSY LAKE is at 550 meters, also less than a hectare in size, found as a tiny pond north of Gwendoline Lake. It is close to the main trail that cuts through the central reserve ten kilometers from the parking lot.

EUNICE LAKE is another good-sized lake at 12 hectares. It resides at an elevation of 500 meters, accessible from a branch trail off the main trail close to the north end of Gwendoline Lake. The branch (at 9.7 kilometers from the parking lot) is about 600 meters long, taking you to the south end of the lake.

SHIRLEY LAKE measures one hectare and sits at 555 meters. The lake is beside the main central trail system 12 kilometers from the parking lot.

ROSE LAKE at 500 meters in elevation is another tiny pond of less than a hectare, just off the main central trail system. This is found 12.8 kilometers north of the parking lot.

KATHERINE LAKE is a large lake of 20 hectares with several smaller lakes meandering around the southwest end. It is at an elevation of 510 meters, accessible via several spur paths that take off from the main trail surrounding the lake. This the most northerly lake, its north end being 13 kilometers from the parking lot.

MIRROR LAKE is another small pond at less than a hectare, at 270 meters. It is accessed from the southeast trail system crossing the north Alouette River. The trek is three kilometers from the parking lot.

JACOBS (Marion) LAKE is four hectares in size and sits at 520 meters. It is 5.4 kilometers from the parking lot accessed via the eastern trail system.

PEACEFUL LAKE is around a hectare in size, at 685 meters. It sits on the border between the reserve and Golden Ears Park. It is probably called *peaceful* because there is no trail to it and it is left in peace. The distance is about 10 kilometers.

MIKE LAKE 6-20

MIKE LAKE is located *on* Maple Ridge (yes there actually is a ridge called Maple Ridge there) at the southwest portion of Golden Ears Provincial Park. Mike is a small lake of four hectares at an elevation of 236 meters. For anyone frustrated at not being able to fish in the UBC Research Forest, this lake, right next door, would be a good alternative, so you won't feel cheated. Mike Lake is set very elegantly in a small heavily forested bowl. Relatively shallow, the lake is mostly surrounded by marsh and marshland vegetation but it gives way quickly to the surrounding forest. Some special attention has been given to Mike, making it an excellent canoeing and fishing lake.

MIKE LAKE at a GLANCE

ACTIVITIES	FISHING, HIKING, CANOEING, RIDING	
LAKE STATS	Elevation & Size	: 236 meters, four hectares
	Lake Setting	: Golden Ears Provincial Park
ACCESS	Vehicle Type	: car
	Nearest Highway	: 10.3 kilometers from Dewdney Trunk Road
FACILITIES	Type & Class	: developed
	Camping	: not permitted, day use only
	Boat Launch	: canoe from wharf
FISHING	Fish Stocked	: 15,000
	Size Reports	: rainbows around 30 centimeters
	Restrictions	: no power boats

FINDING the LAKE

To get to the lake you will travel east on Dewdney Trunk Road out of Maple Ridge, then look for 232nd Street less than two kilometers from the downtown area centered on 224th Street. Set the odometer to zero as you turn left onto 232nd Street and continue over the bridge, turning right onto Fern Road at 2.4 kilometers. Stay on Fern Road paralleling the Alouette River until 4.0 kilometers where you will reach Golden Ears Park limits and the main road into the park. At 8.4 kilometers turn left into the park headquarters then take a quick left onto the gravel road that will get you onto the Maple Ridge bench. The Mike Lake parking lot is at 10.3 kilometers. The lake is close to the parking lot.

RECREATION

Facilities at the lake are basic but adequate. The parking lot is good-sized with men's and ladies' biffies across the road just before the lot. The trail to the lake is a short 100 meters with access right off the lot. It is a gradual slope with no obstacles leading right to a swampy area of the lake where a 30-meter wharf reaches into the deeper water providing an excellent means of plopping in a canoe. A horse hitching rail is also provided for equestrian buffs galloping up from the lower Incline Trail.

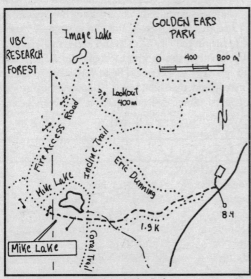

Finding Mike Lake

Trails There is a well-developed trail system around the lake and these connect with the main trail system into both the UBC Research Forest and Golden Ears Park. The Mike Lake Loop Trail will take you around the lake in less than an hour, providing a few access points around the perimeter. To see the connection to the other trail system, check out the Alouette Lake and Golden Ears Trail maps (6-22) where they are covered in more detail.

Fishing This is a great place to plop in your canoe because the parking lot is close and the dock makes it easy. It is also possible to cast a line from the end of the wharf but the water is only two to three meters deep. The lake is shallow with marsh surrounding most of the shoreline. Fisheries have regularly stocked the lake with catchables since 1986. Note that power boats are prohibited.

FISH STOCKED	YEAR	TYPE	NUMBER
Rainbow	1986 to 1990	catchables	3000/ year

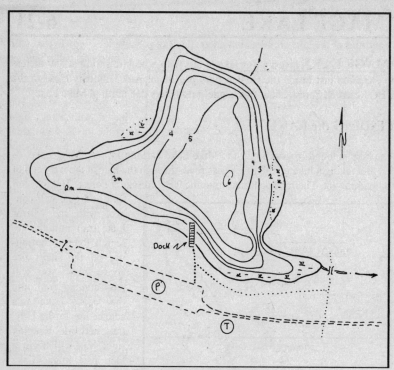

Detailed map of Mike Lake

IMAGE LAKE

IMAGE LAKE is just a tiny lake of less than a hectare sitting at 350 meters in elevation just inside the Golden Ears provincial park boundary close to the UBC Research Forest, about two 'eagle' kilometers due north of Mike Lake.

FINDING the LAKE

The lake is found by parking at the Mike Lake parking lot (see Mike Lake, 6-20) and taking a hike up the fire access road, through the gate at the west end of the parking lot. The road continues into the UBC Research Forest. The first left

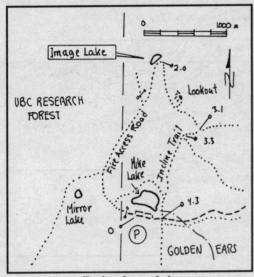

Finding Image Lake

fork and gate will connect with the Mirror Lake trail into the research forest. Continuing on the main fire access road, you will pass another trail into the Jacobs Lake area connecting to the UBC trail network. Keeping right, you will begin a loop past Image Lake about two kilometers from the Mike Lake parking lot. The trail continues down and around past the bluffs where you can take a short diversion up to a viewpoint. Keeping right will connect you with the Incline Trail leading back to the parking lot. You will have covered 4.3 kilometers. Allow a few hours if you include the lookout.

RECREATION

From a recreation standpoint the main feature is the hike of 4.3 kilometers and the great scenery. The trails are good, with slight elevation gain. Mike Lake is at 240 meters while Image Lake is at 350 meters. The diversion to the lookout is at 440 meters.

ALOUETTE LAKE is located in the south section of Golden Ears Provincial Park, which extends 55 kilometers north into mountain wilderness all the way to the southern boundary of Garibaldi Provincial Park. Between these two massive parks is a section of steep rugged mountains dominated by glaciers and wilderness so rough it is virtually impossible to access, except by plane. Needless to say, the most accessible portion of the park lies to the south in the less-rugged Alouette valley. In this respect, the impressive Alouette River and Alouette Lake have had some special attention paid to them by the provincial parks board. Alouette Lake is actually part of a Hydro project with a tunnel cutting through the mountain down to the powerhouse on Stave Lake. A dam at the south end of Alouette holds the waters back.

ALOUETTE LAKE at a GLANCE

ACTIVITIES	BOATING, CAMPING, HIKING, RIDING, FISHING	
LAKE STATS	Elevation & Size	: 106 meters, 1644 hectares
	Lake Setting	: Golden Ears Provincial Park
ACCESS	Vehicle Type	: car
	Nearest Highway	: 11 kilometers to Dewdney Trunk Road
FACILITIES	Type & Class	: well developed
	Camping	: excellent facilities
	Boat Launch	: large concrete
FISHING	Fish Stocked	: natural
	Size Reports	: 40-centimeter rainbows two-kilogram dollys
	Restrictions	: none

At 1644 hectares, elevation 106 meters, Alouette Lake is easy to find by car. Easy access and the striking beauty of the area have contributed to making this the most popular recreation spot in the region. The lake extends about 15 kilometers in a northeast direction from the lower dam. The north side is the most developed, offering a long list of recreational highlights. The park has some of the best camping and boating in the Fraser Valley, but it also caters well to hikers and equestrians, providing a vast network of mountain trails that take you into some of the most incredible country in the valley.

In its early days, prior to the 1930s, the area was one of the largest rail-logging operations, having a reputation for some of the most sophisticated equipment and techniques available. With the big fire of 1931, operations were wiped out completely and never reopened, so only historical remnants such as old donkeys, steam engines and railways are scattered throughout the area, many of which can be encountered along the trails.

FINDING the LAKE

There is only one way to get to the lake: from Dewdney Trunk Road at 232nd Street. This proceeds due north to cross the south Alouette River at about two kilometers. Turn right at 2.3 kilometers along Fern Road to parallel the river, driving through a lush forest area with well-kept residences along the banks. At four kilometers you will encounter the park entrance and at 8.4 kilometers you will pass the Mike Lake turnoff. The first access point to Alouette Lake is at 11.0 kilometers where you will see the right turnoff to the day use area. This includes the beach area, picnic sites and boat launch

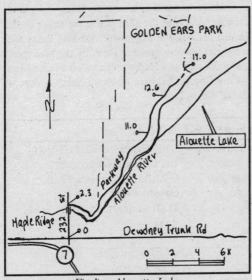

Finding Alouette Lake

(another 3.6 kilometers in). There are two other major access points to the lake, accessed from the main parkway. The next one is at the Alouette campground (turnoff at 12.6 kilometers) and the other at the end of the road at Gold Creek parking lot (14 kilometers). The roads to the lake are mostly paved, so even if you hit gravel, your Ferrari won't suffer greatly.

RECREATION

Facilities at the lake are impressive. If you check out the detailed map you will notice two major campgrounds near Gold Creek. The Alouette campground has 205 units and Gold Creek has 138 units. This may sound like a lot, but the traffic here is heavy, so get there early in the summer camping season. All the campsites have access to water, toilets, showers and wood. Most trailers and recreational vehicles can be accommodated but there are no hookups. Two group campgrounds are also available for non-profit, registered, youth-oriented groups but reserve ahead.

173

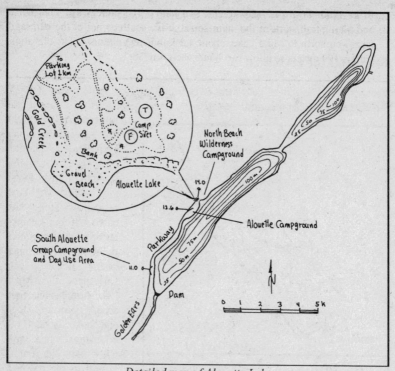

Detailed map of Alouette Lake

A large day-use area is situated at the south end of the lake where you will find a nice sandy beach with change-house and extensive picnic facilities. A superb concrete boat launch is just to the north of the beach. It will allow a good-sized boat to be launched and the trailer-parking area is large. The lake is excellent for swimming with cool, clear waters sparkling all along the beaches but there are no lifeguards. There is also an extensive trail system that caters to hikers, bikers and horses. Corrals and staging areas are provided. A sani-station is available and various self-guided nature trails are featured.

Trails The trails in the park will cater to just about anyone. These can be easy and flat, as with the nature trails or they can be long and tough, like the Golden Ears Trail that takes you up 1500 meters to the highest point on the north side of the valley. The trails are usually well-maintained and are developed to service hikers, horses, even mountain-bikers. In most cases the horse trails are also used by trail-bikes and hikers, but any trails marked for hikers means hikers *only*. I have provided a detailed trail map of the area, noting the elevations and distances between intersections. The main trails are:

174

Mike Lake Trail (4.2 kilometers, two hours, 100 meters up) This horse and hiking trail starts at the main corral at the south corner of the park and takes you north to Mike Lake, about 4.2 kilometers *one way*. The elevation gain is 100 meters so allow two hours each way.

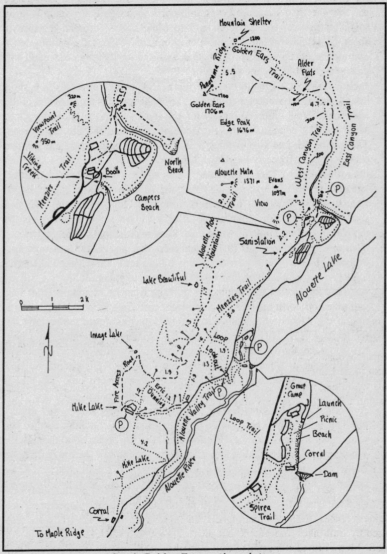

South Golden Ears trails and sites

175

Mike Lake Loop Trail (1.7 kilometers, one hour, flat) This hiking trail connects with the fire access road and Incline Trail to make a complete loop around Mike Lake about 1.7 kilometers total, an easy walk within an hour.

Alouette Mountain fire access road This is not an official trail but you will use it to connect with other trails. Around the Mike Lake area it will take you into the UBC Research Forest and north to Image Lake before it turns south to intersect Incline Trail back to Mike Lake. The total distance is about 4.3 kilometers but note the elevation gains. Mike Lake parking lot is 240 meters, Image Lake is 350 meters, then the lookout area is around 440 meters if you climb up the spur trail.

Incline Trail (1.2 kilometers, one hour, 150 meters up) This is a short hiking and horse connector-trail of 1.2 kilometers that is an extension of the Mike Lake Trail, climbing rapidly for 150 meters from the hitching rack at Mike Lake. It connects with Eric Dunning Trail and the fire access road. The incline was one used by loggers as a route to skyline (using a suspended cable to let gravity carry logs down hill) large logs down to Mike Lake from the railhead above (fire access road). This shortcut eliminated five kilometers of the railroad haul down the mountain. Allow an hour.

Eric Dunning Trail (1.2 kilometers, one hour, 200 meters up) This is a short horse and hiking connector-trail of 1.2 kilometers that intersects the top part of Incline Trail and Mike Lake Road near the park headquarters.

Alouette Mountain Trail (9.7 kilometers, five hours, 1131 meters up!) Probably the best starting point for this hiking trail is the Mike Lake parking lot so you will take Incline Trail (1.2 kilometers) then follow the fire access road for another four kilometers to reach Alouette Mountain Trail. This will take you north another 4.5 kilometers past Lake Beautiful to an elevation at the Alouette Mountain peak of 1371 meters. From the parking lot, the totals will be 1131 meters up and 9.7 kilometers horizontal...you need the whole day for this one but the views will be worth it. Allow 30 minutes per kilometer or 5 hours to get to the top—*one way*! The panoramic view from Alouette Mountain is spectacular. Expect snow until June. The hike is strenuous and proper equipment and experience are needed.

Alouette Mountain Horse Trail (7.3 kilometers, four hours, 400 meters up) This horse trail is best started from the Mike Lake hitching post, so you would take Incline Trail for 1.2 kilometers, the fire access road through the sub-alpine forest for another four kilometers, then follow the lower trail (*not* Alouette Mountain Trail) to the dead-end for a final 2.1 kilometers. The total length is 7.3 kilometers, elevation gain 400 meters and goes through a blown-down area apparently caused by typhoon Freda in 1962.

Alouette Valley Trail (10.5 kilometers, four hours, flat) This horse and hiking trail actually cuts off the Mike Valley Trail about one kilometer north of the main corral then cuts down for 1.4 kilometers across the parkway to parallel the river. From here it is 5.4 kilometers to the main day-use area and the corral. The trail continues another 2.7 kilometers along the parkway where you should be able to cross and connect with Menzies Trail. From the corral this would add up to 10.5 kilometers to the end of the trail, so allow four hours.

Menzies Trail (nine kilometers, 4.5 hours, flat) This horse and hiking trail connects the park Headquarters and the Gold Creek parking lot. It parallels the main parkway for the most part and is nine kilometers long. You will have to cross the parkway twice so, if your horse is shy of cars, beware of this route. The elevation change is minimal but allow 4.5 hours for the one-way jaunt. Note that you will cut back along West Canyon Trail just before getting to the Gold Creek lot.

Lookout and Loop Trail Loop (4.3 kilometers, 1.5 hours, 75m up) These are two connectors best accessed from the Spirea Nature Trail parking lot and used as a complete loop. Loop Trail is a hiking and horse trail 1.9 kilometers long. It climbs to meet Menzies Trail where you take a left for .6 kilometers then cut down Lookout Trail (hiking) for 1.3 kilometers. It crosses the parkway and connects back to the lot. The lookout is at 224 meters so you will have climbed 75 meters. The total length is 4.3 kilometers. Allow 20 minutes per kilometer or about 1.5 hours to loop from the parkway via Lookout Trail to Lookout and return to the parkway via Loop Trail. Park at the Spirea Nature Trail parking lot.

Viewpoint Trail (2.5 kilometers, 1.5 hours, 175 meters up) This is a short hiking trail that gives you a spectacular view of Alouette Lake and Viking Creek best accessed from the West Canyon parking lot. Take West Canyon Trail for about 500 meters north then cut left to start the ascent to the first lake viewpoint (320 meters). This is only about a kilometer but the elevation gain makes up for distance (plus 155 meters!). In wetter seasons a picturesque waterfall tumbles down a cliff just beyond the lake viewpoint. Viking Creek viewpoint is next, another kilometer farther. The final view is from 350 meters, 175 meters gain and 2.5 kilometers distance from the lot. To be safe allow .75 hours to the first lookout and another .75 to Viking lookout.

West Canyon Trail (five kilometers, 2.5 hours, 265 meters up) This trail takes you along the west side of the canyon above Gold Creek and continues to Golden Ears Trail. It is a hiking trail which is accessed from the West Canyon parking lot, taking you five kilometers and gaining 265 meters but this is only the warm-up for the *real* climb! (see Golden Ears Trail below). From the parking lot at an elevation of 175 meters, the trail follows an old logging grade for 3.2 kilometers, then swings uphill. At this point the elevation is only 240 meters and a short trail drops downhill to the lower falls on Gold Creek. This is a nice flat scenic trail so it is very popular, allowing you to come back along Lower Falls Trail. From the junction, however, it is another kilometer to Gold Creek lookout (elevation 320 meters) then Alder Flats and the creek (elevation 440 meters). This is now five kilometers from the parking lot and you should have allowed 2.5 hours to get there.

Golden Ears Trail (12 kilometers, seven hours, 1530 meters up!) Now this is the crowning hiking trail in the area, taking you to the summit of the north Ear (1706 meters!). It is actually a continuation of West Canyon Trail, but let us start the journey back at the West Canyon parking lot (elevation 175 meters). Follow West Canyon Trail from the parking lot to Alder Flats (elevation 440 meters, five kilometers). Fill your water bottle here, for beyond Alder Flats the trail switchbacks upward on an old logging road then heads steeply uphill to Panorama Ridge. Most of the elevation gain is made in this stretch with impressive views of Pitt Lake to the west and mountains to the east and north from Panorama Ridge. The ascent of the north ear and the eventual elevation of 1706 meters is made from the left (east) side across a permanent snowfield (yes, a snowfield!). Extreme caution is advised and proper equipment is recommended. Drinking water may be scarce in dry weather between Alder Flats and the snowfield. The round trip is 24 kilometers so Golden Ears is an overnight expedition for all but the fittest hikers. Overnight campsites are available at Alder Flats and on Panorama Ridge around the mountain shelter which can accommodate up to eight people. *Expect snow on Panorama Ridge even in July. This trail is long and strenuous and should only be attempted by experienced, well-equipped backcountry travelers.* Also remember that open fires are prohibited in the backcountry.

Lower Falls Trail (2.7 kilometers, one hour, minimal gain) This is quite a contrast to Golden Ears Trail; the best access (unless you are taking the West Canyon-Lower Falls Loop) is from the Gold Creek parking lot. The trail is very popular, being an easy walk along Gold Creek to the ten-meter-high lower falls. A beach area found half-way to the falls is a good spot to picnic or sunbathe. Some of the best scenery in the park is here just beyond the beach.

East Canyon Trail (5.5 kilometers, two hours, 100 meters up) The trail is used by both horses and hikers, following the east side of Gold Creek Canyon. It is best accessed from the Gold Creek parking lot where a short jog from the south end gets you onto the trail to the left for 5.5 kilometers up the canyon, right to the north beach, a short 1.2 kilometers away. The parking lot is at about 160 meters. This trail is an old road sloping gradually up to 260 meters in about 2.5 kilometers just above the lower falls. It then drops to the creek at 5.5 kilometers, so you would want to allow about two hours for the one-way trip.

Tiarella and **Spirea Nature Trails** There are two nature trails, one south of the day-use area and the other west of the Alouette campground. These are both well-maintained with informative tidbits everywhere.

There are several information stands along the roads in the park with brochures describing the trails. It is advisable to stop and pick one up if you plan a hike.

Camping Without a doubt, this has to be one of the finest, well-organized campsites in the valley. In fact, this is the first major campsite you will encounter on our eastward journey along the north side of the valley. With almost 350 sites available, you can imagine the effort required to maintain them but they do and the sites are well-laid-out, within easy access to facilities and sandy beaches. If these are not satisfactory, a boat can take you to some very impressive secluded areas of the lake. Every imaginable camping need is covered here, *even a formal tollbooth!*

Another good spot is the **North Beach wilderness campsite area**. These are designed for those who prefer things a bit rougher, classified as primitive, something like some of the night beach-parties here! This is a fantastic area where Gold Creek meets the lake, having carved a deep channel through the rocks and pushed out a nice gravel beach. The deep green water slows down along this section, creating an incredible place to fish and swim. The campsites are distributed in the trees and along the beach with fire pits, toilets, firewood and demarcated spots (see maps). You park at the Gold Creek day-use parking lot and hike about a kilometer down to the lake. The park people will visit to register you for your site. It might seem a bit much but this is really a magic spot and there are no gas fumes from vehicles. You won't find as many conveniences here but the setting will make up for it.

Boating If you have a good-sized boat this lake is indeed an incredible place to explore. It is cool and deep, plunging to over 100 meters mid-lake. The lake-shore is extremely varied with sheer rock bluffs in some areas and spectacular estuaries in others. Multitudes of clear-water streams can be found crashing down the mountains into the lake, many forming incredible natural sandy estuaries popular for overnighters or anglers. With almost 40 kilometers of shoreline to explore, this lake is indeed a choice boating option.

Fishing The lake contains every type of west coast freshwater game fish. Rainbow, cutthroat, dolly, lake trout, kokanee and many other types of sport fish can be found here. A bonus is lake char, thanks to the fisheries. The cutthroat are reportedly the largest fish but dollys have been the focus of some other incredible fish stories. Although an aggressive stocking program has been in effect, as you can see from the table, the lake is huge and deep so are not easy to find.

FISH STOCKED	YEAR	TYPE	NUMBER
Steelhead	1986	yearlings	20600
Cutthroat	1988	catchables	7500
Cutthroat	1990	yearlings	23400
Lake char	1990	fry	10000

The lake is incredibly deep considering it is only a short kilometer wide, reaching a maximum depth of 130 meters, with an average depth of 56 meters. This means that the lake's shoreline dives fast! From a fishing standpoint, the best bet is to stick close to shore or look for the many bays and streams entering the lake. The south end is the shallowest but no fish in his right mind would enter this popular beach area. The shore drops rapidly into the cool depths and has no shelf areas so fishing here is not easy.

LAKE BEAUTIFUL is a small pond high on Alouette Mountain in Golden Ears Park. Less than a hectare in size, the lake sits at an elevation of 750 meters well above Maple Ridge. It is shallow and virtually covered with lily pads in summer. From a recreational standpoint, the lake simply offers a peaceful little spot, tranquil and pure, for nature-lovers and hikers needing a rest, but the hiking and panoramic view at the nearby peak of Alouette Mountain are another thing.

FINDING the LAKE

The easiest route is from the Mike Lake parking lot (6-20) then the Golden Ears trail system. Check out the trail system under Alouette Lake (6-22). From the

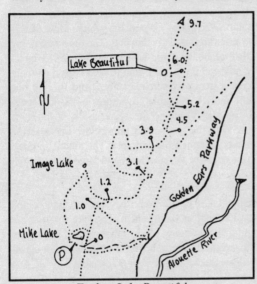

Finding Lake Beautiful

parking lot at 240 meters take Incline Trail climbing to 390 meters after passing Eric Dunning Trail and, at 1.2 kilometers, take the right branch to Alouette Mountain fire access road. At four kilometers you will hit Alouette Mountain Trail. The lower trail is for horses and dead-ends after another two kilometers. Take the upper road to a short trail to Lake Beautiful at .8 kilometers from the start of Alouette Mountain Trail. The tally is six kilometers horizontal and 510 meters up!

If you continue along Alouette Mountain Trail to the peak of the mountain (1371 meters), be prepared to climb *another 621 meters and 3.7 kilometers along the ridge*. You have already climbed 510 meters and traversed six kilometers but the view farther on is spectacular. The return trip is *nine to ten hours* covering 19.4 kilometers and 2262 meters elevation (up and down) **and** expect snow in June. This is a strenuous hike and proper equipment and experience is mandatory.

These **'Fly in'** lakes are for a different type of recreational adventure. From what I have been able to determine these lakes are truly untouched except by prospectors who have wandered the hills (and they have) and fly-in adventurers looking for the ultimate in fishing and camping privacy. These are large lakes, tucked away in the central to north section of Golden Ears Park. Most of this region is so rugged and remote it is rarely seen by anyone. The only way to get there is to fly in with a small float plane, so if you have access to one, try buzzing these lakes. I admit I have not seen them but I plan to next season so there is no information to offer except a map of where they are. I did fly into one years ago and it was one of the most memorable adventures but I do not remember which one it was. I can still visualize the scene as the float-plane skimmed over the lip of the lake with the spectacular falls below, into a scenic alpine wonderland I had never even dreamed was possible. The mountain goats were on the snow line, there were deer in the meadows and large vicious trout in those glassy waters.

Although there are many smaller lakes in the area, they are too remote and probably too small to land in so I am not including them. The lake statistics are described briefly...but as any pilot should know, **always** fly over and **look carefully** at the debris, water depth, exit and approach first. Due to the high elevation, cool air, snow and high ridges, the wind is *very* unpredictable.

RAVEN LAKE is 13 kilometers due north of the south end of Alouette Lake, sitting at an elevation of 927 meters. The lake is 1.1 kilometers long and 400 meters wide, 36 hectares in size. The lake strikes north-south, shaped like a sausage so you have to sneak in from the Pitt Lake side and turn northeast up Raven Creek, then quickly turn due north for the approach.

HECTOR FERGUSON LAKE is 13 kilometers due north of the Gold Creek area, where the creek empties into Alouette Lake. It is at an elevation of 780 meters and about ten hectares in size. The lake is shaped like a wedge with the approach-end thin. It is only 900 meters long and 200 meters wide so take a buzz before attempting anything. The approach must be from the south up Gold Creek, taking the Hector tributary and turning northeast on the approach.

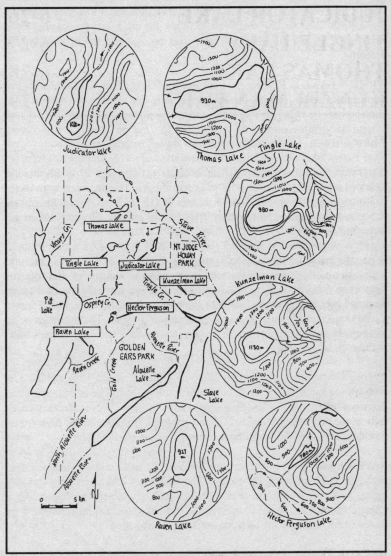

North Golden Ears Park fly in lakes

JUDICATOR LAKE is 16 kilometers northwest (heading 345 degrees) of the Alouette divide (thin passage between the south and north sections) on Alouette Lake. It is at 1020 meters, 24 hectares in size, an odd tadpole-shaped lake about 1.6 kilometers long, 150 meters wide on average. To complicate things, it has a dogleg in it before the large end. Approach is from the north after following Stave River, then turning southwest to follow the creek into the lakes. This is pretty high up and the U-shaped valley buttress is a real dead-end so buzz it carefully.

TINGLE LAKE is 23 kilometers due north of Gold Creek. It is a large lake at 980 meters and 60 hectares. 1.6 kilometers long and average 600 meters wide, the approach is tricky in that you come in by dipping into the Tingle Creek system through the canyon. So it's up Tingle Creek in a northwest direction, then a turn west into the creek gorge, over the lip and into the lake.

THOMAS LAKE is the largest lake of about 141 hectares, 27 kilometers due north of the divide. It is fairly high at 930 meters. The approach is from the Stave River side coming in from the north, flying south where you have about 1.2 kilometers before you hit shore. The lake is actually about 2.6 kilometers along the dogleg.

KUNZELMAN LAKE is in the adjoining Judge Howay Provincial Park, 15 kilometers northeast (azimuth of 025 degrees) of the Alouette divide. It is at a lofty 1120 meters, about 30 hectares in size, shaped like an almond. The approach length is 800 meters with no escape from the ridge encircling it, rising to 1400 meters. The only way in is from the west following the exit creek up from the Stave River.

REGION SEVEN
STAVE FALLS

THE STAVE FALLS REGION is a the next eastward slice of mountainous terrain adjacent to the Maple Ridge region. This particular region covers a ten by 45 kilometer strip of terrain reaching into the Mission district municipality on the east. The south area of the region includes a fairly rural section just north of the Fraser River. To the north the situation changes rapidly, reaching into the vast area of virtually untouched wilderness around the north end of Stave Lake. Within the southern portion are the rural communities of Whonnock, Ruskin, Websters Corners, Stave Falls and Steelhead, all distributed along the lowlands of the river fringe. Unlike the more western regions, there are no massive parks or reserves, only a few smaller parks containing the lakes. Another difference from earlier regions is that northern access is through logging and Hydro roads. The majority of area is Crown forest, part of the massive Douglas forest but within this region are quite a range of interesting lakes with a diverse range of recreation possibilities. Centered in this region is a thrust of rock between the Alouette and Stave valleys containing the majority of lakes. Right in the middle of this region, along the main access route, is a chain of manmade lakes created by damming up the flow of the Stave River. The upper dam holding back the massive Stave Lake is known as Stave Falls, the topmost in the two-dam sequence. The next dam at Ruskin holds back the waters of Hayward Lake. From Ruskin the water flows into the Fraser River.

Significantly, the lakes in this region are reasonably accessible, all a decent size and within a relatively small area. The main feature is that these lakes offer a fantastic variety of size, setting and recreational options that should satisfy the widest range of appetites. A few of these lakes have just recently been made accessible and offer a most interesting range of wilderness fishing opportunities. For the campers, the range is also good, varying from the excellent facilities at Rolley Lake to the remote natural wilds and dangers of Stave Lake. In this region you can begin to get away from crowds and exercise your vehicle or motor bike instead of your cardiovascular system.

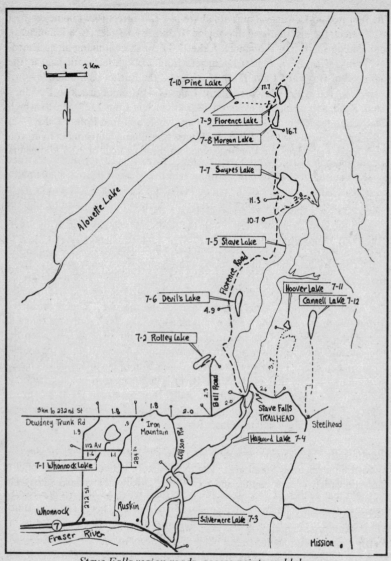

Stave Falls region roads, access points and lakes

ROADS, ACCESS POINTS AND LAKES

Looking at the regional map, note there are 12 lakes. The easiest line of reference is *Dewdney Trunk Road,* which continues due east from the previous region. It has six key access points.

The first two on Dewdney Trunk Road are at 272nd Street (9.0 kilometers past 232nd Street, the last trailhead into region 6) and 284th Street (10.8 kilometers), both leading south into **Whonnock Lake (7-1)**. Next, continuing along Dewdney Trunk, *Wilson Road* (12.6 kilometers from 232nd Street) will lead to the south end of **Hayward Lake (7-3)**. If you cross the Ruskin dam onto *Hayward Lake Road* you will get to **Silvermere Lake (7-4)**. Coming back to Dewdney Trunk Road, you reach *Bell Road* (at 14.6 kilometers from 232nd Street) which takes you to the Rolley Lake Provincial Park where you find **Rolley Lake (7-2)** and some excellent facilities for overnighters. Continuing on the main road, you reach Stave Falls dam and the first major trailhead, a total of 16.5 kilometers from the previous Maple Ridge access point at *232nd Street*.

From the trailhead you can take a short drop to the north end of **Hayward Lake (7-3)** via a short BC Hydro road or take the *Florence Lake Service Road* to reach the next string of lakes. From the trailhead, you can start with **Stave Lake (7-5)**, then drive to **Devil's Lake (7-6)** at 4.9 kilometers; **Sayres Lake (7-7)** at 11.3 kilometers; **Morgan Lake (7-8)** at 16.7 kilometers and **Florence Lake (7-9)** at 17.7 kilometers. **Pine Lake (7-10)** is reached from this same road system but the penitentiary gate prevents access. This chain of lakes is accessible via a good gravel road usable by truck or even high-slung cars.

The next trailhead is back on *Dewdney Trunk Road* a short 2.6 kilometers traveling farther northeast past the Stave Falls dam toward Steelhead where you take a 3.7-kilometer hike into the wilderness to find **Hoover Lake (7-11)**. **Cannell Lake (7-12)** is found farther, in Steelhead, but it is in the Mission watershed, so access is restricted.

CRUCIAL AMENITIES

The southern region can be classified as rural, so there are no major shops to buy goodies. There is a gas station and a small store at Iron Mountain and another small store just before the Stave Falls dam where you can get bait, supplies and rent canoes. If you are heading up the Florence Lake Service Road, remember this is a wilderness area so gas up and stock up here. The next store is at Steelhead to the east or there is gas station and store in the south at Ruskin on Highway 7. There is a local store with groceries and other interesting things around Whonnock Lake on 272nd Street. Most of these rural corner stores stock various fishing items but, if you need anything more serious, Haney is your best bet. Sorry, no watering holes in the area, so drive back to the Black Sheep in region 6 near Maple Ridge Park or head for Mission.

WHONNOCK LAKE is pretty, almost perfectly round, set right in the rural Whonnock Lake Park. This portion of terrain is a flat plateau area between the Fraser River and the more steeply inclined mountains to the north. The lake is therefore relatively low at an elevation of 170 meters in a protected basin. Measuring 50 hectares, the lake is a decent size, able to support a good variety of water activities such as fishing, canoeing and swimming. It is big enough to allow one to get away from the summer crowds.

WHONNOCK LAKE at a GLANCE		
ACTIVITIES	BOATING, FISHING, SWIMMING, PICNICKING	
LAKE STATS	Elevation & Size	: 170 meters, 50 hectares
	Lake Setting	: Whonnock Lake Park
ACCESS	Vehicle Type	: car
	Nearest Highway	: four kilometers to Dewdney Trunk Road
FACILITIES	Type & Class	: developed
	Camping	: not permitted, day use only
	Boat Launch	: wide gravel launch
FISHING	Fish Stocked	: 20,000
	Size Reports	: rainbows 25 centimeters 20-centimeter crappies
	Restrictions	: no motors, day use only

Only ten meters deep in the middle, its waters are dark but clean. The algae is prolific, creating a natural haven for water life, especially crappies. The perimeter, except for the south park area, is mostly swamps and brush. At night the giant bullfrogs inhabiting these swamps in great abundance create an incredible resounding drone, an eerie sound that makes you feel you have entered some prehistoric world. Fed only by small streams, the lake is somewhat dependent for its size on the beaver dams at the southwest exit into Whonnock Creek. Despite its shallowness, the lake contains a variety of fish that give any angler a good opportunity to try their skills. The lake is designed to accommodate a family, offering a well-rounded list of facilities including picnicking, swimming, fishing and boating.

FINDING the LAKE

If you are proceeding from Haney along Dewdney Trunk Road, drive nine kilometers from 232nd Street (region 6 trailhead). There you would reach 272nd Street on your right. After your turn, make a dogleg westward, then turn south to reach 112th Avenue at about 1.9 kilometers from Dewdney Trunk Road. Turn left and travel another 1.6 kilometers to reach the Whonnock Lake turnoff on

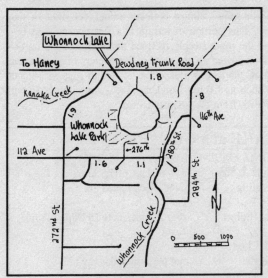

Finding Whonnock Lake

the left to the parking lot situated at the southwest end of the lake, .5 kilometers in. If you were coming from the Stave Falls trailhead, you take a left onto 284th Street which would be the 5.8 kilometer mark traveling west, just as you pass the Iron Mountain store. You would then take 284th and get onto 112th Avenue to get to the same turnoff to the lake.

Upon entering the park you will drive to a good-sized parking lot near the recreation center, through the main gate and circle around in a loop through the trees. There is a large, open, gravel area at the far eastern end of the loop and another gravel area near the lake and boat launch. Alternatively, you can park beneath the trees in several picnic areas that used to be the old campsites when camping was allowed.

RECREATION

Facilities The park includes a decent parking lot, toilets, docks, picnic tables and a beach area where the sand slopes gently into the clear water. Much of the south end is wooded but still offering several open grassed areas. The facilities are well developed but available for day use only.

Although there are a few docks, power boats are prohibited so these are used for showing off bikinis, swimming and fishing. There is an open gravel area to the left side of the beach where you can drive to the shore for an easy launch of the cartop or canoe. The picnic area and playground flank the beach where you will find a gazebo set nicely in the trees for large barbecue parties. There are several open areas under the trees where you can park and enjoy a picnic while the others enjoy the lake. The feature of the area is the new Whonnock Club facilities, catering to canoe clubs, offering training rooms and facilities for social functions. A well-designed dock system used for classes on rowing and canoeing pokes out well past the weeds. This is the local 'beach' for residents of Whonnock so the summer crowds can be large.

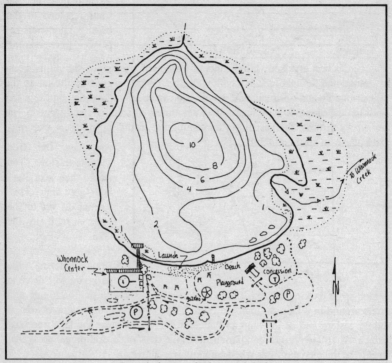

Detailed map of Whonnock Lake

Boating A feature of the lake is the vast marshland surrounding it. The majority of its perimeter is inaccessible except by boat making the lake a fantastic place to explore by canoe. You can row quietly, fish or just observe the natural aquatic ecosystem. Launching a canoe at the south beach is very easy and the lake is usually very calm, making this a magic place to spend a day.

Fishing The lake contains several species of fish including cutthroat, juvenile coho and crappies and has been subjected to an aggressive stocking program as shown in the table below. In a short period of four years, over 25,000 rainbows have gone into this lake, so given its size, this is virtually a fish-farm but, even with these impressive statistics, I believe the crappies outnumber the trout. They are very abundant here so if you are at all picky about catching trout, your challenge will be avoiding the crappies. They do put up a great fight reaching sizes of 20 centimeters…and that is a big crappie!

FISH STOCKED	YEAR	TYPE	NUMBER
Rainbow	1986	yearlings	6500
Rainbow	1987	yearlings	3200
Rainbow	1988	yearlings	3200
Rainbow	1989	yearlings	6400
Rainbow	1990	yearlings	6500

The lake is best attacked with a canoe or small rowboat, since shoreline access is limited and the lake is very shallow. With a canoe it is possible to get to the deeper middle and north channel where you can spend a great day on the water with the girlfriend, kids or buddy to catch a mess of smaller-sized trout. If you are shy of crowds, the best times for fishing are in the mornings or evenings, particularly in spring and fall.

ROLLEY LAKE is a premium place for campers. Situated dead-center of the Rolley Lake provincial park, this small wilderness park has been carefully preserved for the public to enjoy. At a mere 115 hectares in size, the park is not large by any means but is still large enough to contain a power-packed list of interesting recreational goodies, all set in a lush forest dominated by tall timbers. This place really makes you wonder how many shades of dark green there are. The forest completely surrounds the lake creating a nice wooded setting.

ROLLEY LAKE at a GLANCE		
ACTIVITIES	CAMPING, FISHING, BOATING, HIKING, SWIMMING, PICNICKING	
LAKE STATS	Elevation & Size	: 221 meters, 23 hectares
	Lake Setting	: Rolley Lake Provincial Park
ACCESS	Vehicle Type	: car
	Nearest Highway	: 2.9 kilometers to Dewdney Trunk Road
FACILITIES	Type & Class	: developed
	Camping	: 64 excellent sites
	Boat Launch	: open gravel area
FISHING	Fish Stocked	: 46,000
	Size Reports	: rainbows to 35 centimeters
	Restrictions	: no motors

The lake itself is small at only 23 hectares set nicely at a low elevation of 221 meters on a flat plateau area. The main park is also relatively flat, making this a favorite place for the whole family. Even the seniors can wander safely through most of the area while the kids swim and mom and pop catch dinner. The park itself is compact and very well-maintained, providing an excellent 'rural' fishing and recreational alternative to the more residential Whonnock Lake. In fact, Rolley Lake is the only formal campground in this region and, due to its central location, has become quite popular.

FINDING the LAKE

Take Bell Road off Dewdney Trunk Road 5.6 kilometers from 272nd Street or 14.6 from 232nd Street out of Maple Ridge. If you were coming from Stave Falls trailhead, you would be two kilometers along Dewdney Trunk Road traveling west.

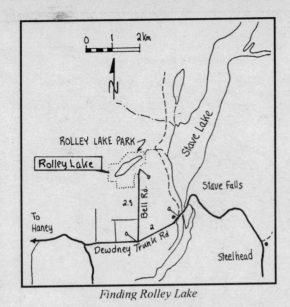

Finding Rolley Lake

Bell Road is also paved, taking you due north for 2.3 kilometers where you turn left onto the short gravel road. As you enter the park the vegetation instantly transforms into lush forest and stands of tall trees, a rather sharp contrast to the drive along Bell. It only gets better from here as the trees rise to block out the sun. The lake and day use area, along with good parking facilities are a short .6 kilometers along the gravel road.

Just before the parking lot the road splits at the information board. The right branch leads to the campgrounds. Straight through is the day use area.

RECREATION

Facilities at the lake are split nicely to service both the day user and the overnighter, providing day use on the west and overnight use on the east. The camp facilities include 64 excellent campsites close to the lake, set in the tall trees. There are a variety of outdoor conveniences and facilities, including good walking trails and well-organized sites. There is good access to toilets, wood, water and a shower in the central area. There is even a sani-station and amphitheater to top the list.

A large day-use area on the west end offers ample parking. There is access to trails, toilets, gravel launch area, picnic sites and an open beach area. Access to the lake itself is primarily from the parking lot or the campgrounds.

Camping The feature here is the camping facilities which include 64 excellent spots set gracefully in the tall timbers close to the lake. The sites are well-organized, with good access to toilets, wood, water and even a shower in the central area. No hookups are available. Camping fees are collected. Facilities are closed mid-fall to early spring.

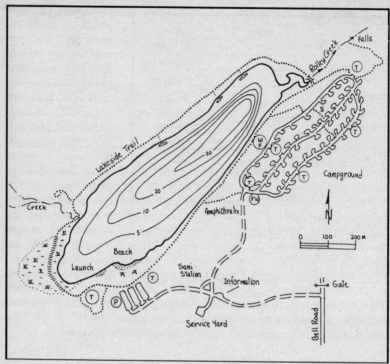

Detailed map of Rolley Lake

Trails Access to the lake itself is primarily from the parking lot or the campgrounds, both of which border the Lakeside Trail. This 1.5 kilometer trail surrounds the lake, providing several access points around the perimeter, an easy 45-minute walk through a variety of vegetation. At the west end, an interesting boardwalk takes you over a marsh where the water from the entry creek spills through the curious swampy habitat. The trail also loops from the campsite to Rolley Creek Falls at the northeast end of the lake. Falls Trail is a short 15-minute hike to a good view area of Stave Lake. This trail can be taken all the way down the creek to the Florence Lake service road.

Fishing at the lake is another feature attraction, providing great opportunity for the whole family including the expert who craves the big action. The lake contains a variety of game fish and is being aggressively stocked. Since 1986, almost 50,000 rainbows have been placed in this lake, most of which are classified as catchable. Power boats are prohibited so this means those catchables planted in 1986 should be whoppers by now! The stocking table is shown below:

194

FISH STOCKED	YEAR	TYPE	NUMBER
Rainbow	1986	yearlings	3000
Rainbow	1986	catchables	3000
Rainbow	1987	catchables	4500
Rainbow	1987	yearlings	10000
Rainbow	1988	catchables	3000
Rainbow	1988	yearlings	10000
Rainbow	1989	yearlings	10000
Rainbow	1990	catchables	3000

The Lake is deepest at the far end, reaching almost 30 meters quite close to shore. The 1.5 kilometer trail is nice and level and takes you completely around the lake, requiring about 45 minutes. Several access trails are provided to reach the shore in that area, as well as to three jetties that allow you to cast into the deeper water. The south end is shallow, with swamps and mud common but this type of environment provides excellent feed for trout so the big ones will be illusive and picky. There are other fish in the lake including dollys, cutthroat, catfish, bullheads and crappies. The lake is long enough for trolling, but motors are not permitted. The launch area is an easy, sloped gravel bar just off to the left of the beach with easy access from the parking lot. You just need to haul the boat about 100 meters so think small!

HAYWARD LAKE is a large manmade lake sitting at an elevation of 44 meters. It is 276 hectares in size, created by the second Stave Lake Hydro dam at Ruskin in 1929. The regional map shows a chain of lakes starting with upper Stave Lake created by damming the Stave River at the Stave Falls dam (our main reference point). Hayward Lake was created below this dam by the formation of the Ruskin dam. It holds Hayward Lake back from cascading into the Fraser River at the bottom. Originally, the area just at the head of Hayward Lake was a private BC Hydro community, housing the work-force for the project. Over the last few decades, as mechanization increased, the area was slowly opened to the public. In addition, Hydro decided to further open the area by creating a park around the north end of the lake where they have developed a variety of recreational facilities. A bonus is some of the remnants that take you back into some interesting history in the area.

HAYWARD LAKE at a GLANCE

ACTIVITIES	BOATING, PICNICKING, FISHING, SWIMMING, HIKING, NATURE	
LAKE STATS	Elevation & Size	: 44 meters, 276 hectares
	Lake Setting	: Hayward Lake recreation area
ACCESS	Vehicle Type	: car
	Nearest Highway	: one kilometer to Dewdney Trunk Road
FACILITIES	Type & Class	: developed
	Camping	: none, day use only
	Boat Launch	: small concrete launch
FISHING	Fish Stocked	: 46,000
	Size Reports	: rainbows to 35 centimeters
	Restrictions	: electric motors only

FINDING the LAKE

There are two ways to access the lake. One is at the Ruskin dam and the other, more developed area at the Stave Falls dam. Both can be reached by taking Dewdney Trunk Road east from Maple Ridge. Alternatively, if you were using Highway 7 you would take the Ruskin turnoff (see map).

The lower Ruskin area has a parking lot just above the dam (see the map). Take a right on Wilson Road at 12.6 kilometers from 232nd Street in Maple Ridge.

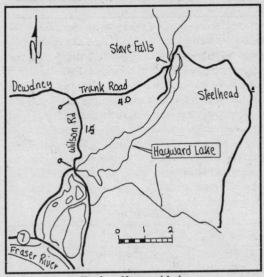

Finding Hayward Lake

Just as you start to the see the lake there is a parking lot to the left. This is not a place for a lot of facilities but it is a place where hikers or anglers can park and head up Railway Trail along the lake. If you missed the lot you will quickly see the Ruskin dam and a place for two cars to park at the old railhead.

The upper Hayward Lake Park is found by continuing on Dewdney Trunk Road all the way to the trailhead at the Stave Falls dam 16.6 kilometers from Maple Ridge. Access the north end of the lake via a paved road that cuts sharply up over the dam hump then plunges into the little valley, snaking down the side of the hill to the flat open area that once was the village. You will see the Stave River, a deep clear green waterway gushing through a beautiful park-like setting as it pours into the lake below. Keeping to the right takes you to the 90-car parking lot.

RECREATION

Facilities at the lake are very good at the main Hayward recreation area at the north. The park offers paved parking for 90 vehicles, a small boat ramp, picnic tables, beach, nature walks, toilets, extensive trails, historical sites and other day-use conveniences. This is a great place to put in a canoe or small boat. You should note that the lake is reserved for canoes and non-motorized (except electric) boats.

This site is a day-use park so do not leave your vehicle behind with the idea of camping overnight somewhere in the wilderness. Rolley Lake has excellent campsites and is close by, to the north, if you need to camp (see Rolley Lake). Just before you reach the parking area, the old road crosses Stave River where

you will find an incredibly beautiful spot. The south end of the lake is barren of
facilities except for the parking lot, a toilet and the south end of Railway Trail.

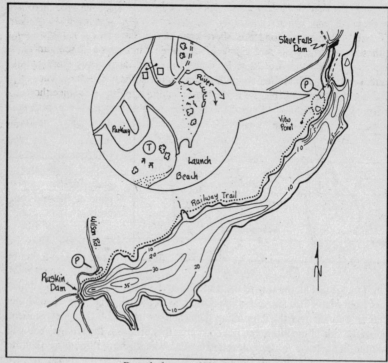

Detailed map of Hayward Lake

Trails Excellent interpretive trails are provided for nature-lovers and hikers.
The interpretive trail is situated at the north park area, looping around a small
pond. The main Railway Trail parallels the shoreline all the way to the other
dam (about six kilometers) offering many access points to the lake and opportunities to rest and ponder. Several streams enter the lake along the shoreline
providing the shoreline angler with some very nice places to try out some flies
or spinners offshore. The trail follows the old railway line with its interesting
history. The trail is not steep and is a pleasant place to spend a day.

Boating The lake is an extremely good place to launch a canoe or a small boat.
The flood waters have inundated into a maze of coves so there are endless
places to take a canoe away from crowds and paddle quietly. Since no gas motors are allowed, you will always be in quiet company undisturbed by noisy
motors. The north area under the bridge will even give you a little white-water

run if you feel up to it…but be careful since there are some strong undercurrents that literally boil when water is high.

Fishing The lake has been heavily-stocked, as you can see from the table. Just at the north end, you can also walk along the river and fish from the bridge. The park-like setting along this short span of the Stave River is impressive, with several deep pools and channels accessible from shore. When runoff is heavy or when Hydro decides to let water out of the dam above, there can be quite a set of rapids boiling through this channel, so boater beware. The river channel at the top probably offers the better fishing opportunities since the lake is actually quite shallow. As noted on the map, the lake deepens at the south end to over 35 meters so if you have a boat and are after giants, that is probably where they are.

FISH STOCKED	YEAR	TYPE	NUMBER
Steelhead	1986	fry	13800
Steelhead	1987	fry	48000
Steelhead	1988	fry	8700
Rainbow	1988	fry	15200

If you do not have a boat, there are plenty of angling places along Railway Trail or at the top end where the Stave River empties into the lake.

SILVERMERE LAKE

SILVERMERE LAKE is another manmade lake, but with a different twist. The area was once a swampy backwater marsh, just below the Ruskin dam then some wealthy individual who purchased the little knoll set in the middle decided to make an isolated island of the knoll. He created a roadway to the island off the main highway which acted as a dam, allowing the area to be flooded. A private northern back road was also completed to enclose a lake now known as Silvermere. Naturally, any property bordering the lake suddenly gained recreational value and lakeside homes popped up along the one accessible shoreline. So most of the accessible shoreline is private with the exception of a few spots where you can still gain access.

SILVERMERE LAKE at a GLANCE

ACTIVITIES	FISHING, BOATING	
LAKE STATS	Elevation & Size	: 35 meters, 110 hectares
	Lake Setting	: residential, private mix
ACCESS	Vehicle Type	: car
	Nearest Highway	: on Highway 7
FACILITIES	Type & Class	: none, mostly private
	Camping	: none
	Boat Launch	: canoe possible
FISHING	Fish Stocked	: unknown
	Size Reports	: rainbows to 30 centimeters
	Restrictions	: limited access

FINDING the LAKE

The lake is found along Highway 7 just a short kilometer past Ruskin. If you are proceeding from the Stave Falls trailhead on Dewdney Trunk Road, you will have taken Wilson Road south to cross Ruskin dam onto Hayward Lake Road. From the dam you would spot the lake just after a short 1.5 kilometers heading south. At 2.8 kilometers from the dam (1.4 kilometers north of the Highway 7 intersection) there is a wide shoulder area large enough for a few vehicles to park. A short trail drops off the road taking you to an open grassy area (about the size of a city lot) on the lakeshore. This is a pretty spot with no signs posted to warn you of trespassing. This will undoubtedly change so I cannot guarantee its state, but it is obviously the spot the locals use to get to the water. A canoe could easily be carried in from the road since the trail is only about 70 meters long.

Continuing south for 4.2 kilometers on Hayward Lake Road, turn right on Highway 7 and drive back along the highway that acts as a dike at the southern shore. This is the only other access since the rest of the lake is surrounded by the private roads (dikes) and the island. Since the Stave River and its flood area bounds these dikes, there is no access from the west or north but if you are really keen to get to the water, you can park a bit farther past the gate to the island off Highway 7 and walk along the shoulder over the lake. This can be hazardous since this is a busy highway so it is best to take only your fishing rod and sneakers so you can move swiftly.

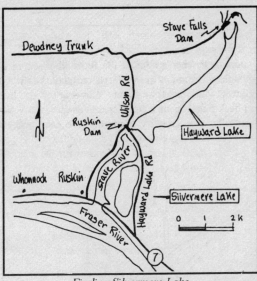

Finding Silvermere Lake

RECREATION

Facilities at the lake are non-existent because it is slowly being surrounded by private residences and summer homes. Thus there are great facilities but they are private. The lake is used quite extensively by the residents for swimming, fishing and boating, particularly water-skiing. There is an inviting ski ramp in the middle of the lake but public use is limited unless you know one of the residents or you have a secret spot to launch a power boat.

Fishing Water circulates through the lake, leaving through a culvert past the gate guarding the island off Highway 7, but the streams are small. There are various fish in the lake but because the area was originally a massive marsh it is shallow. Odds are you will catch smaller trout along with the usual list of bullheads, catfish and so on. Most fishing is done along the highway if you can't launch a canoe. Before the flooding there was a ditch along the road much like the one on the south side of the road so there is a deeper channel paralleling the road. Parking is a problem since the shoulder is narrow and the highway is always busy.

As you approach the Stave River bridge the road shoulder widens enough to park safely.

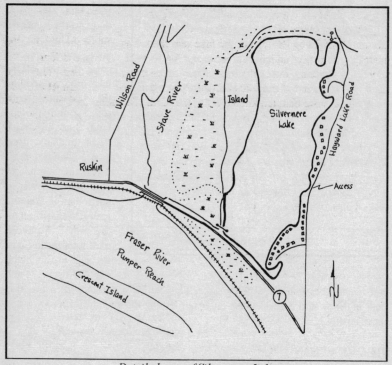

Detailed map of Silvermere Lake

If you insist on fishing, there are two more exciting spots close by; one just under the Stave River bridge on Highway 7 a bit farther along or the other, more exciting is the Ruskin recreation site (.6 kilometers south of Ruskin dam along Hayward Lake Road). No stocking program is in effect.

STAVE LAKE is the largest lake in this region covering 4410 hectares and is the topmost lake created by the Stave Falls dam. It sits at an elevation of 82 meters. Managed by BC Hydro, the lake was created as part of the Stave Falls hydroelectric project undertaken between 1908 to 1921. The lake is long at 27 kilometers reaching into wilderness areas accessible only by boat. The map shows the south end of the lake is actually just a dammed river channel and the main lake is more than ten kilometers to the north. The main body of this lake is quite enormous and mostly inaccessible. The lake was created several decades ago, before pre-clearing was enforced and the flooding process created vast areas where sinister-looking dead trees poke up through the surface waters causing a hazard for the unwary boater. In recent years, while the waters have been unusually low, the labor force at the nearby penitentiary has been efficiently used to clear most of the southern area so it is beginning to look more like a natural lake.

STAVE LAKE West at a GLANCE

ACTIVITIES	BOATING, FISHING, NATURAL CAMPING	
LAKE STATS	Elevation & Size	: 82 meters, 4410 hectares
	Lake Setting	: Crown forest
ACCESS	Vehicle Type	: car and truck
	Nearest Highway	: on Dewdney Trunk Road
FACILITIES	Type & Class	: developed launch, natural
	Camping	: natural
	Boat Launch	: good concrete
FISHING	Fish Stocked	: 8200, not required
	Size Reports	: 50 centimeter cutthroat
	Restrictions	: none

Due to its size and its rugged, remote quality this is a dangerous lake to those not wilderness-skilled but it still offers some dramatic scenery and great recreational opportunities, particularly for those prepared to rough it.

FINDING the LAKE

Stave Lake is first encountered at the Stave Falls dam along Dewdney Trunk Road 16.6 kilometers east of Maple Ridge. This is where you will find the Stave Falls dam and the flooded river section that joins Stave Lake. Although the river channel is large, this is not really the main body of the lake. Stave Lake sits to the north in remote wilderness and it must be respected as a dangerous body of water. Despite the lake's size, there are very few formal access points to the shore. In this southern area the shoreline changes dramatically with the level of the water in the lake. Most of the west shore is exposed during low water, allowing 4X4 access onto the gravel bars but, during high water, this whole area is flooded.

To get to the lake itself, launch a boat. There are two ways of getting to the lake from the Stave Falls reference point. The third is much more remote, on the other side of the main lake, at Cypress Point where you will find a forest service recreational site as described under Stave Lake east in the next region because it is accessible along a different chain of lakes.

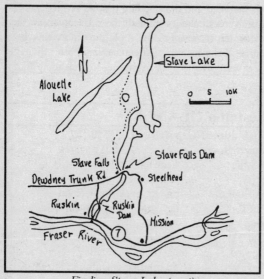

Finding Stave Lake (west)

There is a boat launch at this end of the lake just .8 kilometers along the Florence Lake service road, a good gravel road proceeding north from the main access point at the dam. A sign marks a quick jog to lakeside. Boat up the channel from here to the main lake.

The second access point is also along the Florence Lake Road. Drive 10.7 kilometers, then make a cut to your right, driving towards the lake and to encounter the shoreline of the floodplain. This section of road is not quite as good and requires a truck because of a few rough spots. The road continues for a further 2.8 kilometers where you will end up on the sandy shore of the bottom of Stave Lake. Drive along the beach about 500 meters to get to the lakeshore and the main lake is just around the point. There is no *formal* boat launch here but this is the popular place used by the locals. The beach is used for camping or as a launch for a small boat. This tactic avoids the long haul up the river channel. Note that the sand is soft so a four-wheel drive is recommended.

RECREATION

Facilities at the lake include a formal gravel boat launch at the Stave Falls site and a less formal launch area to the north. There is a good concrete launch, parking lot, a few picnic tables and a few biffies at the south site. If you are looking for formal, organized camping facilities, this is not the lake for you. Although it has many sand beaches, hidden coves, incredible estuaries and secret places that will surprise you, these are essentially natural, untouched by parks and forestry. There is a formal campsite set in quite a spectacular site but it is across the lake at Cypress Point (see Stave Lake east), so access is from the other side.

A popular spot for campers has evolved along the sand/gravel floodplain at the southwest end of the river. When the water is low this area is exposed, allowing access from the Florence Lake Service Road to a vast open area.

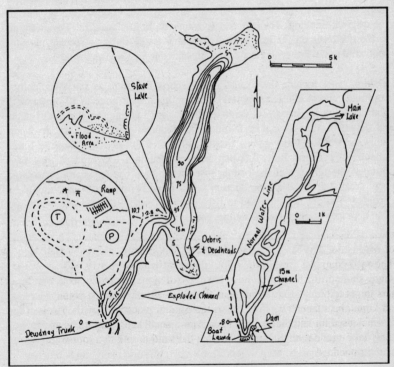

Detailed map of Stave Lake

Boating is, of course, the best way to enjoy Stave Lake so it is the prime activity here. If you are launching a boat via trailer, the formal launch is just at the .8-

kilometer mark along Florence Lake Road where you can launch a good-sized boat directly into the lower arm of the lake. The ramp is a double-wide launch for pleasure boats only. There is a small parking lot with a couple of toilets and a tiny picnic area here. It is worthwhile to keep in mind that this is a flooded river channel and that you navigate almost ten kilometers to get to the main lake. Although efforts have eliminated many of the dangerous deadheads, stumps and submerged trees, these are still a danger if the water is low or visibility is not good. Remember that, if you go up, you must also come back this way. The inset map shows the original river channel, the deepest part, so try to stay in it.

If you want to avoid the long haul through the channel, you can drive (by truck) to the second access point at the north end of the channel. Remember, once you pass this point you are in a spectacular but remote wilderness and on your own. This lake is vast, mostly rugged wilderness with **no** civilization along the shoreline. The wind can get fierce as it blows down from the north and there are many areas where the lake is filled with vast expanses of deadheads because of the original flooding. The lake can be as hostile as it is beautiful. Pay attention to the distances on the map—there are many tragic stories of people meeting foul wind and weather so always go with someone who knows the lake.

Fishing types include the regular list of sports fish such as rainbows, dollys, cutthroats and steelhead. Apparently the cutthroat can range to 50 centimeters and the dollys are massive. Essentially the lake is so huge that it is a vast natural fishery. Large fish can be found at the Alouette powerhouse and diversion tunnel where the water comes roaring through a tunnel from Alouette Lake, sometimes carrying little fish that get mangled into fish food as they pass through the turbines at the bottom just across from Cypress Point. The large pool created at the discharge area provides some boiling water that should be avoided. You are not supposed to fish, swim or boat in these waters so, if you fish here, pay attention to the danger zone.

FISH STOCKED	YEAR	TYPE	NUMBER
Steelhead	1986	yearlings	8200

As far as a formal stocking program is concerned, the table is shown. The lake is large and supports its own fishery so there is probably not much reason for formal stocking and the steelhead program was obviously experimental. To fish this lake you definitely need a boat. It will allow you to visit multitudes of streams and estuaries, deep waters, sheer rock cliffs and many sandy beaches.

DEVIL'S LAKE is a small lake for this region at 46 hectares a mere five kilometers north of Stave Falls dam nestled in a small valley above Stave Lake, easily accessed by car. Situated at an elevation of 106 meters, this is an elongated picturesque lake located in a small timbered valley. The lake has recently received some attention from the Mission municipality, who have improved access and developed a few facilities at lakeshore. Devil's Lake is nicely protected from winds and easily accessible but it requires a short walk down the hill to the shoreline. Although a good-sized lake, there is very limited access to the shore. You will find this an interesting place to camp, swim or fish, not yet too crowded so it is indeed an excellent easily-accessible piece of wilderness.

FINDING the LAKE

Drive along the Florence Lake service road at 4.9 kilometers from the Stave

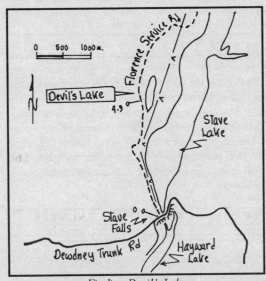

Finding Devil's Lake

Falls trailhead, a good gravel road suitable for cars. As you reach the 4.7 kilometer mark, you will begin to catch glimpses of the lake on the right through the tall timbers. Keep your eyes focused from this point on because there is no great asphalt parking lot or signs to give you landing details.

At 4.9 kilometers, as you just begin to climb, you should see a small gravel shoulder area, large enough for three cars, on the right. The district of Mission has recently posted a small sign on the tree, marking the trailhead. The trail is an easy grade dropping perhaps 20 to 30 meters total in its 330-meter length. The trail is well groomed with little footbridges taking you through a pleasant, enchanted forest right to lakeside.

RECREATION

Facilities There are just a few facilities at this lake, the formal ones including the new biffy and the trail itself. The short trail has been carefully carved into the landscape in an attempt to keep things natural. The rest are all natural facilities formed by campers and picnickers who, by virtue of their shoe leather and need for firewood, make their particular contribution to the open campsites. Once at the shore the trail continues to parallel the lake for a short distance, providing lake access to a few pristine gravel beach areas, both on the southwest shore. The first is the larger with a gravel-sand beach about 100 meters long and 30 meters wide making it a nice open area to swim or to launch your floating device. It is easy to cast a line here where a small stream trickles its way into the lake. It is possible to have a cool swim here and camp in the trees if you so desire. The beach area and the timbered area behind it offer a flat campsite that will support several groups. If this area is full you might follow the trail a little farther to a second smaller and well-hidden gravel beach with a fire pit. The main beach area is perfect for launching a small boat or canoe. Although the 330-meter haul is a fair distance, the trail is wide and clear and having a boat here is certainly an advantage.

DEVIL'S LAKE at a GLANCE		
ACTIVITIES	FISHING, CAMPING, BOATING, SWIMMING	
LAKE STATS	Elevation & Size	: 106 meters, 46 hectares
	Lake Setting	: Crown forest
ACCESS	Vehicle Type	: car plus 330 meter hike
	Nearest Highway	: 4.9 kilometers to Dewdney Trunk Road
FACILITIES	Type & Class	: primitive
	Camping	: natural
	Boat Launch	: on gravel beach
FISHING	Fish Stocked	: 8600
	Size Reports	: small cutthroat
	Restrictions	: none

Fishing Access to the lake is best from the main gravel beach area where the water deepens at a moderate rate but it is most likely you may catch a camper via your back-cast more readily here. A boat is a definite advantage, with the deeper section of the lake against the east rocky shoreline. Unfortunately lake contours are not available. The shoreline on the west side is dominantly brush, making access difficult for shore fishing, so think about carrying a small boat.

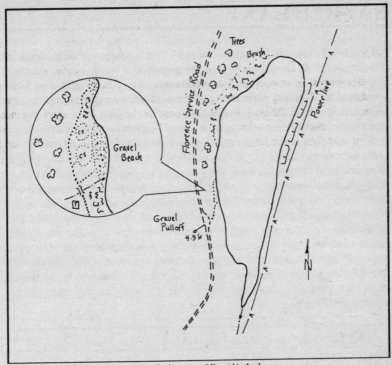

Detailed map of Devil's Lake

down the 330-meter trail. This will be less of an effort than carrying the boat back up again! There are various signs of footpaths farther from the campsite where the anglers' boots have beaten the brush northward in the quest for fishing hotspots. The stocking table is shown below, indicating that fisheries have taken some interest in this lake, beginning in 1986.

FISH STOCKED	YEAR	TYPE	NUMBER
Cutthroat	1986, 1989	yearlings	4300/year

If there are large cutthroat in the lake, they are undoubtedly hiding in the northeast shores where you need a boat to coax them out.

SAYRES LAKE is a complete change of pace, situated at an elevation of 230 meters. A nice-sized lake covering 78 hectares it is set in a wilderness area just recently made more accessible to the public. The lake is almost perfectly round, totally protected by steep hills that completely surround the lake except the southern lip. The mountains plunge steeply into this lake, dropping rapidly to 80 meters below surface but there is another interesting story about this little lake. It has been strictly controlled in the past by the local penitentiary that previously restricted access. At the same time, a small hatchery has existed, spawning trout into the lake and down Sayres Creek at the south end. This has no doubt added credibility to the stories that place two- to four-kilogram trout in these waters. In recent years the road has been changed to avoid the access restrictions imposed by the penitentiary. This, and removal of the access gate around Devil's Lake, has resulted in opening the area to allow the average angler to try his hand at these legends. What is restricted, however, is how you get to the lake fish and the means by which you may catch these monsters! At this lake the feature is fishing...nothing else. The surrounding roads provide good back road and hiking options but this is where you find some unique angling challenges.

SAYRES LAKE at a GLANCE

ACTIVITIES	FISHING	
LAKE STATS	Elevation & Size	: 230 meters, 78 hectares
	Lake Setting	: Crown forest
ACCESS	Vehicle Type	: car
	Nearest Highway	: 11.3 kilometers to Dewdney Trunk
FACILITIES	Type & Class	: developed dock
	Camping	: not permitted
	Boat Launch	: from dock
FISHING	Fish Stocked	: fish hatchery on lake
	Size Reports	: rainbows to four kilograms
	Restrictions	: two fish maximum, barbless hooks no live bait, no motors

FINDING the LAKE

Follow the Florence Lake service road from the Stave Falls dam trailhead. The inset map shows that this road has several little branches that may mislead you but essentially you will be able to distinguish which is the main road. At 10.7 kilometers, you will have started to climb sharply into the mountains but the road is still good gravel, suitable for a car.

At 11.3 kilometers, you will reach a small open gravel area, with a fork turning to the right. This is the service road leading to the lake. Take this right fork and just around the turn, to your left, you will see a gravel pit. The road actually continues climbing gradually for a kilometer straight up the hill to the lip of the lake. Unfortunately there is a control gate about 150 meters from the gravel pit so you might as well park. The lake is actually just at the crest of the hill, so this is not a difficult walk. It is, however, enough to discourage you from taking a large boat with you—specifically what it is designed to do.

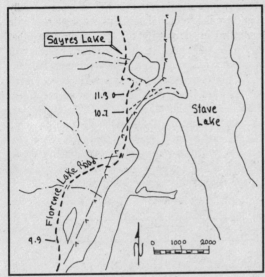

Finding Sayres Lake

There is another access point to the lake at 12.7 kilometers along Florence Lake Road. You would have continued up the main road past a forest service camp at 12.4 kilometers, then, just beyond that as you begin to climb again, there is a 'road' diving off to the right. This is a short road that will end abruptly within 200 meters above the creek gorge so don't think about speeding! You can park here and the lake is a short climb down to the outlet of the creek that empties into the lake below. It is a hardy climb down the rocks and gravel bed (about 60 meters in elevation change) but it is more direct than the other south road. It is not a good idea to consider any flotation device larger than a belly-boat here.

RECREATION

Facilities at the lake include a wharf to fish from, a gravel parking lot, the road and the infinite supply of fish, summing up the list of facilities. After parking and walking to the crest of the road, a rather spectacular little lake is right in front of you. The log booms on the right contain the spawning pens and a cabin that houses the two old codgers, an old pair of characters who guard the lake, living on the log boom and feeding the fish to make them huge. Other than that, there are no facilities. A short trail has been beaten through the trees by hyperactive anglers attempting to find other access to the deeper water.

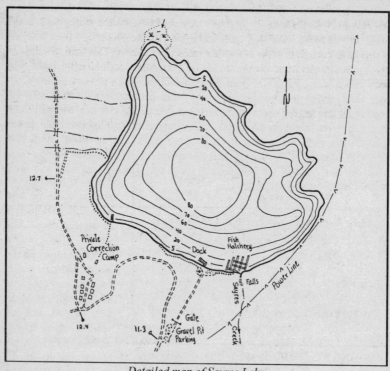

Detailed map of Sayres Lake

Fishing Reports are that the lake contains very large trout for this area—up to four kilograms! Although the lake is not stocked by fisheries, it is not required since it has the fish hatchery run by the prison right on the lake. The lake appears to be a perfect habitat for giant fish. The lake drops to 80 meters in the middle, offering giant trout a safe, deep haven. It is a long walk for a boat so most anglers stick to shore fishing, leaving the deep lake trout safe. I believe these trout are also fed by the old codgers so they may be more interested in fish pellets, further limiting your chances by using artificial stuff but there are further rules to make this a challenge. Signs tell you the maximum daily quota is *two* trout. They must be caught on a single barbless hook and you cannot use live bait! Now this may well be a scheme to make you think there are large fish in the lake, but somehow I do not think this a hoax. A belly-boat is a valuable device here. The lake is well-protected from wind and it would allow you to get into the deeper waters. The other option would be to carry a canoe up the access road, but you should consider bringing along a well-muscled buddy.

MORGAN LAKE

MORGAN LAKE is 20 hectares in size, found up the ridge west of the main body of Stave Lake. Not quite as large as the neighboring Sayres Lake, it is still large enough to support another interesting fishery. This lake, perched at 318 meters in elevation, on the divide between Stave and Alouette lakes, has been kept a secret for years. With the improvement and extension of the Florence Lake road system, the area has been made reasonably accessible, offering another unique fishing opportunity within easy reach of city life. Morgan Lake is elegantly set in a forested plateau and is connected to Florence Lake at the north. Water spills out via Foam Creek at the south end into Stave Lake. The feature at Morgan is the fishing and a great logging road system for the back roads traveler, but that's it. The lake is rough and undeveloped so if you need comfort, this is not the place for you.

MORGAN LAKE at a GLANCE

ACTIVITIES	FISHING, CANOEING, CAMPING	
LAKE STATS	Elevation & Size	: 318 meters, 20 hectares
	Lake Setting	: Crown forest
ACCESS	Vehicle Type	: car is possible
	Nearest Highway	: 16.6 km to Dewdney Trunk Road
FACILITIES	Type & Class	: natural
	Camping	: in natural open areas
	Boat Launch	: not formal but canoe possible
FISHING	Fish Stocked	: natural
	Size Reports	: two kilograms
	Restrictions	: single barbless hooks
		fish release

FINDING the LAKE

Take the Florence Lake service road from the Stave Falls trailhead. The jaunt is just over 16 kilometers, the last portion is a bit rough but a car can be taken in if you are careful. Finding the lake is not a problem since the road parallels the shoreline. The lake will appear on your right as you pass the 16.4 kilometer mark. From the road the lakeshore is visible through the trees a mere 100 meters away. From the road there is a slight drop of 30 meters but force your way through the brush, brambles and logging debris at road's edge. There are three spots along the road providing reasonable access to the lakeshore. At the 16.4 kilometer mark (from the Stave Falls trailhead), you will see a large rock beside the road on the right. You can pull off just beyond this rock where you will find a rough trail that plunges over the side of the road debris into the tall trees. At this point, the shore is lined with scratchy bushes, logs and mud so although you can get to the shore, you can do little more than perhaps launch your belly-boat or stand and gaze at the scenery.

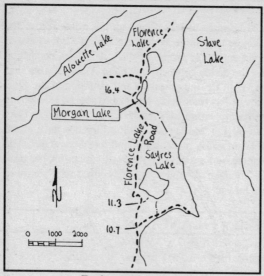

Finding Morgan Lake

The next access point is at 16.6 kilometers where another trail drops quickly to the shoreline with a little open marsh and grass area clear of logs and debris. If you want to plop a canoe in the water this would be the spot since it is only 50 meters from the road. The drop from the road is a bit harsh since you need to clamber over old logging slash, boulders and debris before you break into the wooded forest.

The third access point is at 16.7 kilometers, just past the 16-kilometer forest service marker on the tree where you will see a cedar tree and possibly a stick with a blue ribbon poked into the bank. A rather inconspicuous beaten path can be seen up the bank leading into the bushes beside the cedar tree. This is a good brush-cut trail that takes you to an open, flat projection of land poking into the lake. This is the more popular place, offering an open area with a gravel beach and some large boulders on the shore. The more conspicuous 'big rock' marks the spot; obviously the favorite one for campers. From the road, the lakeshore is about 100 meters away so you could take your boat through here reasonably easily.

RECREATION

Facilities at the lake do not exist in any formal, organized way with the exception of the trails and shoreline access points created by the boots of anglers. Park beside the road then climb down to the lakeshore through the heavily-wooded area. There is a trail that also parallels the lakeshore, but most of it has grown in and it is difficult to find. The trail leads down to the big rock and a little beach area jutting into the lake. There is room for several campsites here, with remnants of rock fire rings. This particular spot was once an old cabin site.

214

This trail intersects the other trail that parallels the lakeshore and used to get you to Foam Creek but it may be easier to find it by charging into the bushes just off the big rock at 16.4 kilometers.

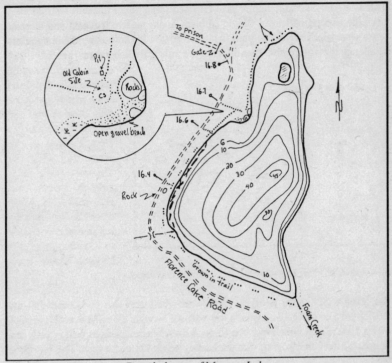

Detailed map of Morgan Lake

The natural campsite area near the big rock is the best location on the west side of the lake, just be careful of the pit in the open area along the trail, left by the old hermit who inhabited the area once-upon-a-time.

Fishing This lake is reported (by fisheries) to contain eastern brook trout. No stocking program is in effect, but the lake definitely does not lack fish, mainly because you are not allowed to take them with you. Opened only recently, the lake has essentially been untouched for decades so fish habitat is natural and the fish are obviously deemed easily-enticed by anglers. The lake is much shallower than Sayres Lake, with the deeper area toward the middle on the opposite side. At that point, a 40-meter-deep channel seems to have been carved out by Foam Creek. Unfortunately, the western shoreline is reasonably difficult to fish from due to logs, marsh, prickly bushes and bog. Most of the shoreline is heavy with sunken logs but the water drops rapidly to ten meters just off the west shore, offering good opportunities for interesting fly fishing as the denizens of the deep surface for bugs in the cool of the evening. The big rock area is more open for casting but the shore does not deepen quickly here.

This is a new lake so fisheries have imposed some rather difficult restrictions—ones the experts will love! Single barbless hook, no live bait and you *must release your catch!* Two-kilogram fish are reported so there is no doubt about the challenge this impressive lake offers to the ardent fly fisherman.

FLORENCE LAKE is the twin to Morgan lake. It is larger, at 32 hectares and a bit higher up at an elevation of 390 meters. Florence is also perched on the divide overlooking Stave Lake, offering the same type of back roads and fishing adventure as its neighbor. It is worthwhile to drive to the 19-kilometer mark past the lake to get a fantastic view from the north end. The road climbs abruptly along a thin ledge about 100 meters above the lake where the mountain literally plunges into the lake. You won't miss the lake as you drive along the ledge! Florence Lake is another one of those super fishing lakes that have been made more accessible by the road system. Development here is non-existent and the brush is thick and mean so access to the water is a challenge. The feature here is the fishing. This lake offers another virgin location to try your new flies.

FINDING the LAKE

To get here, take the Florence Lake service road from the Stave Falls dam trailhead. The road can be a bit rougher in this area so a truck is recommended.

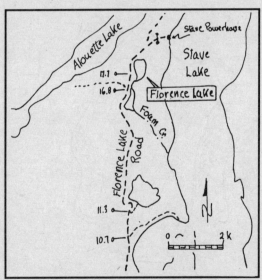

Finding Florence Lake

At 16.7 kilometers you will have passed Morgan Lake and, at 16.8 kilometers, you will encounter the left gated fork to the penitentiary and Pine Lake (close to Alouette Lake) but the boys at the pen may make things uneasy for you should you try to get to it. The right fork proceeds up the hill where you will begin to see a glimpse of the lake and the exit stream as you come to the crest of the hill. At 17.7 kilometers you will level off and see a big rock and stump side-by-side in a small area you can pull off on. You may even see a rock fire pit left by the last camper. There is a wide enough shoulder to park on and just over the bank you may see the old familiar blue ribbon marking the access trail. This trail dives into the tall trees and emerges at lakeshore after about 70 meters, a 30-meter drop and a few tough spots. The bush is rough with some obvious signs of a trail, enough of a path to allow you to take a canoe down (with a bit of sweat). The lakeshore is dominated by logs, debris, prickly bushes and bog. Logs stick into the water in random directions, offering some precarious spots to cast from but essentially this shoreline is difficult to access everywhere.

RECREATION

Facilities at the lake are non-existent, with access to the water a bit of a challenge. There are no open areas on the west side that allow camping at lakeside. This is why the most popular campsite appears to be on the road above the lake. Since it is only a short drop to the lake, this is the most practical alternative. There is enough room at the bottom to launch but be prepared for a good effort over a few windfalls and a few tough spots down a steep grade. It is best to walk down first. If you are fortunate enough to get your boat in, the rocks on the opposite side will undoubtedly provide some excellent campsites.

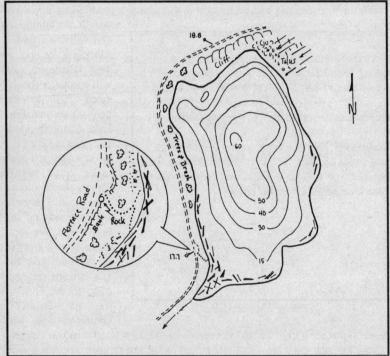

Detailed map of Florence Lake

218

Fishing There are some serious fishing restrictions at this lake, mainly the use of artificial flies only and single barbless hooks. You must also release the fish! There is no formal stocking program here since it is obviously not required; this lake is as natural a fish habitat as you will find. The restrictions simply help ensure the lake, now open to the public, is not over-fished. Little is known or reported about this lake except that there are some big fish here, so the challenges and opportunities are all here for the angler.

FLORENCE LAKE at a GLANCE		
ACTIVITIES	FISHING, CANOEING, BACK ROADS	
LAKE STATS	Elevation & Size	: 390 meters, 32 hectares
	Lake Setting	: Crown forest
ACCESS	Vehicle Type	: truck
	Nearest Highway	: 17.7 km to Dewdney Trunk Road
FACILITIES	Type & Class	: none
	Camping	: on roadway
	Boat Launch	: rough
FISHING	Fish Stocked	: not required
	Size Reports	: rainbows to two kilograms
	Restrictions	: single barbless hooks, fish release

Since the shoreline is essentially hostile, lined with logs, bush and marsh, shore fishing is difficult. Even the outlet is plugged with logs and debris so this is not a good area to cast a fly. The best bet is to launch a belly-boat and head for the other side. A canoe could be carried down by a couple of keen wrestlers. The deeper areas are off to the east where a shelf has formed against the rock bluffs.

Back roads This is a super area to explore with a dirt-bike. Many of the logging roads are new, literally blasted through the rocks. If you continue past Florence, you will get to the divide between Alouette and Stave lakes, a visual experience not had by many people.

PINE LAKE

PINE LAKE is a small lake of four hectares situated just above a remote area of Alouette Lake at an elevation of 180 meters above the south shore. The lake is adjacent to the penitentiary site on an isolated area above the lake. Alouette sits at 106 meters so this is not much higher.

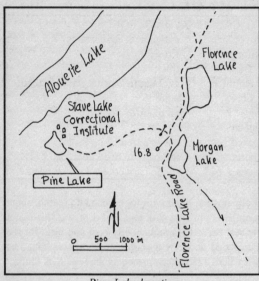

Pine Lake location

To get to the lake take the Florence Lake service road from the Stave Falls dam trailhead. The road can be a bit rougher in this area so a truck is necessary. You will have passed Morgan Lake at 16.7 kilometers and, at 16.8 kilometers, you will encounter the left fork to the penitentiary. This left fork has a gate across it so I do not suggest going any farther unless you know something about the penitentiary and the lake that I do not. The access road goes into a valley and emerges on the lower side of the mountain close to Alouette Lake, Pine Lake and the secret penitentiary. I am including it here because...who knows...you may visit a buddy there one day and go fishing!

HOOVER LAKE is a small lake of four hectares situated on an isolated hill on the east side of Stave Lake just north of the Mission landfill site. It is at an elevation of 440 meters, in the Mission Forest Reserve or an isolated section of it jutting north into the split of Stave Lake. This is the highest of the family of lakes is this region, nestled in the backside of three knolls reaching 600 meters. Hoover has been a secret lake known only by the locals for years. Typical of this area are old grown-in planked logging roads once used to haul shingle bolts (cedar blocks to make shakes) in the old days. These have since all but disappeared, leaving only obscure secret trails, logging roads and Hydro access roads networking the area enough to keep the lake a secret. Hoover requires a serious hike of almost four kilometers from Dewdney Trunk Road but it is a worthwhile experience and the hike is easy. The forest service, in conjunction with the Mission municipality, have recently cut new trails and made a serious attempt to open the lake to boots, backpacks and lures, finally uncloaking the lake from secrecy.

HOOVER LAKE at a GLANCE

ACTIVITIES	HIKING, FISHING, CAMPING	
LAKE STATS	Elevation & Size	: 440 meters, four hectares
	Lake Setting	: Crown forest
ACCESS	Vehicle Type	: car plus 3.7-kilometer hike
	Nearest Highway	: 3.7 kilometers to Dewdney Trunk Road
FACILITIES	Type & Class	: primitive
	Camping	: natural open sites
	Boat Launch	: forget it
FISHING	Fish Stocked	: unknown
	Size Reports	: unknown
	Restrictions	: none

FINDING the LAKE

Take Dewdney Trunk Road over the Stave Falls dam and proceed up to the mountain toward Steelhead. At 2.6 kilometers from the Stave Falls trailhead, you will pass the wire fence guarding the Mission landfill site on the right. Just as you drive past the gate, the open gravel area to the left has the old familiar yellow gate barring entry to the access road to Hoover. From here the trek is 3.7 kilometers with three kilometers of it on a good logging road and .7 of the final trail cut in 1991.

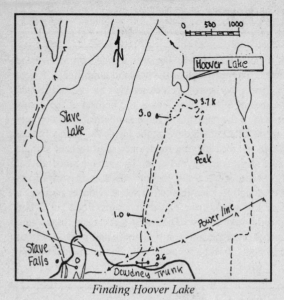

Finding Hoover Lake

Park your vehicle on the gravel area and get ready for a good hike. From the gate, the road takes you into the tall timbers quickly, then cuts to the right to begin the ascent into the valley. The road is of good quality so only the steady climb is the obstacle. You will start at 250 meters in elevation and, after 20 minutes (or about one kilometer) you will reach a marked junction 50 meters higher. Take the lower left fork and enjoy the flat walk for it soon disappears, giving way to five- to ten-percent grades for most of the next two kilometers. After a total of three kilometers and 40 minutes, you reach the divide and encounter the sign marking Hoover Lake Trail. You will have climbed to an elevation of almost 500 meters and the beginning of the descent into the Hoover Lake basin at 440 meters elevation, about 20 minutes. The trail is a footpath through the heavy trees, paralleling the old plank road that formerly went to the lake. Just as you begin to see glimpses of the lake you will pass the old familiar green biffy then emerge at the main, lone campsite area at the south end of the lake. From here the trail continues along the swampy end at the left over a boardwalk and around the west lakeshore to some other open campsites.

RECREATION

Facilities at the lake are mostly those created by ardent campers, hikers and anglers with no formal facilities except the trail, biffy and boardwalk but there are four nice-sized campsites close to or on lakeshore, nicely cleared with remnants of fire circles, set nicely in the trees. The first and largest spot is the open one at the south end, where you first see the lake. This has some logs, a fire pit and a large open area that will support a few tents. There are three other tiny areas, one on the west shore following the lakeside trail and one just above it set in the timbers overlooking the lake. These are the nicest sites; the fourth is small but secluded farther along the trail (which gets a bit rough) just around the point. Lake access is not easy in most of the area and the forest is thick, so

222

open areas and access to them is at a premium. Note the area is known for resident **cougars and bears**. Also remember they were here *first*.

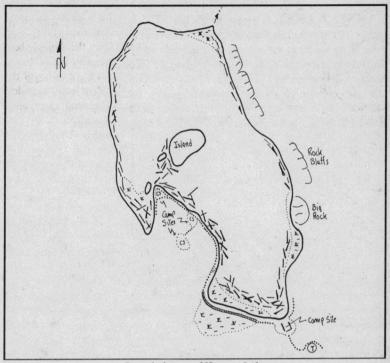

Detailed map of Hoover Lake

Fishing information is rather sparse since this lake has been a well kept secret. Needless to say, the difficulty has been access, limiting any heavy traffic here, leaving the fish to grow. Getting a boat to the lake has been almost impossible. Good entry and exit streams make the lake a natural fishery. The lake itself is difficult to fish, with most of the shore lined with swamp, thick brush and sunken logs left by the cedar and logging operations of the past. A belly-boat would certainly fix that problem. The water is incredibly clear but rich in vegetation. The flies are numerous and, all in all the lake is a perfect haven for rainbows. This is undoubtedly why no formal stocking program is recorded. If you are forced to fish from shore then your best bet would be at a few open access points along the west trail where there are a few precarious log bridges to stand on and cast into the drop-off beyond the logs and debris. Essentially the shore trails are undeveloped, so here is your chance to find your *own* secret spot!

CANNELL LAKE is a long narrow lake of 35 hectares sitting at an elevation of 280 meters. It is situated in the rather rural area of Steelhead. The lake is the main source of water for the municipality of Mission so is out-of-bounds. The lake is just north of the little community of Steelhead, off Dewdney Trunk Road six kilometers east of the Stave Falls dam. From here the local road system takes you north to the big gate that bars entry. The lake is set back in a little valley so you cannot even see it. There are no facilities except for the guardhouse and the dog house for the five Dobermans so forget this one!

FOR MORE INFORMATION

The following list is provided for those who may need to find more information on the lakes, parks, roads and services in the Valley. Please *keep in mind that numbers may change.*

BC HYDRO   **528-1801**
If you need to know more about Hydro's recreation sites on Hayward Lake, Buntzen Lake and Wahleach Lake, this number gets you to the recreation department.

BOOKS on HIKING and LOCAL INTEREST
Vancouver's Famous Stanley Park, by Mike Steele, 1993, published by Heritage House
Fishing Hot Spots of the Upper Fraser Valley, by Richard E. Probert, 1992 published by Hancock House
The Discoverer's Guide Fraser River Delta, by Don Watmough, 1992, published by Lone Pine Publishing
109 Walks in British Columbia's Lower Mainland, by Mary and David Macaree, 1990, published by Douglas & McIntyre
Exploring the Outdoors in Southwestern BC, by Tony Eberts & Al Grass, 1984, published by Hancock House
Easy Hiking Around Vancouver, by Jean Cousins and Heather Robinson, 1990, published by Douglas & McIntyre

BURKE MOUNTAIN NATURALISTS   **936-4108**
These people are very active in the Port Moody and Port Coquitlam area so they may be able to give you new information on the status of trails in the area.

CANADIAN FOREST PRODUCTS (CANFOR, Harrison Mills)   796-2757
This number is useful to determine the logging road states, closures, times open, and to get general information on access in the Harrison Mills Region.

GVRD REGIONAL PARKS (Head Office-bookings)   **432-6350**
Central Area Parks   520-6442
East Area Parks   530-4983
West Area Parks   224 5739
The Greater Vancouver Regional District (GVRD) has as one of their functions the responsibility to Developedop and maintain the smaller, local regional parks. These numbers are useful to get further information on the parks.

HUNTING and FISHING (Surrey Office)   **582-5243**
Maple Ridge office   465-4011
Chilliwack office   795-8422
Squamish office   892-5971

These are conservation offices that will give you up to date information on fishing regulations and other information.

PROVINCIAL PARKS
Golden Ears (Lower Fraser Valley) in Maple Ridge   463-3513
Cultus Lake (Upper Fraser Valley) in Sardis   858-7161
Mount Seymour in North Vancouver   929-4818
These numbers are useful to get up to date information on the provincial parks, facilities, trails, camping costs, bookings, etc.

LYNN HEADWATERS PARK (trail advisory)   985-1690

MAPS
Surveys and Resource Mapping in Victoria   387-1441
Ministry of Forests in Burnaby   660-7500
Forestry Maps in Victoria   387-5181
Outdoor Recreation Council of BC   737-3058
Geological Survey of Canada   666-0271

MINISTRY OF THE ENVIRONMENT
Fisheries Branch Surrey   582-5200
Fisheries Branch Victoria   387-9561

MINISTRY OF FORESTS (Main Office, Burnaby)   660-7500
Vancouver recreation   775-1661
Lower Mainland (Chilliwack)   685-5972
Upper Valley   858-7161
Central Valley   820-2055
Main Office (BC Parks)   929-1291

NORTH SHORE HIKERS ASSOCIATION   925-9312

RESCUE COORDINATION CENTER   1-800-567-5111

ROYAL CANADIAN MOUNTED POLICE
Vancouver   264-3111
Maple Ridge   463-6251
Agassiz   796-2211
Hope   869-2432
Mission   862-7161
Chilliwack   792-4611
North Vancouver   985-1311
You may need these numbers if you have any troubles that require police attention.

SEYMOUR DEMONSTRATION FOREST   432-6410
This number will connect you with the GVRD section that will give you up to date information on the park.

UBC RESEARCH FOREST   463-8148
For information on trails, access, programs and special events in the park, use this number in Maple Ridge.

WATERSHED MANAGEMENT   432-6286
This is actually a GVRD number but it connects you with the people who manage the watershed. They will tell you about the areas to avoid.

WEATHER FORECASTS (Environment Canada)
General information   664-9032
Vancouver and vicinity   664-9010
Vancouver/mountain forecasts   664-9021

WESTERN CANADA WILDERNESS ASSOCIATION   683-8220
These people have an office and store in Vancouver, offering maps, books and information on the area, dedicated to the preservation of wilderness.

INDEX TABLE

The following pages provide a special *table index* that also summarizes all the key information in the book. All 195 lakes are listed in alphabetical order with a direct reference to the page number and the lake region-number code. The following information is provided in the tables:

LAKE REFERENCE and STATISTICS is the first, left page focused on lake and area statistics.

Lake Name This is the actual, most popular name of the lake. This name is used at the beginning of each lake section.

Lake Refer This is the reference number given to each lake identifying the *region* and sequential lake *number* (i.e. 13-10 refers to region 13, HOPE and lake number 10, KAWKAWA).

Region The region name is identified here. Remember this is a *general* region central to a strip of land and not necessarily the exact location of the lake.

Elev The elevation, in meters, is given here. This is the value taken from the government 1:50,000 contour maps. In many cases these conflict with published elevations. It is assumed that the government maps are correct.

Size The size of the lake, in hectares, is given here. In some case these have been measured from 1:50,000 maps and may be approximate (<1 is less than 1).

Area Use This identifies the main land use such as Crown, Private, Park, Watershed, or Multi use for example.

Vehicle Type This identifies the mode of transport needed to get you *closest to the lakeshore.* If a hike is required thereafter there will be an entry in the hike column. *Restr* means that access is *restricted.*

Hike reflects the distance *one way* in kilometers to the lake from the point where your vehicle (whatever it is) is parked. A '*?*' indicates *unknown*, or that several questionable routes are possible.

FACILITIES and RECREATION SUMMARY The second page is focused on facilities and recreation information.

Facilities Type These are either developed, primitive, natural or private, referring to the camping, launch, toilets, or other facilities.

Recreation A series of standard recreational activities are summarized here indicating whether they *exist* (marked with an X) or whether they are the *feature* attraction (marked with an F). The abbreviations in the table are:

CP Camping	**BT** Boating	**HI** Hiking	**PK** Picnicking
EQ Equestrian	**BR** Backroads	**OT** Other	

Fish Stocked This identifies the total number of fished stocked up to 1990. Although the stocking program continues to date, the figures were not included. The word 'natural' indicates a *natural habitat* for fish...no stocking needed.

Page is the actual page number in the book where detailed information is found.

INDEX TABLE

LAKE REFERENCE and STATISTICS						ACCESS	
Lake Name	Lake Refer	Region	Elev (Mt)	Size (Ha)	Area Use	Vehicle Type	Hike km
Aldergrove	3-6	Burnaby	50	<1	Reg. Park	Car	0
Allan	8-2	Dewdney	100	20	Private	Car	0
Alouette	6-22	Maple Ridge	106	1644	Prov. Park	Car	0
Bear	10-1	Harrison	920	2	Crown	Car	5.5
Beaver	1-26	West Van	20	4	City Park	Car	0
Beaver Pond	10-5	Harrison	205	2	Prov. Park	Car	0
Betsy	6-12	Maple Ridge	550	< 1	Reserve	Car	10.0
Blaney	6-4	Maple Ridge	335	8	Reserve	Car	4.0
Bird	6-8	Maple Ridge	465	< 1	Reserve	Car	7.4
Blinch	8-13	Dewdney	765	50	Crown	4X4	1.0?
Blue Gentian	1-9	West Van	810	< 1	Park	Car	2.5
Brunswick	1-5	West Van	1270	3	Park	Car	9.9
Buntzen	4-2	Pt Moody	123	182	BC Hydro	Car	0
Burnaby	3-3	Burnaby	14	5	Park	Car	0
Burwell	2-22	North Van	1765	25	Watershed	Restr	
Cabin	1-13	West Van	1170	<1	Park	Car\lift	.5
Cannell	7-12	Stave Falls	280	35	Watershed	Restr	
Campbell	9-17	Harrison M	650	3	Crown	4X4	0
Capilano	1-23	West Van	144	200	Watershed	Restr	
Chadsey	11-4	Sumas	620	9	Crown	Truck	.8
Chehalis	9-4	Harrison M	227	629	Crown	Car	0
Chicadee	4-7	Port Moody	950	<1	Crown	Car	5.2
Chilliwack	12-10	Chilliwack R	620	1198	Multi use	Car	0
Clegg	2-18	North Van	1190	<1	Park	Car	7.0?
Clerf	13-5	Hope	1260	7	Crown	4X4	2.0
Coquitlam	5-2	Pt Coquitlam	154	1100	Watershed	Restr	
Como	4-14	Port Moody	150	5	Park	Car	0
Consolation U	5-10	Pt Coquitlam	1325	52	Crown	Boat	20?
Consolation L	5-10	Pt Coquitlam	1142	28	Crown	Boat	20?
Cornett	2-23	North Van	1605	2	Watershed	Restr	
Cougar	1-17	West Van	1120	<1	Park	Car\lift	1.7
Cranberry	6-2	Maple Ridge	140	<1	Reserve	Car	.6
Cultus	11-7	Sumas	43	624	Multi use	Car	0
Cypress	4-3	Pt Coquitlam	770	4	Crown	Car	4.7
Davis	8-3	Hatzic	166	32	Park	Car	.4
Deeks	1-3	West Van	1080	25	Park	Car	6.7
Deer	3-2	Burnaby	20	30	Park	Car	0
Deer	10-7	Harrison	190	54	Park	Car	0
Demelza	4-8	Port Moody	950	<1	Crown	Car	5.2
Dennett	5-5	Pt Coquitlam	950	8	Private	Car	5.2
De Pencier	2-14	North Van	1020	<1	Park	Car	3.0?
Devil	13-8	Hope	76	4	Crown	Car	0
Devil's	7-6	Stave Falls	106	46	Crown	Car	.3
Dick	1-24	West Van	390	9	Watershed	Restr	
Dickson	8-11	Dewdney	638	78	Watershed	Truck	1.0
Disc	5-9	Pt Coquitlam	870	25	Crown	Boat	18?
Eaton	13-3	Hope	1318	44	Crown	Car	6.5
Echo	9-2	Harrison M	106	6	Private	Restr	0
Elbow	9-3	Harrison M	167	14	Crown	Car	0
Enchantment	1-22	West Van	1030	24	Watershed	Restr	

INDEX TABLE

FACILITIES and RECREATION SUMMARY

CP= CAMPING, BT= BOATING, HI=HIKING, FI= FISHING, PK=PICNICKING, EQ= EQUESTRIAN, BR= BACKROADS, OT=OTHER

Lake Refer	Facilities Type	C P	B T	H I	F I	P K	E Q	B R	O T	Fish Stocked	Vol 1 Page	Vol 2 Page
3-6	Developed			X		X	X		X	No fish	100	
8-2	Private		X		X					Natural		31
6-22	Developed	F	F	F	F	F	F		F	61500	172	
10-1	Natural	X		X						Natural		132
1-26	Developed			F		X			X	Natural	49	
10-5	Developed	X	X	X	F	X			X	Natural		145
6-12	Natural			X						Natural	162	
6-4	Natural			X						Natural	162	
6-8	Natural			X						Natural	162	
8-13	Natural	F		X	X			X		Natural		62
1-9	Developed			X		X			X	No fish	36	
1-5	Primitive	X		F	X					Natural	29	
4-2	Developed		F	F	F	F	X		X	75000	111	
3-3	Developed		F	F	X	X	X		F	Natural	89	
2-22	Natural									Natural	77	
1-13	Natural			X					X	No fish	44	
7-12	Natural									Natural	224	
9-17	Natural	F	X	X	F			X		2000		126
1-23	Natural									Natural	48	
11-4	Primitive	F		F	F					3000		168
9-4	Developed	F	F	X	F			F		Natural		78
4-7	Natural			F						No fish	118	
12-10	Developed	F	F	F	F	F		X		Natural		218
2-18	Natural			F						Natural	68	
13-5	Natural			X				X		Natural		243
5-2	Natural									Natural	138	
4-14	Developed				F	F			X	28600	123	
5-10	Natural	X		F	X					Natural	149	
5-10	Natural	X		F	X					Natural	149	
2-23	Natural									Natural	77	
1-17	Natural			F						No fish	44	
6-2	Natural			X						Natural	161	
11-7	Developed	F	F	F	F	F	X		X	20000		177
4-3	Natural			X						Natural	118	
8-3	Primitive	F	F	X	F			X		4800		33
1-3	Natural	F		F	X					Natural	29	
3-2	Developed		F	F	F	X			X	75630	85	
10-7	Developed	F	F	X	F	X		X		45000		149
4-8	Natural			F						No fish	118	
5-5	Natural	X		F	X					Natural	139	
2-14	Natural			X						No fish	68	
13-8	Natural				F					Natural		250
7-6	Natural	F	X		F				X	8700	208	
1-24	Natural									Natural	48	
8-11	Natural									Natural		57
5-9	Natural	X		X	X					Natural	149	
13-3	Primitive	F		F	F					Natural		238
9-2	Private									Natural		72
9-3	Natural		F		F					10000		74
1-22	Natural									Natural	48	

INDEX TABLE

LAKE REFERENCE and STATISTICS						ACCESS	

Lake Name	Lake Refer	Region	Elev (Mt)	Size (Ha)	Area Use	Vehicle Type	Hike km
Elsay	2-17	North Van	765	20	Park	Car	7.0
Eunice	6-13	Maple Ridge	500	12	Reserve	Car	10.5
Fannin	2-24	North Van	700	8	Watershed	Restr	
First	1-6	West Van	960	<1	Park	Car	.9
First	2-12	North Van	1020	<1	Park	Car	1.0
Flora	12-7	Chilliwack R	1356	16	Crown	Car	6.0
Florence	7-9	Stave Falls	390	32	Crown	Truck	.1
Flower	2-8	North Van	950	<1	Park	Car	1.0
Foley	12-3	Chilliwack R	550	11	Crown	Car	0
Fourth	1-7	West Van	1010	<1	Park	Car	1.1
Francis	9-11	Harrison M	366	4	Crown	4X4	0
Galene	13-6	Hope	1873	1	Park	Car	16.0
Goldie	2-7	North Van	950	1	Park	Car	1.0
Goose	6-3	Maple Ridge	140	6	Reserve	Car	5.2
Gopher	2-16	North Van	790	1	Park	Car	5?
Grace	9-9	Harrison M	106	6	Crown	Car	0
Greendrop	12-9	Chilliwack R	1021	21	Crown	Car	5.2
Gwendoline	6-11	Maple Ridge	550	10	Reserve	Car	9.0
Hanging	1-21	West Van	1110	4	Watershed	Restr	
Hanging	12-11	Chilliwack R	1417	25	Crown	Car	4.0
Hanover	1-4	West Van	1170	3	Park	Car	8.9
Harrison west	9-15	Harrison	20	21780	Variable	Truck	0
Harrison east	10-2	Harrison	20	21780	Multi use	Car	0
Hatzic	8-1	Dewdney	12	365	Multi use	Car	0
Hayward	7-3	Stave Falls	44	276	BC Hydro	Car	0
Hector Fergus	6-25	Maple Ridge	780	10	Park	Fly In	0
Hicks	10-4	Harrison	210	104	Park	Car	0
Hidden	2-11	North Van	1100	<1	Park	Car	1.0
Hoover	7-11	Stave Falls	440	4	Crown	Car	3.7
Hour Glass	5-6	Port Coquit	1000	<1	Reg. Park	Car	6.0
Image	6-21	Maple Ridge	350	<1	Park	Car	2.0
Irmy	6-7	Maple Ridge	470	<1	Reserve	Car	7.0
Jacobs	6-18	Maple Ridge	520	4	Reserve	Car	5.4
Jay	4-11	Port Moody	960	<1	Crown	Car	5.2
Jessica	4-12	Port Moody	998	<1	Crown	Car	5.2
Judicator	6-26	Maple Ridge	1020	24	Prov. Park	Fly in	0
Judson	11-1	Sumas	40	30	Private	Car	0
Katherine	6-16	Maple Ridge	510	20	Reserve	Car	13.0
Kawkawa	13-10	Hope	45	77	Multi use	Car	0
Kennedy	2-1	North Van	1015	4	Watershed	Restr	
Kenyon	8-8	Dewdney	700	26	Crown	Truck	0
Kunzelman	6-29	Maple Ridge	1120	30	Prov. Park	Fly in	0
Lafarge	5-1	P Coquitlam	45	5	Park	Car	0
L. Beautiful	6-23	Maple Ridge	750	<1	Park	Car	6.0
Lake Errock	9-1	Harrison M	30	26	Multi use	Car	0
Latimer Pond	3-4	Burnaby	45	6	Park	Car	0
Laxton	11-2	Sumas	40	20	Private	Car	0
Lindsay	4-13	Port Moody	1150	<1	Crown	Car	6.7
Ling	12-5	Chilliwack R	1365	14	Crown	4X4	4
Lindeman	12-8	Chilliwack R	838	12	Crown	Car	1.2

INDEX TABLE

FACILITIES and RECREATION SUMMARY

CP= CAMPING, BT= BOATING, HI=HIKING, FI= FISHING, PK=PICNICKING, EQ= EQUESTRIAN, BR= BACKROADS, OT=OTHER

Lake Refer	Facilities Type	C P	B T	H I	F I	P K	E Q	B R	O T	Fish Stocked	Vol 1 Page	Vol 2 Page
2-17	Natural	X		F	X					Natural	68	
6-13	Natural			X						Natural	162	
2-24	Natural									Natural	77	
1-6	Natural			X		X			X	No fish	36	
2-12	Natural			X						No fish	68	
12-7	Natural	X		F	X					Natural		209
7-9	Natural	X	X		F			F		Natural	217	
2-8	Natural			F						No fish	68	
12-3	Primitive	F	X	X	F			X		7500		197
1-7	Natural			X					X	No fish	36	
9-11	Primitive	F	F		F			X		2500		105
13-6	Primitive	X		F	X					Natural		245
2-7	Natural			X					X	No fish	68	
6-3	Natural			X						Natural	162	
2-16	Natural			X						No fish	68	
9-9	Primitive	X	X		F					6000		98
12-9	Primitive	X		F	F					Natural		215
6-11	Natural			F						Natural	162	
1-21	Natural									Natural	48	
12-11	Natural	X		F	X					Natural		223
1-4	Natural	X		H	X					Natural	29	
9-15	Developed	F	F	F	F			F		Natural		119
10-2	Developed	F	F	F	F	F		F		Natural		134
8-1	Developed		F	X	F	X				Natural		27
7-3	Developed		F	F	F	X			X	85700	196	
6-25	Natural									Natural	182	
10-4	Developed	F	F	F	F	F			X	60000		141
2-11	Natural			X						No fish	68	
7-11	Natural	F		F	F					Natural	221	
5-6	Natural			F						No fish	139	
6-21	Natural			F						Natural	171	
6-7	Natural			F						Natural	162	
6-18	Natural			F						Natural	162	
4-11	Natural			F						No fish	118	
4-12	Natural			F						No fish	118	
6-26	Natural	X			X					Natural	182	
11-1	Private									Natural		162
6-16	Natural			F						Natural	162	
13-10	Developed		F		F	F			X	Natural		256
2-1	Natural									Natural	56	
8-8	Primitive	X	F		F			F		6000		50
6-29	Natural	X			X					Natural	182	
5-1	Developed		X	X	F				X	42400	134	
6-23	Natural			F						Natural	181	
9-1	Developed		F		X	X				5000		69
3-4	Natural		F	X	F		X			43400	94	
11-2	Private									Natural		162
4-13	Natural			F						No fish	118	
12-5	Natural			F	X			X		Natural		203
12-8	Primitive	F		F	F					Natural		212

233

INDEX TABLE

LAKE REFERENCE and STATISTICS						ACCESS	
Lake Name	Lake Refer	Region	Elev (Mt)	Size (Ha)	Area Use	Vehicle Type	Hike km
Little Capilano	2-19	North Van	290	1	Watershed	Restr	
Liumchen	11-8	Sumas	1380	2	Crown	Truck	4.7
Lookout	9-14	Harrison M	650	11	Crown	4X4	0
Lookout	10-9	Harrison	1390	9	Crown	4X4	.3
Loon	6-5	Maple Ridge	350	45	Reserve	Car	5.8
Lost	1-10	West Van	770	<1	Prov. Park	Car	3.2
Lost	6-6	Maple Ridge	350	<1	Reserve	Car	7.5
Lost	4-16	Port Moody	130	<1	Mun. Park	Car	.4
Lost Lagoon	1-27	West Van	0	20	City Park	Car	0
Lynn	2-3	North Van	790	1	Park	Car	11.7
Mac	4-10	Port Moody	952	<1	Crown	Car	5.2
Macklin	1-20	West Van	900	5	Watershed	Restr	
Marion	1-1	West Van	520	4	Crown	Car	5.6
McKay	8-4	Dewdney	830	2	Crown	Car	3.0
Meech	2-2	North Van	1170	<1	Park	Car\lift	3.5
Mike	6-20	Maple Ridge	236	4	Prov. Park	Car	0
Mill	11-3	Sumas	60	18	Mun. Park	Car	0
Mirror	6-17	Maple Ridge	270	<1	Reserve	Car	3.0
Morgan	7-8	Stave Falls	318	20	Crown	Truck	.1
Morris	9-7	Harrison M	24	8	Crown	Car	0
Moss	10-6	Harrison	518	4	Crown	Car	2.8
Mundy	4-15	Port Moody	122	1	Mun. Park	Car	.5
Munro	5-4	P Coquitlam	830	9	Reg. Park	Car	4.0
Mystery	2-10	North Van	1150	<1	Prov. Park	Car	1.5
Nancy	2-9	North Van	1070	<1	Prov. Park	Car	.5
Obelisk	5-8	Pt Coquitlam	1150	20	Crown	Boat	18.0?
Olive	8-12	Dewdney	1015	8	Watershed	4X4	3.0
Orchid	1-18	North Van	1054	4	Watershed	Restr	
Owen	1-16	West Van	1160	<1	Park	Car\lift	1.4
Pallisade	2-21	North Van	876	42	Watershed	Restr	
Peaceful	6-19	Maple Ridge	685	<1	Reserve	Car	10.0
Peacock	1-19	West Van	1180	4	Watershed	Restr	
Peneplain	5-3	Pt Coquitlam	990	23	Watershed	Restr	
Phyllis	1-2	West Van	530	6	Crown	Car	6.5
Pierce	12-1	Chilliwack R	1350	18	Crown	Car	4.0
Pine	7-10	Maple Ridge	180	4	Penal Area	Restr	
Pitt	6-1	Maple Ridge	50	5380	Multi use	Car	0
Placid	6-10	Maple Ridge	503	1.5	Reserve	Car	9.5
Radium	12-6	Chilliwack R	1480	<1	Crown	Car	5.5
Raven	6-24	Maple Ridge	927	36	Prov. Park	Fly In	0
Rice	2-4	North Van	190	7	Reserve	Car	1.0
Robin	4-6	Port Moody	945	<1	Crown	Car	5.2
Rodgers	2-20	North Van	650	14	Watershed	Restr	
Rolf (Lost)	2-5	North Van	230	2	Reserve	Car	8.5
Rolley	7-2	Stave Falls	221	23	Park	Car	0
Rose	6-15	Maple Ridge	500	<1	Reserve	Car	12.8
Ross	13-7	Hope	511	5000	Park	Car	0
Ryder	11-6	Sumas	230	1	Private	Restr	
Salsbury	8-7	Dewdney	409	79	Crown	Truck	0

FACILITIES and RECREATION SUMMARY

CP= CAMPING, BT= BOATING, HI=HIKING, FI= FISHING, PK=PICNICKING, EQ= EQUESTRIAN, BR= BACKROADS, OT=OTHER

Lake Refer	Facilities Type	C P	B T	H I	F I	P K	E Q	B R	O T	Fish Stocked	Vol 1 Page	Vol 2 Page
2-19	Natural									Natural	77	
11-8	Natural	X		F	F			F		Natural		181
9-14	Natural	X	X		F			F		2500		115
10-9	Natural			X	X			F		Natural		157
6-5	Natural			F						Natural	162	
1-10	Natural			F					X	No fish	36	
6-6	Natural			F						Natural	162	
4-16	Developed			X	F					Natural	129	
1-27	Developed			F	X				X	Natural	49	
2-3	Natural			F						Natural	56	
4-10	Natural			F						No fish	118	
1-20	Natural									Natural	48	
1-1	Natural	X		F	X					Natural	27	
8-4	Natural			F						Natural		37
2-2	Natural			F						No fish	56	
6-20	Developed		X	F	F		F			15000	168	
11-3	Developed		F	X	F	F			X	41000		164
6-17	Natural			F						Natural	162	
7-8	Natural	X	X		F					Natural	213	
9-7	Natural	X	F		F					Natural		90
10-6	Natural			F	X					2000		147
4-15	Developed			F	X	X			X	Natural	126	
5-4	Natural	X		F	X					Natural	139	
2-10	Natural			F						No fish	68	
2-9	Natural			F						No fish	68	
5-8	Natural	X		X	X					Natural	149	
8-12	Natural			X				F		2000		60
1-18	Natural									Natural	48	
1-16	Natural			F						No fish	44	
2-21	Natural									Natural	77	
6-19	Natural			F						No fish	162	
1-19	Natural									Natural	48	
5-3	Natural									Natural	138	
1-2	Natural	X		F	X					Natural	27	
12-1	Natural	X		F	X					Natural		189
7-10	Developed									Natural	220	
6-1	Developed	X	F	F	F				X	Natural	156	
6-10	Natural			F						Natural	162	
12-6	Natural	X		F						Natural		206
6-24	Natural	X			X					Natural	182	
2-4	Developed			F	F	X	X		X	Natural	61	
4-6	Natural			F						No fish	118	
2-20	Natural									Natural	77	
2-5	Natural			X			X			Natural	67	
7-2	Developed	F	F	X	F	F				46500	192	
6-15	Natural			F						Natural	162	
13-7	Developed	F	F	X	F	F			X	Natural		247
11-6	Private									Natural		175
8-7	Primitive	F	F		F			F		38000		46

INDEX TABLE

LAKE REFERENCE and STATISTICS						ACCESS	
Lake Name	Lake Refer	Region	Elev (Mt)	Size (Ha)	Area Use	Vehicle Type	Hike km
Sam	1-15	West Van	1150	<1	Park	Car	.7
Sardis Pond	11-5	Sumas	12	2	Park	Car	0
Sasamat	4-1	Port Moody	70	45	Park	Car	0
Sayres	7-7	Stave Falls	230	78	Crown	Car	1.0
Schkam	13-9	Hope	166	17	Multi use	Car	0
Second	2-13	North Van	1100	<1	Park	Car	1.0
Seymour	2-6	North Van	495	89	Watershed	Car	11.0
Shirley	6-14	Maple Ridge	555	1	Reserve	Car	12.0
Silver	13-2	Hope	350	40	Prov. Park	Car	0
Silvermere	7-4	Stave Falls	35	110	Multi use	Car	0
Sisken	4-5	Port Moody	940	<1	Crown	Car	5.2
Slollicum	10-8	Harrison	1280	26	Crown	4X4	1.7
Sonny	8-10	Dewdney	890	6	Watershed	4X4	1.0
Spindle	5-11	Pt Coquitlam	780	4	Crown	Boat	17?
Spoon	12-2	Sumas	1480	<1	Crown	4X4	1.5
Stacey	9-16	Harrison M	803	3	Crown	4X4	0
Statlu	9-6	Harrison M	600	37	Crown	4X4	1.0
Stave west	7-5	Stave Falls	82	4410	Multi use	Car	0
Stave east	8-6	Dewdney	82	4410	Crown	Truck	0
St. Mary's	4-9	Port Moody	950	<1	Crown	Car	5.2
Surprise	6-9	Maple Ridge	555	<1	Reserve	Car	9.0
Sunrise	3-5	Burnaby	36	35	Private	Car	0
Sunrise	9-13	Harrison M	396	5	Crown	4X4	0
Swanee	13-4	Hope	1290	30	Crown	Car	3.0
Theagill	1-14	West Van	1150	<1	Park	Car\lift	.7
Theta	2-15	North Van	900	<1	Park	Car	4?
Thomas	6-28	Maple Ridge	930	141	Crown	Fly in	0
Thurston	8-9	Dewdney	1070	2	Crown	4X4	7.5
Tingle	6-27	Maple Ridge	980	60	Prov. Park	Fly in	0
Trout	3-1	Burnaby	53	4	Park	Car	0
Trout	10-3	Harrison	76	12	Park	Car	0
Turtle	1-12	West Van	1130	<1	Park	Car\lift	1.9
Twin	8-5	Dewdney	450	6	Crown	4X4	0
Vicar	2-25	North Van	990	<1	Watershed	Restr	
Wahleach	13-1	Hope	655	498	BC Hydro	Car	0
Weaver	9-8	Harrison M	258	81	Crown	Truck	0
West	1-8	West Van	870	1	Park	Car	2.0
Whonnock	7-1	Stave Falls	170	50	Park	Car	0
Whyte	1-25	West Van	325	<1	Watershed	Restr	
Widgeon	5-7	Pt Coquitlam	770	773	Reserve	Boat	8.0
Williamson	12-4	Chilliwack R	1650	2	Crown	Car	3.6
Wilson	9-5	Harrison M	817	47	Crown	4X4	0
Wolf	9-10	Harrison M	106	2	Crown	Truck	0
Wood	9-12	Harrison M	167	5	Crown	Car	0
Wren	4-4	Port Moody	940	<1	Crown	Car	5.2
Yew	1-11	West Van	930	2	Park	Car	.8

INDEX TABLE

FACILITIES and RECREATION SUMMARY

CP= CAMPING, BT= BOATING, HI=HIKING. FI= FISHING, PK=PICNICKING, EQ= EQUESTRIAN. BR= BACKROADS, OT=OTHER

Lake Refer	Facilities Type	C P	B T	H I	F I	P K	E Q	B R	O T	Fish Stocked	Vol 1 Page	Vol 2 Page
1-15	Natural			F						No fish	44	
11-5	Developed			X	F	X				21000		172
4-1	Developed		F	X	F	X			X	13100	106	
7-7	Natural				F					Natural	210	
13-9	Developed		X		F	F			X	15000		253
2-13	Natural			X						No fish	68	
2-6	Developed			X	F	X	X		X	Natural	67	
6-14	Natural			F						No fish	162	
13-2	Primitive	F	F		F	X				Natural		234
7-4	Private		X		X					Natural	200	
4-5	Natural			F						No fish	118	
10-8	Natural	F		F	F			F		Natural		153
8-10	Natural			F				F		Natural		55
5-11	Natural	X		F	X					Natural	149	
12-2	Natural			F				F		No fish		193
9-16	Natural	F	X		F			X		10000		123
9-6	Natural	F		F	F					Natural		86
7-5	Developed	X	F		F					8200	203	
8-6	Primitive	F	F	X	F	X		F		8200		42
4-9	Natural			F						No fish	118	
6-9	Natural			F						Natural	162	
3-5	Private									Natural	98	
9-13	Primitive	F	X		F			X		Natural		111
13-4	Natural	X		F	X					Natural		241
1-14	Natural			X						No fish	44	
2-15	Natural			X						No fish	68	
6-28	Natural	X			X					19000	182	
8-9	Natural	X		X				X		Natural		53
6-27	Natural	X			X					Natural	182	
3-1	Developed			X	X	X			X	1970	82	
10-3	Developed		F		F					Natural		138
1-12	Natural			X						No fish	44	
8-5	Natural							F		Natural		39
2-25	Natural									Natural	77	
13-1	Developed	F	F	X	F	X				Natural		230
9-8	Primitive	F	F	X	F	X				30000		138
1-8	Natural			X					X	No fish	36	
7-1	Developed		F		F	F			X	20900	188	
1-25	Natural									Natural	49	
5-7	Primitive	F		F	F					20000	144	
12-4	Natural			F						Natural		200
9-5	Natural	F	X	X	F			F		40000		82
9-10	Primitive	F	X		F					1500		102
9-12	Primitive	F			F			F		2500		108
4-4	Natural			F						No fish	118	
1-11	Developed			F		X			F	No fish	41	

WESTERN GUIDES

**Alpine
Wildflowers**
J. E. (Ted) Underhill
ISBN 0-88839-975-8
5½ x 8½ SC   6.95

**Coastal Lowland
Wildflowers**
J. E. (Ted) Underhill
ISBN 0-88839-973-1
5½ X 8½ SC   6.95

**Sagebrush
Wildflowers**
J. E. (Ted) Underhill
ISBN 0-88839-171-4
5½ x 8 ½ SC   6.95

**Upland Field & Forest
Wildflowers**
J. E. (Ted) Underhill
ISBN 0-88839-174-9
5½ x 8½ SC   6.95

**Northwestern
Wild Berries**
J. E. (Ted) Underhill
ISBN 0-88839-027-0
5½ x 8½ SC   8.95

Wild Harvest
Edible Plants of the Pacific Northwest
Terry Domico
ISBN 0-88839-022-X
5½ x 8½ SC   7.95

**Rocks & Minerals
of the Northwest**
Stan & Chris Learning
ISBN 0-88839-053-X
5½ x 8½ SC   4.95

**Western
Mushrooms**
J. E. (Ted) Underhill
ISBN 0-88839-031-9
5 ½ x 8½ SC   4.95

**Wildlife
of the Rockies**
David Hancock
ISBN 0-919654-33-9
5½ x 8½ SC   3.50

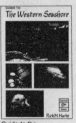

**Guide to the
Western Seashore**
Rick M. Harbo
ISBN 0-88839-201-X
5 1/2 x 8 1/2, SC   5.95

**Tidepool
& Reef**
Rick M. Harbo
ISBN 0-88839-039-4
5 1/2 x 8 1/2, SC   6.95

**The Edible
Seashore**
Rick M. Harbo
ISBN 0-88839-199-4
5½ X 8½ SC $5.95